A Place
Among The Nations
Issues of Irish Foreign Policy

PATRICK KEATINGE

Institute of Public Administration
Dublin

Published by
Institute of Public Administration
57-61 Lansdowne Road
Dublin 4
Ireland

ISBN 0 902173 81 2

First published 1978

Printed in Ireland by
Mount Salus Press
Sandymount, Dublin 4

CONTENTS

Preface   vi

Glossary of Irish Terms   viii

Introduction: **The Scope of Foreign Policy**   1

PART I: THE HISTORICAL LEGACY

Chapter 1. **Britain's Ireland in International Relations**   9

Chapter 2. **The Foreign Policies of Irish Nationalism, 1798-1913**   22

Chapter 3. **From Images to Realities, 1914-1922**   42

PART II: ASPIRATIONS AND POLICIES: THE MAJOR ISSUE-AREAS

Chapter 4. **Independence and Identity**   61

Chapter 5. **Security**   81

Chapter 6. **Unity**   100

Chapter 7. **Prosperity**   127

Chapter 8. **The International Milieu: Order**   149

Chapter 9. **The International Milieu: Justice**   170

PART III: PROBLEMS OF PURPOSE IN FOREIGN POLICY

Chapter 10. **The Problem of Design**   193

Chapter 11. **The Problem of the Policy-Making Process**   203

Chapter 12. **The Problem of the Future**   223

Notes   231

Appendix One   268

Appendix Two   270

Select Bibliography   272

Index   277

PREFACE

The nineteen-seventies have seen the broadening of the horizons of Irish diplomacy and a quickening in the pace of transactions across our borders. The consequent need not merely to understand the immediate effects of these developments but to place them in their historical perspective is becoming more pronounced, but at the same time more difficult to meet. During this period I have been engaged both in introducing Irish students to the study of the international system and in providing foreign scholars with a background to Irish experience in that system; in both these tasks I have encountered much difficulty with the existing literature on the subject. Although, in sum, many words have been written on various aspects of Irish foreign policy, they are for the most part scattered over a broad range of works of varying quality. The best are often embedded in surveys of more general scope and the worst are repetitive assertions or slogans. While academic specialisation in Ireland has advanced far enough to provide more than one frame of reference, whether it be history, economics, political science or the law, it has not yet advanced far enough to pull these together and to give shape and consistency to the external dimension of Irish public life. Thus Irish students confront international relations with little clear idea of their own country's place in this scheme of things, and the foreigner looks in vain for a concise but comprehensive survey of the substance of Irish foreign policy.

I have written this book in an attempt to remedy these defects. Much of importance remains to be uncovered in this field, but in the meantime it is necessary to reassess the information we already possess, to suggest possible ways of interpreting it, and to try to present a coherent view of the subject as a whole. To cover such ground within one book has necessarily entailed a very condensed exposition of complex trends and events which may do no more than scratch the surface. To assist those readers who wish to go further I have provided two sorts of references; some are among the better-known academic works in the field of international relations in general, while the bulk are (mostly published) sources relating to the case of Ireland.

While I remain responsible for errors of fact and interpretation, I am most grateful for the help I have received on this project. Stephen Barcroft assisted me in researching some of the more recent developments, and officials in the Departments of Foreign Affairs, Agriculture and Finance have been a patient and positive source of information. Earlier drafts of the text were read in whole or in part by John Bowman, David Harkness, Dennis Kennedy, Dermot McAleese and Fergus Pyle; I am indebted to them for their time and comments. I received some financial support from the Joint TCD/UCD Postgraduate Course in European Studies, funded by the Commission of the European Community. Jim O'Donnell and Jonathan Williams guided me through the minefield of publication and our task was made all the easier by the typing of Carol O'Sullivan, Hilary Tyrrell and, for an impeccable final draft, Mary Cotter.

GLOSSARY OF IRISH TERMS IN GENERAL USAGE

Aontacht Éireann: Republican Unity. (Political party founded in 1971).
Bunreacht na hÉireann: Constitution of Ireland. (Enacted in 1937).
Bord Fáilte: Tourist Board.
Clan na Gael: United Brotherhood. (Irish-American nationalist group).
Clann na Poblachta: Republican Party.
Córas Tráchtála Teoranta: Export Board.
Cumann na nGaedheal: League of Gaels. (Political party supporting the Anglo-Irish Treaty of 1921).
Dáil Éireann: Lower House in the national legislature. Between 1919 and 1922 this title was also used loosely to refer the revolutionary government responsible to the Dáil.
Éire: Ireland.
Fianna Fáil: Soldiers of Destiny. (Political party opposing the Anglo-Irish Treaty of 1921. Founded in 1926).
Fine Gael: Tribe of Gaels. (Political party succeeding Cumann na nGaedheal in 1933).
Gorta: Famine. (Name of the Irish National Committee of the United Nations Freedom from Hunger Campaign).
Saorstát Éireann: Irish Free State. (Official name of the Irish state from 1922 to 1937).
Seanad: Senate.
Sinn Féin: Ourselves. (Separatist movement founded in 1905. In 1917 the title was adopted by a coalition of the major separatist bodies. After the civil war it was retained by unconditional opponents of the Anglo-Irish Treaty of 1921).
Taoiseach: Prime Minister. (Prior to 1937 called President of the Executive Council).
Teachta Dála (TD): Member of the Dáil (or Dáil Deputy).
Trócaire: Mercy. (Fund-raising body for development aid).

Introduction
The Scope of Foreign Policy

Ireland's 'foreign relations' *in the true sense are broader than anything done by my Department.*

> Dr Patrick Hillery,
> Minister for Foreign Affairs, 1972

There has been in Ireland a tradition of looking at foreign policy through the wrong end of the telescope. The image thereby perceived may not always be quite as nebulous as that of the Dáil deputy who in 1923 opposed the establishment of the Department of External Affairs with the complaint that

> . . . we are concerned with no foreign affairs. We have no colonies and have no interests to clash with any other nation . . . it is ridiculous to be playing with theatricals like this.[1]

Nevertheless, even though reluctantly accepting the existence of something called 'foreign policy', the general public and its parliamentary representatives have often been happy to assign it to the outer limits of public life.[2]

This dismissive view of foreign policy is not altogether surprising and can arise from several sources. In the first place, the involvement of Irish governments in international relations has generally been geographically limited and the state has been to a large extent insulated from the more traumatic consequences of the large-scale international violence characteristic of this century. It has been too easy, perhaps, to conclude that because Ireland has enjoyed this measure of insulation there is no need to be concerned with the follies of the outside world. This head-in-the-sand posture is also arrived at by quite a different route, where external pressures are not seen as being remote, but rather as being so overwhelming that there is little point in trying to modify them through government action. Ireland, it is pointed out, is a small, weak state and as such can only respond to the unpredictable and usually disagreeable forces 'out there'. The world sneezes and Ireland catches double pneumonia — the best any government can do is to keep the patient alive.

A false sense of security or of pessimistic fatalism can thus lead to the view that to seek to control the state's external actions is futile. Such pessimism about foreign policy is not of course a characteristic peculiar to Ireland or even to other states which occupy the humbler ranks of the hierarchy of state strength, for even superpowers are 'small' in relation to their external environment and the problems it contains. But in the Irish case, where pessimism about the possibility of formulating and implementing foreign policy often takes the form of indifference towards it, there is also a tendency to reduce the significance of foreign policy by taking a narrow view of what the term entails. This is only to be expected at the level of general public debate: when a newspaper editorial proclaims that 'at last Ireland has a foreign policy', it often means little more than the fact that the leader writer approves of the government's condemnation of the actions of state X in increasing the number of its international ballistic missiles, or invading state Y or expelling the nationals of state Z from its territory. Such condemnations are a part of foreign policy, but only a part.

What is rather more surprising is the extent to which the practitioners of Irish diplomacy have been content to take a restricted view of the content of foreign policy. Although this attitude has weakened in recent years, particularly since Ireland joined the European Community, it has been firmly embedded in Irish political thinking. During the nineteen-sixties, for example, the Minister for External Affairs, Frank Aiken, argued that the issues of membership of the EEC and that of Northern Ireland were 'constitutional issues' and therefore not primarily his business. Such modesty concerning the foreign minister's role is not to be explained solely by reference to party or governmental demarcation disputes; it also reflected the view that foreign policy was above all concerned with issues of global consequence. This usage of the term could be seen among professional diplomats as well as in the cabinet. A senior official in the Department of Foreign Affairs remarked to the author in 1971 that he had never, during his whole career, had anything to do with foreign policy. At the time he had responsibility for one of the most pressing diplomatic problems facing the Irish government; what he meant was merely that he had never worked in the Department's General Political and United Nations Section, which had the task of helping the minister formulate policy positions on the large issues of world politics encountered in the United Nations.

Confining the definition of foreign policy to such matters amounts to a semantic confusion whereby 'foreign policy' is taken to be synonymous with 'world politics'. Seen in this light, Irish foreign policy is indeed of little import since the actions of a small state, insulated from major 'flash points', have only a marginal bearing on the outcomes of international politics. Such actions as are taken can thus be safely left to a small group of individuals belonging to that rather theatrical species, diplomatic man, who can perform his dated rituals behind the walls of parliamentary bipartisanship.

This book is based on the contention that it is both misleading and dangerous to regard foreign policy as being restricted in this way. It is misleading because the state's foreign policy is more use- fully seen as encompassing all governmental objectives, decisions and actions which impinge on human behaviour outside its borders. International relationships are bilateral as well as global and are concerned with relatively humdrum economic, social and cultural transactions between states as well as with the more dramatic issues arising from attempts to impose order on a near-anarchic system of states. The greater part of most states' foreign policies is concerned with bilateral transactions and this is no less true of Ireland's case, in which bilateral relations with the United Kingdom have loomed so large. If the term 'foreign policy' is not used to include such transactions, under what conceptual label will they be considered? The danger is that in general public debate, and perhaps in closed governmental discussions, many of them will not be considered at all, until they emerge suddenly as an 'unforeseen problem'.

Foreign policy is, therefore, seen here as a broad field of govern- ment concern and as containing a wide range of diverse features. The purpose of this book is to provide a map of this field, in which the major features are identified and their evolution is described. With this end in view foreign policy is conceived of as being composed of different 'issue-areas'. Although this term has been widely used by students of foreign policy, it has been defined and employed in different ways and it is therefore necessary to comment on its application here.[3] The issues which confront statesmen are grouped according to the very broad types of values upon which the existence of the state is held to depend.[4] These values — independence, security, unity, prosperity, global order and global justice — are vague and general expressions of purpose. It is true that in themselves they do not explain how or why particular policies emerge, and are often a cloak for sectional or personal ambitions. Nor do they necessarily indicate the extent to which a statesman pursues precise objectives purposefully or merely responds to external events. Nevertheless the persistence of the statesman's appeal to such values, from government to government and from generation to generation, is striking, and is often associated with distinctive patterns of behaviour and different groups of actors. External security, for example, remains a general concern from one century to the next and the issues arising from this concern impinge directly on particular groups within society, such as the military establishment, the armaments industry and potential conscripts. Prosperity is likewise a recurring theme, with its own range of interested groups and its own patterns of activity.

By separately considering these sets of related issues, i.e. issue-areas, it is possible to describe in a manageable way what would otherwise appear to be a rather heterogeneous collection of governmental activities taking place in a complex and unpredictable political setting. When examined in its historical context, each issue-area can be seen to produce patterns of deliberate action or mere response, and of success or failure. The broad value it represents may continue to be elusive, but alternative strategies which have been adopted can be identified and assessed. The extent to which attitudes and commitments towards specific goals and policies persist, or are modified under changed circumstances, may be discerned; policies can be seen to depend on traditional perceptions (and mis-perceptions) as well as on the immediate pressure of events.

Indeed, the strength of tradition in the shaping of these issue-areas is often pronounced. The realities of today's international system are accepted or rejected by minds which have been moulded both by actual historical experience and by simplified images of historical experience. In this respect Irish foreign policy does not start from scratch with the creation of an Irish state during the winter of 1921-22. Therefore, in the first part of the book an attempt is made to trace through the past the fortunes of Ireland as an object rather than an actor in international relations; particular attention is paid to the ways in which Irish nationalists, often implicitly, thought and acted in terms of a 'pre-foreign policy'.

With the establishment of the Irish Free State, however, these general tendencies can be more readily grouped and examined as separate issue-areas. The historical evidence so far available is unevenly distributed, both between the issue-areas and with regard to chronological periods, though there are signs that over the next decade this situation may improve significantly.[5] But historical revision is a lengthy process, depending on the accumulation of detailed case-studies; in the meantime the general surveys of each issue-area in the second part of this book can at least provide a map of the surface and the contours of the foreign policy field, even if it is only possible to speculate about what may be seen as the field's geological structure.

Finally, there is the problem of the field's boundaries. The division of foreign policy into issue-areas admits a degree of heterogeneity in what might otherwise be assumed to be a distinctive and unified segment of public policy.[6] It is important, therefore, to identify the connections between different issue-areas and to see the ways in which governments are constrained by or able to manipulate or ignore such connections. Thus the third part of the book is concerned with the government's perception of foreign policy as a whole − first with the manner in which it is designed and then with the manner in which it is made and implemented − and attempts to show that the foreign policy field is an increasingly important one, and certainly not 'playing with theatricals'. At the same time, the scope of foreign policy is so broad that the boundaries which mark it off from what are normally conceived to be different parts of public policy are becoming increasingly blurred. This gives rise to problems concerning the way in which foreign policy is conceived, co-ordinated and implemented in an unpredictable world.

PART I

The Historical Legacy

Where are our ambassadors? What treaties do we enter into? With what nation do we make peace or war? Are we not a mere cipher in all these, and are not these what give a nation consequence and fame?

Sir Lawrence Parsons in the Irish House of Commons, 1790

Chapter 1
Britain's Ireland
in International Relations

*. . . English policy is determined to retain Ireland as a barren
bulwark for English aggrandisement, and the unique geographical
position of this island, far from being a benefit and safeguard to
Europe and America, is subjected to the purposes of England's
policy of world domination.*

Message to the Free Nations of the World,
issued by Dáil Éireann, 21 January 1919

In the early hours of 6 December 1921, Irish and British delegations signed the 'Articles of Agreement for a Treaty between Great
Britain and Ireland', the document generally to be known as the
Anglo-Irish Treaty, or in Ireland simply as the Treaty. A year later,
the Irish Provisional Government, which had been established
under the Treaty, became the official government of the new
state, the Irish Free State. In the autumn of the following year,
1923, the Irish Free State was admitted to membership of the
League of Nations. Internationally recognised as the government
of a sovereign independent state, with responsibility for conducting
its external relations, the Irish government during this period
started to concern itself with issues of foreign policy.

Yet these apparently straightforward formalities mark not a
climax of achievement in Irish political life, but rather a period of
confusion and often despair. The new Irish state got off to a bad
start and an acute division over the terms of the Treaty led to a
civil war in a little over six months. In the debate leading to this
outbreak of violence and even more clearly in the negotiations
which led to the Treaty, can be seen the crystallisation of most of
the major issues that were to persist in Irish foreign policy for
decades to come. But these issues did not emerge for the first time
in the Treaty negotiations although, in the context in which they
arose then, they sometimes assumed new forms; in this sense the
Treaty represents not so much the beginning of a new state as a
new stage in an old and often tortuous relationship.

No state is created without reference to the past, but in the case of Ireland reference to the past is notoriously marked. Although there was no Irish state until the twentieth century, Ireland had been involved in international relations well before the early seventeenth century when the territorial state was finally accepted as the primary political unit. Ireland, in this respect, means two things. First, there is Ireland as a territorial unit, and, being an island, a territorial unit with unusually clear geographical definition. But Ireland, too, is a people, although clear definition of this idea is often conspicuously lacking. In both these senses, Ireland was bound up with the harsh world of international, that is to say inter-state, politics long before she herself achieved statehood. Moreover, this experience lay at the very basis of the Treaty of 1921, and has continued to be reflected in the substance of Irish foreign policy.

*   *   *

'The geographical propinquity of Ireland to the British Isles is a fundamental fact', wrote the British prime minister, David Lloyd George.[1] It had been a fact with important implications for British (and indeed before Britain existed as a political unit for English) policy for centuries. The most striking implication was that the island of Ireland lay within the larger island's strategic orbit, and for that reason British leaders felt compelled to exert a measure of control over the neighbouring territory. The extent of this control, and the forms it took, varied greatly, according to the threats which Ireland appeared to pose to British interests and to the energy with which British governments responded to the situation as they saw it. From the first intervention, under the Norman kings, until the Tudors came to power in the sixteenth century, British control was often nominal, for military conquest was anything but complete. The Tudor conquest was fiercely resisted in the following century, and, although this resistance was broken by the eighteenth century, conditions had been created which ultimately were to make the political integration of the two islands impossible. British rule became associated with the ascendancy of a small protestant minority, based for the most part on colonial settlements during the sixteenth and seventeenth centuries. The catholic majority was repressed and its economic standing, its political influence and its religious and cultural traditions were effectively diminished.

Military conquest had been bought at the price of political disaffection; not for the last time in the quest for security did the means employed by a government tend to contradict the ends it was pursuing. Even a conquered Ireland would prove to be a strategic irritant for British policy-makers. On the one hand it served, as it had done in medieval times, as a base for the subversion of British regimes, while on the other hand, it represented an opportunity for Britain's continental enemies to strike her where her domination seemed to be least secure. Thus Ireland became a factor in the strategic designs of the great European powers, and from the end of the sixteenth century can be discerned a pattern of military intervention in Ireland by Britain's rivals.[2]

At the time of the final Tudor conquest, no less than three such interventions occurred, in 1579, 1580 and 1601. The invading troops were mainly Italian and Spanish, sometimes with papal backing; indeed the intervention of 1579 was declared a religious crusade. The number of foreign troops was never greater than 3,500, and the defeat of the largest expedition alongside its Irish allies at the Battle of Kinsale in 1601 marked the culmination of British military conquest in Ireland.

Less than a hundred years later a more important foreign element had a hand in the efforts of the Stuart king, James II, to regain his crown. In 1689, a large French fleet landed James and his entourage at Kinsale in county Cork, with considerable equipment, and the following year 7,000 French troops were added to the expedition (though these were in exchange for more than 5,000 Irish soldiers who had been sent to France). The arrival of a French Marshal, St Ruth, in 1691 was a token of the extent of Louis XIV's ambitions in Ireland, but the intervention failed. In a campaign lasting from 1689 to 1691, Ireland was in effect the cockpit of Europe as international armies resolved one of the major dynastic and religious issues of the day. England's new Dutch king, William of Orange, assisted by his countrymen (both English and Dutch) and by Scots, Germans and Danes, defeated the Irish and French at the Boyne (1690) and at Aughrim (1691). The future of Britain's protestant monarchy was consolidated, as was that of religious division in Ireland.

Apart from a small French raid on Carrickfergus in 1760 during the Seven Years War, another interval of about one hundred years elapsed before the next intervention. The intervening power was revolutionary France, acting at the instigation of the Irish nationalist leader, Wolfe Tone. The most serious military effort was mounted in 1796 when a large fleet, with 15,000 troops led by General Hoche, set sail for Ireland. Given the military and naval technology of the day, not to mention the vagaries of Irish weather, the month of December was not the most auspicious in which to mount such an expedition. This fact was appreciated by those in the few ships which reached Bantry Bay, and no landing was made. In 1798, a much smaller force of 1,100 men under General Humbert did succeed in landing at Killala Bay, but were eventually defeated, while a month later another fleet, with about 3,000 troops, was dispersed or taken near county Donegal, and Wolfe Tone was captured. The latter's promised conjunction with an internal rising had already come to nothing with the defeat of the insurgents at Vinegar Hill outside Enniscorthy in June 1798.

Somewhat more than a century had elapsed, and the intervening power had changed from France to Germany, when in 1916 the final continental military intervention was made on 'John Bull's Other Island'. It consisted of two incidents – the arrival of a ship-load of military supplies which were eventually deposited on the bottom of Queenstown harbour (now Cobh) in county Cork, and the return to Ireland by submarine of Sir Roger Casement, who wished to urge his compatriots to abandon their insurrection because of the paucity of German aid.[3] German thoroughness was no more than French naval prowess the answer to the impregnability of Britain's Ireland.

However, the strategic significance of these events does not lie in the military outcome of specific incursions, nor even in the historian's easy perception of unbroken failure, coloured by comedies of mismanagement rather than the martial virtues. What was important was the effect on British policy towards Ireland of not only actual invasions but the *possibility* of invasions; the threat was as important as the reality, and was given a new lease of life every time an invasion took place. Precisely what seemed to be threatened varied with different British governments. During the early centuries of British rule it was the dynastic *status quo,* which after the Reformation came to be entangled with the question of religious allegiance. Later, with the development of the territorial state in Europe, Britain's position in the balance of power was at risk, and more particularly her increasing reliance on naval power. In the nineteenth century this latter aspect loomed much larger; British naval power held together an empire and no challenge could be tolerated in home waters. With the emergence of Britain as an industrialised state in the middle of the nineteenth century, control of the seas seemed vital, not merely to maintain trade routes, but in time of danger to preserve the import of essential supplies, especially food. 'Ireland', said Lord Salisbury in 1872, 'must be kept, like India, at all hazards: by persuasion, if possible; if not, by force.'[4]

The control of Ireland, therefore, was a basic principle of British strategic policy, and the simplest means of control seemed to be possession. This gave rise to support of the settler minority's privileged position and the maintenance of a garrison which could be reinforced with relative ease — the 'ownership of Ireland simply minimized risks.'[5] However, for the disaffected Irish, the mirror-image of this principle had more relevance. If Britain held on to Ireland in order to maintain her position in international politics, a deterioration of that position, however it might occur, would be an occasion for attempting to reduce the stranglehold of British domination; thus the dictum, 'England's difficulty is Ireland's opportunity.'

But Ireland's position as an object of British concern did not derive solely from considerations of British security and the associated policies of strategic diplomacy and military power. Geographical propinquity did not imply only a military burden; it equally represented the occasion for economic exploitation. The part played by British governments in this respect was not always so overt as it was in the strategic sphere. British economic intervention in Ireland was often the consequence of private interests, and for considerable periods the role of government was the rather passive one of guaranteeing, with varying degrees of enthusiasm, the continued survival of such groups and individuals. Nor were the economic benefits to the British state — as opposed to private British landowners or merchants — always an obvious and satisfying recompense for the costs of maintaining Ireland as an offshore garrison. Ireland did not prove to be an El Dorado of economic imperialism.

Yet in two respects, at least, British governments were closely

involved in the economic exploitation and control of their neighbouring island.[6] First, strategic control implied a minimum degree
of economic control. At the very least the garrison had to be fed.
And if by 'garrison' is understood, not merely the military establishment, but a class of colonial settlers, whose task it was to
maintain British domination on the spot, the maintenance of the
garrison can be seen as a vital concern. Moreover, the creation of
this colonial class was the direct consequence of government
policies. The 'plantation' of specific regions was first tried, with
varying success, under the Tudors, while at the beginning of the
seventeenth century James I was responsible for introducing large
numbers of mainly Scottish immigrants into the northern province
of Ulster. Shortly afterwards large tracts of land became the booty
of Cromwell's soldiers.

The policy of settlement encompassed both political and
economic objectives. Their political purpose — to introduce into
Ireland a population more responsive to British rule — was only
partly achieved, but they did lead to the development of economic
interests in Ireland which in the last resort would seek the protection of the British government. The consequences for Anglo-Irish
relationships could be seen in most of the important issues which
arose over the next two hundred and fifty years, long after the
policy of settlement had ceased.

In the nineteenth century, ownership of the land became the
most pervasive political question in what was still a predominantly
rural economy. The outcome of Irish agitation and parliamentary
representation was British legislation which eventually undermined
the position of the protestant aristocracy to a considerable degree,
but the political implications of this economic revolution were
not always perceived either by its victors or its victims by the time
the final struggle for independence had been engaged in the
second decade of the twentieth century. The landowning class,
traditionally an important tie between Ireland and Britain, was
economically down but by no means politically out.

British economic interests were also involved in Irish industrial
development and trade. The pace of the former, however, was
severely restricted when the large-scale production unit, based on
local energy resources, became the norm in Britain at the beginning
of the nineteenth century. Yet the successful development of a
modernised linen industry, and later a shipping industry, in and

around Belfast led to the existence of an industrialised region in the north-east. This was not only a contrast to the overwhelming agricultural bias of the Irish economy, but, since the north-east's interests were broadly compatible with those of industrialised Britain, at a time when the economic interests of the two islands were opposed to each other, the area was in effect an economic, as well as a religious, Trojan horse in the Irish camp.

Patterns of trade between Ireland and the outside world were also seriously affected by British policies. In the late seventeenth and early eighteenth centuries any threat to the interests of British producers was eliminated by government action; for example, in the face of competition in wool, not only were prohibitive duties imposed on exports to England, but in 1699 exports of wool to any market were prevented by act of parliament. The irony of this situation was that the major victims of Britain's thorough-going mercantilism were to be found in the colonial class upon which Britain relied to maintain her presence in Ireland. By the end of the eighteenth century when they showed some disturbing signs of imitating their American counterparts, their grievances were answered by the creation of an Irish parliament in Dublin; the garrison had to be maintained. Nonetheless, Irish overseas trade remained vulnerable. Much of this trade was overdependent on one type of product – agricultural produce – and a large part was dependent on the British market (to which British policy had directed it in 1776). Trade, and indeed the Irish economy as a whole, was subjected to the vagaries not only of the market but of nature, with devastating consequences: in the Great Famine of the eighteen-forties the Irish population fell by about twenty per cent. About a million died of fever and starvation and another million emigrated. This experience was further corroboration that British management of the Irish economy did not work; governments steeped in a *laissez-faire* economic philosophy which was harsh but successful in England simply could not grasp the fact that the Irish economy was different. 'In the final analysis it was less the lack of mineral than of mental resources that inflicted on Ireland the slowest rate of growth of national income in western Europe, about 0.5 per cent per annum, between 1848 and 1914.'[7]

But of course by the nineteenth century, Ireland had been a British dependency for hundreds of years. Britain's strategic fears had not diminished, and a complex pattern of economic motivation and vested interests permeated relations between the two islands. British control of Ireland was a constant of Westminster policy; all that varied were the constitutional forms under which it might operate. Before the defeat of James II in 1691 these had been 'almost chaotic'[8], but under the new regime Ireland was kept on a tight rein, so tight in fact that Britain ran the risk of antagonising not only the catholic majority, which had been firmly placed in a position of inferiority by the penal laws introduced at the end of the seventeenth century, but the loyal protestant settler class as well. The latter formed militia groups — the Volunteers — in the seventeen-seventies in order to counter threats of invasion from the continent, but these soon became the vehicle of colonial interests, inspired by the American example. Consequently, the British felt it necessary to accede to the demand for a separate Irish parliament in 1782. This body, known as 'Grattan's Parliament' after its principal advocate Henry Grattan, was restricted in its representation to the wealthy protestant class and its legislation was enacted only on the advice of British ministers. It was in effect a device whereby Britain gave her colonists continued protection and a measure of local freedom in exchange for the latter's guarantee of Irish quiescence.

However, the abortive rising of 1798 and the French military intervention of that year demonstrated the failure of the Irish colonists to maintain order in their own house. In spite of the swift and inexpensive military response by the government, the seriousness of the threat posed to British security should not be under-estimated. At that time Ireland contained one-third of the population of the British Isles and the catholics — three-quarters of the Irish population — were disaffected[9]; what is more, the intervening power represented not a traditional dynastic rivalry but the new and potent ideology of popular sovereignty. A more direct form of control was deemed necessary, and in 1800 the Act of Union was passed, thereby bringing Ireland under the control of the British parliament and government.

With this measure of constitutional integration, Ireland formally became merely a part of the United Kingdom of Great Britain and Ireland. But in practice she remained in the position of a political dependency.[10] Moreover, the form of this constitutional arrangement contained serious obstacles to any future change in her status. As a parliamentary statute, its repeal could be, and was, blocked by a conservative House of Lords, until the eve of World War I, while at the same time it was presented as a final settlement of the Anglo-Irish constitutional relationship, thereby arousing expectations of 'perpetual security' on the part of the protestant minority in Ireland.[11]

The Act of Union was the setting for Anglo-Irish relations up to 1921, and was a powerful influence in determining the forms of the Irish nationalist response to British rule. On the one hand, with its focus on parliamentary representation in London rather than Dublin, the Act encouraged parliamentary agitation at Westminster in order eventually to regain the now idealised *status quo ante* — domestic parliamentary autonomy. On the other hand, given the inherent constitutional obstacles the Act offered to the attainment of this objective, it encouraged more radical forms of nationalism, whose goal was complete separation. That Irish nationalists continually found it difficult to decide on their ultimate objective, or on the means they could employ to attain it, is hardly surprising, the more so given the increasing disparity in power which developed between Ireland and Britain during the nineteenth century. 'The experience of being assimilated by, and resisting assimilation into, a powerful and alien empire — perhaps the master-culture of the nineteenth century — was truly traumatic.'[12]

*   *   *

Ireland, then, was by virtue of location closely bound up in British strategic and economic interests to the extent that she was treated as a political dependency and even formally integrated with Britain. In this sense she was an object of inter-state politics, an often inconvenient but, for some, profitable piece of territory which at the very least had to be denied to others. But Ireland was also concerned in international relations as a people, a people which maintained a strong cultural identity even when living far from the land with which this identity was associated. 'Emigrant Ireland' played an important role in the achievement of statehood, and to some degree still does in the external policies of the Irish state.

The Great Famine of the eighteen-forties was the high-water mark of Irish emigration, yet for centuries before, emigration had been a persistent feature of Irish life.[13] Seasonal migration to Britain was established by the seventeenth century, and Irishmen with military or religious vocations often went further afield. In the eighteenth century a combination of religious persecution (of protestant dissenters as well as catholics) and poverty saw the beginnings of regular emigration to North America. But continental Europe was still a major destination, and large numbers of Irishmen were recruited to serve in continental armies, particularly that of France. The wealthier catholics, denied educational opportunities at home, sought them at the Irish colleges, mainly in France, Spain and Italy.

After the Napoleonic wars, North America became a more attractive destination with cheaper fares and a more ready acceptance of catholics, and the Famine years confirmed this change in the pattern of emigration. But, more than that, the Famine raised the phenomenon of emigration to a different level; it is no exaggeration to speak in terms of the 'Irish diaspora' from this time on. Between 1845 and 1855, 70,000 Irish went to Australia, 340,000 to Canada, and 1,481,000 to the United States. Reliable figures for emigration to Britain are not available, though one estimate puts the number of Irish in Britain in 1855 at over a quarter of a million.[14] Emigration continued throughout the nineteenth and early twentieth centuries, and a population which stood at about eight million in 1841 was reduced to under four and a half million by the time the Anglo-Irish Treaty was signed eighty years later.

Emigration to the United States was to have particular significance for Ireland's political future. While Irish communities in Australia, New Zealand and Canada — and indeed in Britain — often displayed similar characteristics, the sheer extent of the development of the Irish community in the United States, in conjunction with that country's emergence as the first great centre of power outside Europe, makes it a case apart.[15] During the fifty years following the Great Famine, about three million Irish men and women arrived in the United States. They formed readily identifiable communities which made considerable demands on the loyalties of their members. The Irish immigrant generally brought few material possessions and few skills beyond those of the peasant who had lived at subsistence level on another man's land. He was equipped not for the life of the expanding frontier, but for unskilled labour in the vast urban centres on the east coast.

His intense catholicism gave him and his fellows a distinctive cultural identity.

These characteristics, and the fact that immigration was often of large numbers over short periods, frequently aroused hostility from other Americans. At first the Irish responded by organising their lives around their own community and, in so doing, many of them whose outlook in Ireland had been limited to the parish became aware of their common national origins. They were able to reconcile their nationality with several important American political values. Both Irish and Americans had a tradition of hostility to England; they rejected the notion of English superiority and both enjoyed a history of liberal revolution. They were confronted by the challenge of moving from a position of obvious and humiliating inferiority to one of respectability in American society.

Promoting the cause of Irish nationalism was one of the principal means by which the new immigrants could meet this challenge. They did not lack memories of misery under British rule and it was immaterial to them whether these tribulations were the result of malice or stupidity. Their hatred of Britain and support for Irish independence provided them with an issue which could transcend the concerns of ward politics in which their more ambitious fellows generally made their mark. They had the means to act, to raise funds, provide men and leadership, disseminate propaganda, and to press their own government, safely outside the reach of British coercion. They could help their relatives in Ireland – and, by so doing, improve their own political and social standing. It was not until the early twentieth century that the tension inherent in this 'hyphenated loyalty' would resolve itself one way or the other.[16]

The emergence of Irish-American nationalism as a political force naturally served to stimulate nationalism in Ireland. But it also served to make Anglo-Irish relations, in spite of their formal constitutional setting, an international issue. 'However much successive British governments affected to regard the condition of Ireland as essentially a domestic issue, the great migration ensured that a domestic issue was precisely what it would never be again.'[17] It would provide increased temptations for Britain's enemies to intervene, and would complicate her relations with her friends and particularly with the United States. Irish nationalism now had an external lever which would at least partly compensate for its lack of military power.

But if 'Ireland overseas' became an important element in the politics of Irish nationalism in the second half of the nineteenth century, it also represented in broader terms the development of an external aspect of Irish cultural identity which can later be traced in some aspects of Irish foreign policy. Briefly, it led the Irish to regard themselves as an important influence in international affairs. Ireland, just as much as Britain, was seen as a 'mother country'; 'she owned, perhaps still owns, a ghostly empire of a sort.'[18] This image was to make it difficult for many Irish nationalists to accept the relationship with Britain which was to be offered to them in 1921 — that of dominion status. Having repudiated their own settler class (in the form of protestant unionism), they did not see their position as analogous to that of Australian or Canadian settlers. At the same time, the notion of possessing 'an empire of a sort' also sometimes sat uneasily with the image of Ireland as a pioneer of modern anti-colonialism.[19]

However ambiguous the international influence of the Irish people may now seem to be, it was sometimes represented as a distinctive contribution to the moral education of the rest of the world. Thus Professor Eoin MacNeill, a leading nationalist intellectual in the first decades of the twentieth century, conceived of Ireland as a propagator of exemplary values.[20] This rather vague idea perhaps finds its most concrete manifestation in the long tradition of overseas missionary activity. Such missionary endeavour expanded as a consequence of the diaspora, but later in the nineteenth and early twentieth centuries Irish missionaries were to be found beyond the geographical limits of the diaspora, in Africa, India and the Far East.[21] This has been seen as a form of 'religious imperialism'.[22] It is difficult to assess the political consequences of the phenomenon, but it was certainly to have a general influence on attitudes, and sometimes on policies, when the Irish state was established.[23]

*   *   *

It was during the nineteenth century that Ireland's participation in international relations — whether as a territory or as a people — became a persistent feature of Anglo-Irish relations. During the same period, Irish nationalism assumed the diverse, sometimes disorganised, forms which were ultimately to clash, both over objectives and methods, in the years surrounding the Treaty of 1921. These nationalist movements devised and pursued their own 'foreign policies', and the attitudes they held towards international issues and the relationships they established as it were 'under the diplomatic counter', were to provide the foundations for the development of Irish foreign policy after 1921. World War I was to demonstrate the inadequacy of some of these attitudes and relationships, but before seeing how this occurred, the long, often frustrating years in which they were developed must be examined.

Chapter 2

The Foreign Policies of Irish Nationalism 1798-1913

When we have undermined English misgovernment we have paved the way for Ireland to take her place among the nations of the earth. And let us not forget that that is the ultimate goal at which all we Irishmen aim.

Charles Stewart Parnell, 1880

Placed by nature in the shadow of one of the great powers of Europe – the cradle of modern international relations – Ireland had been involved in strategic and diplomatic rivalries for centuries before she became an independent state; moreover, the mass emigration of the mid-nineteenth century ensured that Anglo-Irish relations became and remained an international issue. These facts, beyond the control of human agencies, were important elements in the development of the Irish variants of the major political phenomenon of nineteenth-century Europe – the rise of the national state in the place of its dynastic predecessor.

Irish nationalism during that century was anything but monolithic, either in its goals, methods or organisations. But underlying the thought and actions of all nationalist groups was the central problem of Anglo-Irish relations. Strictly speaking, this problem was a conflict between centralising and peripheral interests within a single state, the United Kingdom, to be resolved either by negotiation or force or by some combination of the two. Yet in so far as Irish nationalists perceived the central government to be alien and neglectful of the values which they professed, and wished to replace it with some form of government of their own, they tended to behave in many respects as representatives of a government *de jure*. In this sense their behaviour *vis-à-vis* Anglo-Irish relations may be seen as a sort of 'foreign policy in embryo', with consequences which were ultimately reflected not only in the creation of a new state, but also in the foreign policy of that state towards its nearest neighbour.

But Anglo-Irish relations were also an international issue; that is to say, the aims and actions of Irish nationalists were not contained within the boundaries of the United Kingdom but impinged on the behaviour of governments of other states and of groups and individuals within them. Many Irish nationalist groups were what are now known as 'transnational actors'. Transnational relations have been defined as 'contacts, coalitions, and interactions across state boundaries that are not controlled by the central foreign policy organs of governments.'[1] Such relations involve bodies such as multinational business, churches, trade unions — and revolutionary organisations — which operate in more than one state. They may seek to influence, or resist the influence of, governments, but the latter do not necessarily participate in all their dealings. Transnational relations form the bulk of all international interactions; indeed, the formal intergovernmental interactions, whether diplomatic, military or economic, may be seen as the tip of an iceberg of transnational relationships.

Transnational actors often pursue their own foreign policies, and this was the case with the most important Irish nationalist groups which sought external support in the shape of funds, arms, men or diplomatic and public pressure. These nationalist bodies approached governments outside the United Kingdom as well as other non-governmental groups with similar interests. In this way, like governments, they maintained foreign relations, though they were often unable to employ similar procedures. But Irish nationalists, unlike multinational oil companies or the great religious movements, did not see themselves as being transnational actors in perpetuity. It was hoped to be a transitory status, to be replaced by national independence, and this ultimately (though not always) meant an aspiration towards statehood. It is relevant, therefore, to ask what inheritance nationalists left to their governmental successors, in the form of guidelines, aspirations and expectations regarding the external purposes of Irish statehood. What was their vision of Ireland's place in the world? In so far as such a vision did exist, and was articulated, it is possible to conceive of a 'foreign policy image' of Irish nationalism, as well as the external relationships which were actually established.

*   *   *

Before World War I, Irish nationalism pursued almost as many foreign policies, in the senses outlined above, as it contained different groups, objectives and strategies. It is necessary therefore to identify the major developments in Anglo-Irish relations under the Act of Union and to examine the ways in which the various groups contrived to formulate and execute their foreign policies in their struggle with British governments.[2]

The Act of Union of 1800 was itself the result of a sequence of events[3] which foreshadowed future developments in two respects. It marked the end of Grattan's parliament, an experiment in 'settler nationalism', in which legislative independence, or domestic autonomy, had been granted, but in which the question of an Irish role in foreign affairs had been avoided. This model was to influence some nationalists, in totally different situations, right up to 1918. On the other hand, the Act of Union was the response to one of the most celebrated examples of the nationalist perception of the possibilities of foreign support. In the event, Wolfe Tone's alliance with republican France in 1798 showed some of the limitations of this strategy. Quite apart from errors of timing and organisation, both within Ireland and between Ireland and France, there was the obvious difficulty of creating and sustaining a really effective commitment by the foreign ally. Tone did achieve a more significant military commitment than any of his successors but, without a solid political base in France, the alliance relied overmuch on the one man. Ironically, before the revolution there had been an Irish-French community of sorts, with influence in the army and the church, but this potential lever on French support had been broken by the very force with which Tone was subsequently allied. Tone's example was to be followed by later nationalists, but not before half a century had passed.

The major figure in Irish politics in the fifty years after Tone's rising was Daniel O'Connell. Following his success in mobilising mass opinion in Ireland to gain catholic emancipation in 1829, he turned his attention to the question of Anglo-Irish relations. In 1830 he advocated the repeal of the Act of Union, though it was not until ten years later that he founded the National Repeal Association, and embarked on a campaign of parliamentary and non-violent mass agitation, a political technique of which he was one of the greatest pioneers. But, throughout, his objective remained vague, if not negative; if the Union were to be repealed, what would take its place? When challenged that he sought no more than a return to the domestic autonomy of Grattan's parliament, albeit reformed and based on catholic as well as protestant representation, O'Connell's response was veiled in generalities.[4]

A notable feature of O'Connell's approach was that it was contained within a United Kingdom political framework. In spite of the fact that he was a figure of international repute and possessed a cosmopolitan outlook, O'Connell took the line that repeal 'sought no foreign alliance'.[5] Sympathisers in France and the United States, and they were not lacking[6], were not cossetted, and the repeal movement was essentially self-supporting financially. Indeed, such external leverage as was employed when O'Connell was alive was performed by his opponents, the British government, which tried to erode the Irish clerical support by mobilising the influence of the Vatican.[7]

However, associated with O'Connell's campaign was a small group of more radical nationalists, the Young Ireland movement. Their initial emphasis was to create a sense of national identity and this led them eventually to espouse the goal of separation. Even before they came together as a group in 1842, some of them considered the implications for Ireland of war between Britain and France[8], and they had no inhibitions about seeking foreign support. In 1845, with O'Connell's movement losing its impetus, the Young Irelanders began to mark their distance from their former leader. When John Mitchel took over the editorship of the Young Ireland paper, the *Nation,* following the death of Thomas Davis, one of his first articles was based on the theme, 'England's difficulty is Ireland's opportunity'.[9] Angered by British neglect of Ireland during the Great Famine, Mitchel advocated total separation from Britain, to be won by whatever means came to hand.

Mitchel was often more radical than his colleagues in the Irish Confederation which was formed in 1847, but in the following year England experienced a 'difficulty' which gave him the chance to put into practice what he had preached. The revolution in France saw the establishment of the Second Republic which posed a threat to monarchies throughout Europe. Irish nationalists saw France as 'a deliverer of oppressed nations'[10], and in the Spring of 1848 a delegation was sent to Paris.[11] Although warmly received in the revolutionary clubs, the Irishmen were to be frustrated by diplomatic realities. The new French premier and foreign minister, Lamartine, was eager for British support to forestall a possible intervention by governments which wanted to snuff out the revolutionary infection at its source. Although he allowed himself some ambiguous oratory on the occasion of St Patrick's Day (to appease his left wing, rather than the Irish), he was happy to be pulled into line by the British ambassador, and the Irish delegation eventually left empty-handed. Although there was still talk of sending representatives to France and the United States later that year, the Irish 'revolution' of 1848 ended ingloriously in a Tipperary village. Mitchel had earlier expressed the disillusion which Irish nationalists felt with foreign support: 'we are well pleased that M. Lamartine has let us know distinctly we must rely on ourselves'.[12] It was to be the last significant appeal to continental Europe for over sixty years; subsequently, the anti-clerical tone of many continental nationalists made it difficult for Irish nationalists to establish any substantial contacts.[13]

However, 1848 does not mark the end of the quest for foreign support, but rather a change in the direction from which it was to be sought. Ten years later, Irish America had become an external resource to be exploited. A conspiratorial organisation, the Fenian movement or Irish Republican Brotherhood (IRB), was set up to link nationalists on both sides of the Atlantic.[14] Fenianism was unequivocally separatist in its aims and its association of separatism with a republican form of government and the use of physical force against British domination were subsequently to mould the behaviour of many nationalists, who refused to allow that any distinction could be made between these three different ideas. Moreover, the IRB regarded itself not as a suppliant nationalist group but as an underground government; thus was created the myth that 'the Republic' already existed *de jure* – a fiction that was to complicate the foreign policies of Irish nationalists in later years.[15]

It may be that Irish nationalists did not regard their Irish-American counterparts as being 'foreign'[16], but the fact remains that 'the opening of a systematic struggle for public opinion overseas, and the effective mobilization of the Irish communities abroad, were radical innovations in the Anglo-Irish conflict.'[17] The United States in particular gave Irish nationalism a safe organisation base, the prospects of further financial support and more active converts, and the American civil war provided many of the latter with military expertise. In 1866 this experience was put to use in a raid on the western flank of the British Empire. To attack Canada was not only a matter of logistical convenience; it also reflected the desire to provoke 'that long cherished Anglo-American war which had become so embedded in Fenian mythology.'[18] This grand strategy proved to be over-ambitious and demonstrated the Achilles heel of reliance on Irish-American support, which was ultimately influenced by American rather than Irish considerations.[19] In any case, the Fenians' military and revolutionary appetites were geater than their means allowed, and their rising in Ireland in 1867 was likewise a military fiasco. Nevertheless, the separatist tradition had been reaffirmed and was not subsequently extinguished.

But the immediate aftermath of this failure of separatism and violence was the re-emergence of the nationalist tradition inherent in the aims of Daniel O'Connell — the tradition of domestic autonomy. Its principal advocate was Isaac Butt, who proposed a federal system for the British Isles: the Irish parliament would control domestic matters, while foreign policy, defence and fiscal policy were to be reserved to an imperial parliament in which Ireland would be represented, as would the other members of the federation, England and Scotland (but not Wales, which was to be subsumed with England).[20] In 1873 the Home Rule League was founded to advance this idea and fifty-nine Home Rule candidates were elected to the Westminster parliament. The pursuit of the limited objectives of domestic autonomy, or Home Rule as it was popularly called, was to persist up to the end of World War I.

However, by the time Charles Stewart Parnell became leader of the Irish Parliamentary Party in 1880, Home Rule had become the rallying point for a much broader range of Irish nationalist opinion. The land question had come to the front of the political stage, thereby mobilising the mass of the population as a source of potential disaffection to supplement the parliamentary campaign. Irish-Americans, notably John Devoy, wished to unite nationalist forces, and some former Fenians, though not the IRB, were prepared to abandon their doctrinal rigidity in order to achieve this aim. But it was Parnell, with a genius for political leadership that owed not a little to ambiguity about the objectives he was pursuing, who became the focus of that *rara avis* of Irish nationalism, a united front.

Nevertheless, Parnell still had to confront the British government on the question of the modest claim for domestic autonomy and on the government's own ground, the Westminster parliament. In this arena, the strictly disciplined Irish Party, with eighty-six members, held the balance after the general election of 1885, and Parnell won the commitment of the Liberal leader, Gladstone, to Home Rule. However, Gladstone's party-leadership was no match for his Irish counterpart, and the defection of Joseph Chamberlain and his followers led to the defeat of the first Home Rule Bill in June 1886, by 343 votes to 313. Even had the result been otherwise, there remained the veto of the conservative House of Lords, now firmly committed to the maintenance of the Union and inclined to view the mildest measure of domestic autonomy for Ireland as an intolerable threat to the survival of the British Empire. In spite of this rebuff, Parnell managed to keep his nationalist coalition intact, until his involvement in divorce proceedings led Gladstone to repudiate him in 1890, thereby splitting the Irish Parliamentary Party.

A significant feature of Parnell's Home Rule coalition was the extent of external support it gained, and on which it depended to finance its parliamentary activities; for unlike British parliamentarians many of the Irish members had inadequate private sources of income. As early as 1879 Parnell had visited the United States and had raised considerable funds for famine relief and the land agitation.[21] In 1883 his lieutenants, John Redmond and John Dillon, made successful tours in Australia, while in the same year the Irish National League of America was set up in order to establish a power base comparable to that which Parnell had organised in Ireland and Britain. Although it never achieved the political cohesion of the latter, it was a valuable source of funds until it started to disintegrate in 1890, just before Parnell's downfall.

Part of Parnell's influence in the United States lay in his ability to attract the support of the more respectable (and wealthy) elements in the Irish-American community because of the constitutional framework of his policies. But he also gained support from some important extremists, and particularly from John Devoy's Clan na Gael (United Brotherhood) which had been founded in 1867. This secret society formed a joint revolutionary directory with the IRB in 1877, which had originally allowed for a representative from Australia and New Zealand, thus forming a sort of 'Irish International'. It also had pretensions to a diplomatic role: its officers made themselves and their cause known to the Russian ambassador in Washington at the height of Anglo-Russian tension in 1875, while two years later they tried in vain to stir up the Spanish government on the question of Gibraltar:

> The Clansmen conducted their affairs as though they represented a great power. They were overwhelmed perhaps by the realization of the enormous numbers of Irish dispersed throughout the world . . . and were convinced that somehow a formula could be hit upon that would unite them all.[22]

But with the fall of Parnell in 1890 and his death a year later, unity was the great absentee from Irish nationalism. The Irish Parliamentary Party did not reconcile its differences until 1900, although, in 1893, the second Home Rule Bill had been defeated in the House of Lords. Under John Redmond the party still claimed to be independent of the British parties, but because of a deepening Conservative commitment to the Union, partly in response to the demands of Ulster protestants, it depended on Liberal support, and it was only in 1910 that the distribution of seats at Westminster compelled the Liberals to give that support. Meanwhile, the party's objective was still the limited one of domestic parliamentary autonomy, though by the time the third Home Rule Bill was published in 1912 some Home Rulers were coming to appreciate the need for full financial autonomy as well.[23]

Redmond renewed the party's links with the Irish-American community.[24] In 1901 he organised the United Irish League to counteract extremist groups such as Clan na Gael. Between 1903 and 1910, either he or his principal lieutenants made annual fund-raising tours in North America, which were 'consistently successful . . . with large audiences and excellent publicity'.[25] Between 1900 and 1910 they raised at least £70,000.[26] These funds were an important asset to the party, enabling it to maintain its electoral activities throughout the country and thus remain the principal organised force in Irish nationalism.

Nevertheless, this revival of limited, parliamentary nationalism occurred against the background of a less cohesive, but ultimately more significant, revival of the separatist tradition. During the

eighteen-nineties there was renewed interest in cultural nationalism; a new generation was introduced to the vision of national
independence through the Gaelic Athletic Association and the
Gaelic League, which proved to be recruiting bases for the IRB.
The socialist leader, James Connolly, arrived in Ireland in 1896 to
found the Irish Socialist Republican Party and to attempt to
synthesise socialist and nationalist aspirations. Two years later
there were reminders both of the militant past of separatism, with
the centenary of Tone's rising, and of the evils of British domination, with the Boer War. The latter event was opposed by Home
Rulers, but separatists went much further in their protests and
publicly discouraged recruiting in the British army.

However, the organisation of separatist forces was chaotic. The
IRB still existed, but was in the throes of a change in leadership
which did not become effective until 1910. The major focus of
activity was a body called Sinn Féin ('Ourselves'), established in
1905 under the leadership of Arthur Griffith. It attempted to
unite separatist opinion on the basis of a policy of withdrawal
from the Westminster parliament and establishing an alternative
administration (following the example of the Hungarians in 1867)
and its 1908 Constitution laid down several 'severely practical
objectives' to further this aim.[27]

In contrast to the success of Redmond in the United States,
separatists received little financial support.[28] The Clan na Gael
had also enjoyed an internal reconciliation in 1900 and made
overtures to the Russian and French ambassadors at the time of
the Boer War, and to the Russian ambassador after the Anglo-
Japanese alliance of 1902. But the attendance of the Russian
ambassador at Irish-American picnics was of no consequence, and
although the Clan gave Sinn Féin some financial support from
1907 on, it did not prevent the latter's decline in the face of what
appeared to be the imminent success of Home Rule from 1910.
The reorganisation of the IRB, however, was aided by Irish-
American sources, especially when Thomas Clarke returned to
Ireland in 1907 and acted as liaison between the two arms of
the movement. The significance of this, however, was not apparent
before 1914.

*   *   *

Thus, by the beginning of the twentieth century, certain elements of the foreign policies of Irish nationalism were firmly established. As far as the quest for external support and the consequent development of relationships outside the United Kingdom were concerned, two points are clear. There was a marked swing away from continental Europe as a source of support and towards the United States. Further, assistance was seen as increasingly important, whether it be to finance political parties or armed revolts. But what was not so clear was a definition of the eventual objective of Irish nationalism, and this affected the ways in which nationalists looked at the role of Ireland in international politics either in the present of the future.

A broad distinction can be made between two ultimate objectives — between domestic autonomy or Home Rule, and separation or 'absolute independence'. Of course history shows many variations of each type; Home Rulers often differed on the nature of the constitutional arrangement, while separatists could simultaneously advance different socialist, republican or 'sinn féin' versions of what they meant by independence. History also shows that these different objectives could become blurred, depending on the prevailing situation and the exigencies of political tactics, not to mention the interplay of changing personalities. Yet it is an important distinction, posing as it did the fundamental question: was Ireland to be a sovereign state or not? Or, in other words, were Irishmen to be 'consumers' of their own foreign policy or of that of another government?

The answers given to these questions by the various elements of Irish nationalism reveal an important aspect of Irish political culture — that 'general pattern of people's attitudes and beliefs about, and their knowledge of, politics and political phenomena' which helps 'explain many of the political institutions in Ireland and much of the political behaviour of the Irish people.'[29] This aspect, the external aspect, may be called the 'foreign policy image'.[30] It is composed of attitudes towards international politics in general, towards the purposes of a state's activity in this sphere, the means such a state would employ and the ways in which its activity would be related to political institutions. Given the fact that there was no Irish state in existence, the foreign policy image can be seen above all in the aspirations and expectations relating to the future exercise of foreign policy. In that future, when statehood had been achieved, decision-makers would be influenced not merely by realities which surrounded them, but by the foreign policy image which had been handed down to them. Indeed, a clearly defined foreign policy image conceivably could be an important determinant of the way in which policy-makers would interpret the world about them.

On the face of it, those nationalists who pursued the goal of domestic autonomy, by virtue of that fact possessed no foreign policy image, or at least their foreign policy image related to the actions of a government whose domain was broader than their nation. Indeed this was the case for some, but by no means all, such nationalists; they found it relatively easy to think of the Irish nation, or 'domestic politics', and international politics as separate spheres of political behaviour. They lived in an age when this assumption was widely held. The dramatic events in the international arena, whether diplomatic or military, did not impinge on national societies in the regular and frequent ways that are characteristic of the twentieth century. Even major wars did not involve all citizens, though the French Revolutionary and Napoleonic campaigns had provided some taste of what was to come. Ireland's geographical isolation could only have reinforced this view: did not the might of Britain, emerging as the world's greatest power, protect the Irish from the vagaries of international anarchy?

Some of the greatest Irish leaders did indeed see Britain in this light. Daniel O'Connell saw the British political system as markedly superior to others and therefore worth defending. No matter how neglectful particular governments might be of Ireland, or India, in which O'Connell was also interested, the potential for good government lay at Westminster. There was no fundamental difficulty about accepting Westminster's direction of imperial affairs; thus, 'on constitutional issues, such as the relations between Great Britain and Ireland in the fields of foreign and military policy . . . [O'Connell] was often vague'.[31] He considered the question of Irish representation in the imperial parliament in order to have some influence on foreign policy, but when this federal solution was attacked by the Young Irelanders, he seems to have acceded to their pressure without much heart-searching.[32] Butt was in the same mould. At Westminster he took a keen interest in British foreign policy and had always acted on a vision of imperial partnership; he 'believed in the empire which Irishmen had helped to create; he believed that they could find a full national expression within its framework; emotionally he was moving towards an ideal of commonwealth which was politically in advance of his time.'[33]

Among the later Home Rule leaders, this tradition had its advocates. When John Redmond visited Australia as a young man in 1883 he maintained that it was 'undesirable that two countries so closely connected geographically and socially, and having so many commercial and international ties, should be wholly separated, or that any dismemberment of the Empire, which Ireland has had her share in building up, should take place.'[34] Although he was later to talk to American audiences rather ambiguously about 'national independence', he was sincere and consistent in insisting that independence should take place within an imperial framework.[35] Redmond's principal lieutenant, John Dillon, was a rather different case. He was by no means so emotionally wedded to the virtues of empire, but he had a keen and well-informed interest in international politics. In the years leading up to World War I he saw himself not so much as an Irish Home Ruler but as 'one of that group of Liberals . . . who were deeply concerned about the peace of the world and the growing likelihood of a clash between the armed alliances.'[36] His frequent parliamentary interventions marked him out as a constructive critic of the foreign policies of particular British governments, rather than a sworn enemy of Britain's status as a great power.

But what of the rank and file of the Home Rule movement? Before the first Home Rule Bill of 1886 some of Parnell's parliamentary colleagues were active in debates on imperial policy, though their views were diverse and their contributions were rarely distinctive. If any common attitude existed it was the often implicit assumption that, once given Home Rule, Ireland would be a loyal member of the British Empire.[37] But it is difficult to find here the positive enthusiasm for empire of a Butt or a Redmond. Later, the parliamentarians in the movement became increasingly constrained by the very nature of the Home Rule strategy. Once domestic autonomy was accepted as the 'final settlement', even if this was only because it seemed the most that could be obtained in the face of British (and Ulster unionist) intransigence, it followed that foreign or imperial affairs were not the proper concern of the

Irish. Moreover, the tightly disciplined Irish Party attempted self-consciously to keep its distance from its Liberal allies, to restrict its attention to what could be seen as purely Irish matters; Dillon's interest in Persia or Morocco did not win him any popularity from his Irish colleagues.

But in addition to these tactical exigencies, supporters of Home Rule often appeared to have an instinctive distaste for anything to do with foreign policy. Isaac Butt's concern for British policy during the crises in the Near East in 1877–78 provoked a revolt by his followers – and especially by the young John Dillon – which was one cause of his replacement as leader of the party. The federal proposals, whereby Irish representatives could attempt to influence external issues through a central parliament, had traditionally been suspect in the eyes of separatists and were anathema to Parnell's more extreme followers. A studied indifference towards foreign policy in its imperial guise became both a manifestation of national dignity and of tactics.

In this respect, as in others, it was Parnell who reflected most faithfully the mood of the supporters of Home Rule. It was a mood, however, shrouded in ambiguity. The first Home Rule Bill of 1886 made no provision for Irish influence on foreign affairs, and Joseph Chamberlain underlined the implications of this: 'Ireland is to have no part in the arrangement of Commercial Treaties by which her interests may be seriously affected . . . and Irishmen under this scheme are to be content to be sent to battle and to death for matters in which Irish members are to have no voice in discussing or determining.'[38] Parnell blandly accepted the Bill as a 'final settlement', without entangling himself in Chamberlain's snare, but much in his behaviour suggests that 'final' did not mean 'forever'.

Parnell had no personal warmth towards England. He could appeal to separatists with sentiments both noble and equivocal: 'No man has the right to set a boundary to the onward march of a nation.'[39] On a more practical level he was concerned with the question of tariff autonomy, but in so far as he did articulate his ideas on the constitutional relationship between Britain and Ireland he moved towards an acceptance of Irish representation at Westminster – the federalism for which he had earlier shown so little enthusiasm.[40] However, his commitment to future policy was always tentative. For a decade he kept everyone guessing as to his ultimate objective – and to a certain extent he still does. To one historian he was 'a Nehru or Makarios working within the British constitution, rather than a precursor of Botha, Smuts or Cosgrave;' [41] to another 'his real object was a new form of empire moderated by dominion status for the old dependencies.' [42] Not the least tragic consequence of his sudden fall in 1890 was that he left the Home Rule movement – a significant link in the Irish parliamentary tradition – in a state of suspended animation. This encouraged an attitude of both studied and instinctive indifference towards international politics which offered few guidelines for parliamentarians of the future apart, perhaps, from a yearning to be untouched by the external environment. Domestic autonomy thus contained two inherently contradictory foreign policy images – participation in an imperial coalition of states and isolation.

It might be thought that adoption of the separatist goal, independent statehood, would have led to more coherent and clearer foreign policy images than this. Yet it was not until the decade before World War I that such images began to emerge, and hesitantly even then. Separatists were sometimes confused and usually content with generalities when they thought about Ireland's diplomatic future. Before the Famine the Young Irelanders flirted with the idea of federalism. Thomas Davis wrote of 'sharing' control of foreign policy with England; however, he did not resolve the difficulties which would arise, firstly, because Irish interests would be in a parliamentary minority and, secondly, because, in any case, foreign affairs tended to elude parliamentary control.[43] In 1845, Michael Joseph Barry 'came close to proposing something like a commonwealth solution'[44], but more typical was the essentially tactical, short-term vision of John Mitchel: 'The Irish people are little concerned in the complicated foreign policy of England, save as it may bring the crisis, big with fate to us and ours, that is assuredly coming upon us . . .'[45] Fenians were if anything less inclined to speculate about the problems of the future they sought; they 'had no programme past violent national revolution.'[46]

This neglect of ancillary goals by separatists was not altogether surprising. They had chosen a difficult, almost impossible, objective and the immensity of their immediate task restricted their vision of what lay beyond its completion; 'even the wisest regarded the achievement of independence as an end and not as a beginning.'[47] The sacrifices to be made for independence could be justified only by regarding independence as the panacea for all Ireland's problems, whether internal or external, and if it were indeed such, why bother about the future? A persistent strain of romanticism reinforced this tendency to neglect the consideration of the future. The rebirth of an idealised past was sufficient for many — 'a nation once again' was Davis's most popular legacy. An inclination towards a doctrinaire way of thinking, focusing on abstract ideals, and encouraging 'an atmosphere . . . hostile to pragmatism and compromise, favourable to visionary idealism'[48], was another element of Irish culture which hindered the development of political realism.

Meanwhile, the consideration of the means to be employed proved all-absorbing; 'only too often, in Ireland, as in other nations, the purpose of nationality was forgotten in the immediate struggle for independence.'[49] Moreover, Irish nationalism was perhaps more self-centred than other nineteenth-century nationalist movements. Nationalists 'rarely compared their political treatment with that of other subject nationalities or of minorities in Europe', and continental Europeans often found it difficult to relate the Irish case to their own views and experience.[50] Emotionally, separatists looked to Irish history for sustenance, to a golden age before the pure Gael had been corrupted by foreign interference. So far as practical politics were concerned, they became preoccupied with internal questions of great consequence, particularly the land question. And then, in the eighteen-eighties, much of separatist opinion allied itself at least temporarily to the Home Rule cause.

So it was not until the separatist revival of the early twentieth century that more attention was paid to the foreign policy image. The principal theorist of this revival was Arthur Griffith. Yet although his goal was separation, his obsession with the model of Hungary's successful bid for a share in the control of what was to become the Austro-Hungarian empire in 1867, a model which he saw principally as a means of gaining independence, obscured his view of what independence, once achieved, would entail internationally. In this respect the Hungarian example offered an inappropriate precedent for Ireland.[51] The Hungarians did exert considerable influence on the foreign policy of the empire to which they belonged, but in size they represented a distinctly more serious counterweight to Austrian power than Ireland did to that of Britain. Moreover, the Hungarians still had to work through imperial ministries of foreign affairs and defence and were also subject to some financial control from Vienna. Griffith might be excused for failing to see that this imposed rigidities which, among other things, were to make the Austro-Hungarian foreign policy system one of the least effective in the European crisis of 1914; it is less easy, however, to accept his implicit assumption that Hungarian autonomy was not seriously diminished by this arrangement.[52] It may be that Griffith justified his position by a belief in the inherent racial superiority of the Irish in an imagined Anglo-Hibernian empire, and his assumption that the 'natural' level of Irish population was in the order of twenty millions.[53]

But if Griffith's adoption of the 'Hungarian model' implied an aspiration towards leadership of an empire with world influence, which was not far removed from the view of Home Rule imperialists such as Redmond, his foreign policy image contained more down-to-earth characteristics. The most important of these was his emphasis on the generally neglected question of economic separatism.[54] In this he picked up the thread of Parnell's interest in the powers relating to economic protection but, for the basis of his arguments, went further back to the work of the German advocate of protection, Friedrich List. Overlooking List's insistence that economic nationalism was not appropriate for small economic units (which should form alliances or merge with larger economies!), Griffith tried to show how industrialisation could be developed. He advocated the import of foreign capital, the establishment of a merchant marine, and trade promotion overseas. While these practical measures were to be instituted before independence was granted by Britain, they were also seen as manifestations of an alternative government which would somehow replace that controlled from London. Thus, the proposal for consuls to promote trade abroad may be seen as an attempt to create an embryonic diplomatic service; although it was not in the event acted on seriously, Sinn Féin did attempt to negotiate with foreign governments, pressing the German government on the question of cattle exports and obtaining an interview with President Taft of the United States.[55]

Griffith's insistence on protection was accompanied by some awareness among Irish business interests of the distinctive nature of their economic problems, while a similar concern with the economic aspects of independence was shown by the socialist leader, James Connolly. Connolly's view of international relations was unambiguously socialist and in his writings he developed an anti-imperialist rationale for opposing British rule in Ireland, as well as pointing to the possibility of a politically independent Ireland remaining economically dependent unless a socialist economy was created. However, this approach did not make much impression on the nationalist leadership as a whole, although it did serve to broaden the economic basis of separatism.[56]

Connolly, like other separatists, shared a further element of the Sinn Féin policy image, which was to be of some consequence in the future – the stress on opposing recruitment to the British army. The Boer War provided much of the stimulus for this opposition. The great mass of Irish opinion was against the war, which was seen as 'organised murder promoted by the insatiable greed of the vampire Empire.'[57] Subsequently, anti-recruitment campaigns became a persistent separatist activity and one which was not unequivocally opposed by many supporters of Home Rule. The objection to participation in what were seen as Britain's rather than Ireland's wars was widespread, a forerunner of an instinctive Irish predilection for neutrality.

All of this did not add up to a very consistent foreign policy image, nor one that was articulated in great depth. When asked what Sinn Féin's foreign policy was, Griffith is alleged to have said: 'In any issue I find out where England stands. Ireland will be found on the other side.'[58] Indeed, it was not Griffith who provided the fullest attempt to spell out the implications of international politics for Irish separatism on the eve of World War I. This was the achievement of Sir Roger Casement. From the earliest days of the Sinn Féin organisation he had tried 'to get some representative Irishmen interested in "foreign policy".'[59] But Casement, as an official in the British Consular Service, well-known for his exposure of atrocities in Africa and South America, could play only an outsider's role until his retirement from the Foreign Office in 1913. On the other hand, his career had given him direct experience of the diplomatic world which no other Irish separatist possessed; he was the nearest thing to an Irish 'foreign policy specialist' at that time.[60]

Casement's foreign policy image can be seen in an article on 'Ireland, Germany and the next war', published under the pseudonym 'Shan Van Vocht' in the summer of 1913.[61] Starting from the assumption that the only hope for Irish independence lay in German victory in a European conflict, he advanced the thesis that 'Ireland, already severed by a sea held by German warships, and temporarily occupied by a German army, might well be permanently and irrevocably severed from Great Britain, and with common assent erected into a neutralised, independent European State under international guarantees.'[62] Ireland would be 'an Atlantic Holland, a maritime Belgium.'[63] The analogies might not prove to be the happiest, but Casement argued that this outcome was in Germany's interests. It would provide her with the freedom of the seas, while Irish neutrality, rather than the alternative of direct German control of Ireland, would make it impossible for Britain to gain international support in any quest to reassert her dominance over Ireland and the western approaches.

This nicely balanced structure of practical and moral considerations was, of course, shortly to be a victim of history. Casement's espousal of a balance of power theory may not have been remarkable in itself, and the emphasis on Ireland's location, as opposed to other strategic factors, is sometimes overdone; nor are the possible restrictions on a neutral Ireland's freedom of action discussed. Yet, taken in the context of 1913, his attempt to work out the implications of the existence of an Irish state in a world of states is a far cry from generalisations about 'Ireland taking her rightful place among the nations.' Several of the ideas which Casement examined in 1913 became important later. The most immediate was the implicit notion of an alliance with Germany; but more important in the long run were the general readiness to see Ireland as a part of European politics and the particular stress on some form of neutral status.[64]

Apart from Casement's views on the politics of grand strategy and Griffith's stress on protection, the only other discernible foreign policy image was a very vague one related to cultural attributes. Eoin MacNeill's notion of Ireland as an 'educator' has already been cited.[65] This view was closely related to the religious values of the catholic majority in Ireland. The one continental European question in which Irishmen had shown considerable interest after their attention had been diverted to the Irish communities in the United States was that of the Vatican, particularly in the uncertainties the latter faced with the establishment of the

Italian state.[66] For some, the activities of Ireland's missionaries were 'the only glory she possesses'; and this could result in 'a concept of Irish imperialism in which the Irish would emerge as rulers of a world-wide spiritual empire.'[67] Alternatively, Irish religious values were seen as part of a movement towards a pre-dominantly catholic united Europe.[68] Such ideas did not, how-ever, receive any overt political expression of significance.

One reason for this lay in the awkward fact that religious values, whether promoted internally or externally, were divisive in Irish politics. So divisive indeed that they posed a fundamental question for Irish separatists; if there were to be an Irish sovereign state, what were its territorial limits to be? Over what people would it exercise jurisdiction? Yet there was a long tradition amongst Irish nationalist leaders, of all persuasions, of speaking of 'Ireland' as a single, indivisible political entity.[69] There was an Irish nation and a territory called Ireland, the latter's boundaries being plainly circumscribed by sea; the island of Ireland was seen as the 'natural' locus for the Irish nation.[70] On the other hand, this view was not shared by the vast majority of protestants and their attitude of 'unconquerable distrust' was increasingly revealed as nationalist fortunes seemed to thrive in the eighteen-eighties.[71]

The focus of this distrust was the northern province of Ulster.[72] Here, and particularly in the north-east, lived the bulk of Ireland's protestants, about one-quarter of the total population. A distinc-tive feeling of cultural identity existed, largely based on religion and amounting to a sense of racial superiority.[73] In addition, there was an awareness of economic interests more akin to those of Britain than to those of the rest of Ireland, which might be threatened if Ireland as a whole were permitted to adopt pro-tectionist policies.[74] Any move that might lead to Irish indepen-dence – and Home Rule was seen as such – was to be opposed.

The reaction of Irish nationalists to this situation took several forms. Sometimes it was simply ignored, at least in the public statements of nationalist leaders.[75] If recognised, it could be dis-cussed as the artificial creation of a conspiracy organised by British imperialists.[76] In any case, it was assumed that, ultimately, British governments – Liberal governments – ruled in Ulster and would enforce the settlement of the Irish question on any local dissidents. Moreover, the nationalists' association of the whole province of Ulster with the unionist reaction allowed a degree of complacency to enter into their political calculations, and for that matter into those of British Liberals; electorally, the province was very finely balanced between nationalists and unionists.[77]

But the rationale of nationalist attitudes towards Ulster unionism was less important than its consequences. That Ulster might receive special treatment and be subtracted from the Irish political entity was, in the words of even so moderate a nationalist as John Redmond, 'an abomination and a blasphemy.'[78] The idea that the partition of the island might be an issue in the foreign policy of any future Irish state was therefore inconceivable; the Ulster question would be solved without any fundamental difficulties, as a matter of internal reconciliation after the whole island's independence, however defined, had been won. This myth of unity accounted for the principal blind spot in the foreign policy images of all Irish nationalists.

*   *   *

On the eve of World War I, therefore, in spite of the increasing dependence of Irish nationalists, whether Home Rulers or separatists, on some degree of external support, the implications of their activities for future foreign policy were perceived only in the most general or fragmentary ways by relatively few individuals in the leadership of the various groups. The attitudes of the mass of their supporters was probably more faithfully reflected in Douglas Hyde's poem, written in 1898:

> Waiting for help from France, waiting for help from Spain; the people who waited long ago for that, they got shame only.
>
> Waiting for help again, help from America, the lot who are now waiting for it, my disgust for ever on them.
>
> It is time for every fool to have knowledge that there is no watchcry worth any heed but one – Sinn Féin amháin – Ourselves Alone! [76]

However, in 1914 this mood of defiant isolation was rudely shaken by two developments, the mounting opposition of Ulster unionists and British Conservatives to Home Rule, and the outbreak of war in Europe. Traditions and images were to be tested by realities imposed by events far beyond Ireland.

Chapter 3

From Images to Reality 1914-1922

*Supported by her exiled children in America and by gallant allies
in Europe, but relying in the first on her own strength [Ireland]
strikes in full confidence of victory.*

Proclamation of the Provisional
Government of the Irish Republic, 1916

When, in 1913, Sir Roger Casement was formulating his vision of a
future Irish state in a Europe dominated by Germany, the forces
which would culminate in independence in the next decade were
already coming to the front of the political stage.[1] This process
had begun in 1910 when, following the Liberal government's
challenge to the veto power of the House of Lords, the Irish Party
found itself in a position of balance between the great British
parties, and to maintain its support, the Liberals were obliged to
introduce the third Home Rule Bill in 1912. This Bill contained
the objective of domestic autonomy as a 'final settlement' of
nationalist claims; Irish participation in foreign and imperial affairs
was to be limited to the almost certainly ineffectual influence of
a reduced number of members in the Westminster parliament.

Given the successful reduction of the House of Lords' veto to a
delaying period of two years, it seemed probable that Irish and
Liberal votes in the lower house would ensure that Home Rule
became a reality from 1914. But this constitutional timetable
proved to be the fuse to a time-bomb. Opposition from Ulster
unionists was quickly mobilised, and in 1912 was underpinned by
the enthusiastic, if not reckless, support of the British Conservative
Party under Bonar Law. This party's championship of the Ulster
unionists' cause was first acknowledged in a series of suggested
modifications to the provisions of the Home Rule Bill which
would allow for the supposedly temporary exclusion of Ulster.
Redmond was confronted with an heretical proposition – the

partition of the island — and was increasingly compelled to move away from the principle of unity.

As Asquith's Liberal government wavered, a more sinister element emerged. In January 1913 the unionists organised a well-drilled paramilitary body, the Ulster Volunteer Force, later to be armed in notorious gun-running exploits. The nationalist reaction was seen in the formation of a similar force, the Irish Volunteers, in November of that year, and this was supplemented by the socialist Irish Citizen Army. Serious threats of violence were thus added to bitter constitutional and parliamentary controversy, which split asunder both Irish and British politics.

Redmond tried to meet the challenge by insisting on controlling the Irish Volunteers through his own nominees. However, the situation was fast developing beyond the capacity of normal constitutional processes. In March 1914, the British army officer corps showed itself to contain at best conditional supporters of government policy, and gun-running and drilling continued; then, on 24 July, a last-ditch effort to reach a constitutional compromise broke down. However, the climacteric of the struggle for Irish nationalism was not to arise in the context of a civil war in the United Kingdom, for within days violence on a far greater scale took place. International war in Europe would be the setting in which the foreign policies of Irish nationalists were most severely tested.

The initial Irish response to the outbreak of war came from Redmond, whose party still represented the bulk of Irish nationalist opinion. The decisions on which his policy was based were, nonetheless, essentially personal; consultation seems to have been limited to a brief and hurried exchange with two colleagues in the House of Commons.[2] Moreover, they reflected the extent of his personal commitment to the British Empire. On 3 August he declared his support for British objectives in the war, and pledged the Irish Volunteers to the defence of Ireland, thereby releasing British garrison troops for front-line service. But on 20 September he went further than this and committed the Volunteers themselves to the front. In effect these decisions formed a bargain with Britain, for on 18 September Home Rule had become law, though its application was suspended for twelve months, or longer if the war persisted.

Apart from Redmond's personal loyalty to Britain and his

views on the morality of the war, his policy has a certain rationale in the context of the Anglo-Irish relations. It marked a continuation of the alliance with the Liberals, which had been central to Home Rule strategy since 1886, and might undermine the emotive charge of the unionists that Irish nationalists were fundamentally disloyal and therefore could not be trusted even with domestic autonomy. Above all, it was a policy based on the commonly held assumption that the war in Europe would be short; the costs of the gesture — as measured by the loss of public support in Ireland — would be relatively low.

Initially, in spite of serious reservations amongst his colleagues and the immediate loss of financial support from Irish-Americans[3], Redmond's gamble looked promising. At a time when war was still seen either as a useful means of character formation or a rare opportunity for employment, the general response was favourable, and was this not a war to preserve 'the rights of small nations'? In September 1914 even the Volunteers on the whole accepted their ticket to destruction with equanimity; about 170,000 of them showed their approval by following Redmond's leadership, under the new name of 'National Volunteers'. Only 11,000, still called the 'Irish Volunteers', showed their separatist instincts by refusing to leave Ireland.[4]

But gradually the bargain collapsed; the war went on beyond the original estimate of twelve months. Redmond's Volunteers, dispersed throughout the British army without any recognition of national identity, were sharing only in mass slaughter and their suffering was reflected in disillusion at home; in 1915 a bishop could say 'it is England's war not Ireland's.' The Irish Party's parliamentary position was gravely weakened in May 1915 when the Liberal government was replaced by a national coalition, including leading unionists such as Sir Edward Carson. Constitutional tampering with the suspended Home Rule Act now became more likely, but, given the traditional view that for an Irishman to serve in a British government was the ultimate in political corruption, Redmond could not fight his battles within the cabinet. In January 1916 he had enough political influence left to prevent conscription being introduced in Ireland — a move which would have made a nonsense of his attempt to deal with the British government as a near equal. Then, three months later, the insurrection in Dublin allowed his opponents to claim that he had failed to deliver his side of the bargain; Irish nationalism was capable of the utmost infamy when Britain was in danger. From that time on, the Home Rule nationalists needed more than their usual share of political miracles.

Separatist foreign policy was the mirror-image of Redmond's 'alliance' with Britain; England's difficulty was to be the occasion of an alliance with England's enemies.[5] In 1914, the initial public response of the separatists could be seen in the split in the Volunteer movement and the formation of an Irish Neutrality League, which for a short period carried out the old Sinn Féin policy of anti-recruitment. But the real focus of policy was the clandestine IRB, which infiltrated the leadership of the dissident Irish Volunteers. The IRB had decided in August 1914 to mount an insurrection during the war and to look for support from Irish-Americans and from the German government, later during the rising to be referred to as Ireland's 'gallant allies in Europe'.[6]

There were widely differing interpretations, however, of the purpose of this German alliance. For the IRB leaders, such as Pearse, Clarke and McDermott, it represented, above all else, a source of military supplies; military decisions and the actual fighting would remain an Irish preserve. For those accepted leaders of the Volunteers who were outside this conspiratorial group, such as Eoin MacNeill, a rising would be only a defensive measure in response to a provocative act by Britain, such as the imposition of conscription in Ireland. Support from Germany was seen in this light. But for Casement an alliance with Germany was critical, not merely in order to obtain military aid, but because he hoped and believed that Germany would be the dominant power in post-war Europe.[7] Hence he took it upon himself to act as the representative of Irish separatists and negotiate the terms of an alliance with the German government.

But the German alliance amounted to very little militarily. At the beginning of the war John Devoy's Clan na Gael in the neutral United States had established relations with the Germans, and the Clan, though pressed for funds, paid for Casement's visit to Germany.[8] This resulted in a German declaration of support for Ireland on 20 November 1914, and on 28 December Casement and the German Under-Secretary for State, Zimmermann, signed a draft treaty. This provided for an Irish brigade, to be recruited from Irish prisoners-of-war in Germany and to be trained and

equipped by the German army for service in the cause of Irish
independence; for Casement (but not Devoy) this would mean
using the brigade to fight British imperialism in the Middle East!

But these plans came to nothing. Although the Irish abcess in
Britain's body politic may have entered the Kaiser's calculations
before 1914[9], in the event Germany did not have sufficient naval
strength to develop a serious Irish strategy. The idea of an Irish
brigade was a fiasco, and Casement's German activities were well
known to British intelligence. On the eve of the rising in 1916 a
disillusioned Casement returned to Ireland to arrest and eventual
execution in England, while a shipload of German arms was prevented from reaching its destination.

This was unfortunate for the IRB but of secondary importance.
They acknowledged the alliance in order to strengthen their
position in any future peace conference which might be dominated
by Germany.[10] And although they discussed the possibility of a
German prince becoming King of Ireland as British shells fell
about them[11], they now saw their rising as a 'blood sacrifice'
which would serve to mobilise nationalist support for their ideal of
an Irish republic. And so it proved to be. Irish-American sympathies
were immediately aroused against the British coercion which
followed the rising[12], and support for the separatist cause at home
was to develop dramatically over the next two years.

The political significance of the rising was not immediately
obvious. The strategies of both Home Rulers and separatists
seemed to be in disarray; the latter were mostly in jail and the
former in political isolation at Westminster. Nevertheless, the
British government felt obliged to make some concessions to Irish
nationalism, partly in order to appease American opinion and
facilitate the entry of the United States into the world war, and
partly to pave the way for the imposition of conscription in
Ireland.[13] So, in July 1917 the Irish Convention was organised
in Dublin, representing Home Rule and unionist opinion; separatist
organisations ignored it. The Convention's deliberations foreshadowed the Treaty negotiations of 1921. It marked a move
away from the traditional form of domestic autonomy to something approaching dominion status, and in particular the nature of
Irish financial autonomy emerged more clearly. This seemed to be
acceptable to unionists outside Ulster, but the latter were as
immovable as ever in their insistence on the exclusion of the

north-eastern six counties.[14] Meanwhile, in October 1917 the separatists created a new national front under the old name of Sinn Féin, avoiding the contentious issue of whether independent Ireland should have a strictly republican form of government.[15]

In April 1918, a time of near-panic for the allies on the western front, the British government decided to impose conscription in Ireland. The Convention had been safely and ineffectually concluded; the United States was now in the war. But the decision, which was never even executed, was momentous for Ireland – 'the decisive moment at which Ireland seceded from the Union.'[16] The Irish Party withdrew from Westminster, a protest which accorded with public opinion but which also demonstrated the failure of the party's traditional strategy.[17] It joined with Sinn Féin in 'the most massive demonstration of nationalist solidarity that had been seen since the beginning of the war.'[18] Indeed, the trauma of this event was to establish significant restrictions on future Irish political leaders faced with the issue of some form of military participation in international politics; the popular basis of Irish neutrality was enshrined in 1918.

A more immediate consequence of the conscription crisis was the final ascendancy of Sinn Féin. In the post-war general election of December 1918, although the Irish Party maintained its traditional vote, the swing of new voters to the separatist party gave it seventy-three seats to the Home Rulers' six, a complete reversal of the previous situation. Anglo-Irish relations would henceforth be conducted in a new way and in a different international setting.

*   *   *

The Sinn Féin parliamentary candidates were pledged to abstain from Westminster and create their own parliament in Dublin. This they did in January 1919 when Dáil Éireann was established, and a 'government' of five ministers was formed including a 'Minister of Foreign Affairs'. The claim for international recognition was made in a 'Declaration of Independence', and more fully in a 'Message to the Free Nations of the World'. The latter, with its emphasis on Ireland's strategic location and the 'freedom of the seas', reflected the martyred Casement's pre-war ideas on foreign policy.[19] A 'Democratic Programme' also contained foreign policy objectives, including the promotion and control of external trade and support for international co-operation in labour and social legislation.[20] Indeed, it is possible that the whole of this list of relatively advanced social aims was accepted mainly to facilitate the recognition of Ireland as a separate political unit at the imminent International Socialist Conference in Berne.[21]

The Message to the Free Nations contained the central declared aim of Sinn Féin's policy: a demand 'to be confronted publicly with England at the Congress of the Nations, that the civilised world having judged between English wrong and Irish right may guarantee to Ireland its permanent support for the maintenance of her national independence.' The origins of this 'peace conference policy' can be seen in the IRB's concern before the 1916 rising to establish a position for Ireland in a 'German' peace conference; although the controlling influence in any conference appeared less certain in 1917, IRB opinion still promoted the idea of Irish representation because 'it gave our public organisation, Sinn Féin, an objective . . . [and] served to put the Irish question on an international footing.'[22] This rather cynical and purely tactical view was not shared by Arthur Griffith, who had a profound distaste for the IRB philosophy of violence, and who had, since the end of 1916, advocated the peace conference formula with enthusiasm and sincerity.[23] As far as the public was concerned, the appeal to the peace conference was presented in the election manifesto of December 1918 as one of the primary objectives of Sinn Féin, as indeed it had appeared in previous by-elections.[24]

A small meeting of the IRB immediately prior to the publication of the Message to the Free Nations concluded that 'it was a waste of time, as the "free nations" would neither recognise our independence nor admit us to the Peace Conference.'[25] But expectations had been aroused; official delegates were appointed and a mission under Seán T. O'Kelly was sent to Paris to press for Irish representation. For those who had faith in the policy, the key to success was the United States. President Woodrow Wilson was committed to the principle of self-determination, his country was the real victor of the war, and, like any American president, he could be subjected to Irish-American pressure. The latter was not long in making itself felt.[26] In February 1919, at an Irish Race Convention in Philadelphia, a new organisation, the Friends of Irish Freedom, emerged as the focus of influence, under the veteran Fenian, John Devoy, and Judge Cohalan. It established a victory fund to ensure financial support. On 4 March its representations resulted in a sympathetic resolution from the House of Representatives, while on 6 June the US Senate voted sixty to one in favour of Irish representation at Versailles.

But where it mattered – the presidency – Irish-American pressure was to no avail. Wilson had Irish antecedents, but of the Ulster Scots variety. More important, he had a general distrust of 'hyphenated Americans' who could not decide where their national loyalties lay. He grudgingly received a delegation in March but refused to put Ireland's case at Paris. A three-man group, appointed by the Philadelphia Convention, followed him to Europe, but in making a highly publicised visit to rebellious Ireland gave him the chance to dismiss them and their cause as irresponsible. Two of them finally met him in June, where he claimed the British had vetoed any discussion of the Irish question. This was not strictly true but the claim reflected his priorities – the creation of the League of Nations and the preservation of solidarity among the allied powers. The Dáil's mission in Paris fared no better than its Irish-American allies.

Thus, by the summer of 1919, Sinn Féin's primary foreign policy strategy had failed, and the struggle for independence increasingly became one of internal terrorism and repression. Nevertheless, the First Dáil's foreign policy continued, and three major activities were pursued. First, funds had to be raised to finance the war of independence; the major source of this was the Irish-American community. Initially the Irish victory fund raised one million dollars, but about three-quarters of this was diverted into the campaign to defeat American membership of the League of Nations. Towards the end of 1920, however, the leader of the Dáil cabinet, Eamon de Valera, raised five million dollars, four million of which were to reach Ireland.[27] The second activity was the dissemination of propaganda. Outside the United Kingdom this provided the bulk of the work of the Dáil's 'diplomatic missions', of which there were eight at the time of the truce in 1921.[28] The propaganda was successfully projected of Ireland as one of several subject nations under British rule which had been cruelly and arbitrarily neglected at the time of the creation of the new world order in 1919.[29] In so far as this propaganda was seen to threaten British prestige overseas, either with regard to her moral stance or her control of other imperial possessions such as

India, it played some part in reducing the British government's will to deny independence.

It was quite another matter, though, to translate general sympathy into official recognition, where Irish representatives, working quasi-diplomatically, attempted to influence the policies of foreign governments. This task was confused by two questions. First, was recognition to be based on the claim that the Irish Republic already existed, or on the principle of self-determination, which argued that it should be allowed to exist? This provided one cause of dissent between the Dáil's American representative, Dr Patrick McCartan, and Irish-American leaders.[30] And then, what governments should be approached in the quest for recognition? McCartan favoured the revolutionary regimes in Mexico and the USSR, for it could be argued that the need for recognition was mutual. In May 1917, he had been appointed as IRB delegate to Russia, but was then diverted to the United States. In 1920 he negotiated a draft treaty with the Russian representatives in Washington, which, as well as providing for recognition and mutual aid, would have made Ireland the representative of the Catholic Church in the USSR and committed her to joining an anti-imperialist league.[31] No one in the Dáil cabinet encouraged this project, and by the time McCartan took it up again with the Russians in 1921 they rejected it because they wanted a trade agreement with Britain.[32]

De Valera's policy was that priority should be given to seeking recognition from the United States, because success there would have more influence with the British government and possibly start a recognition bandwagon. However, he did not achieve any more success than McCartan.[33] In February 1920, he suggested that Ireland's relationship with Britain should be analogous with Cuba's to the USA; this was immediately attacked by the Irish-American leadership (and privately by McCartan) as a betrayal of the claim on which recognition was based. His subsequent attempt to nail an Irish recognition 'plank' to the Republican Party's presidential platform in June 1920 was an embarrassing fiasco and met with little more enthusiasm from the Democrats. Representations to Congress, and to the President in October 1920, were made without conviction and met with no response.

The 'diplomacy' of the First Dáil demonstrated the limits of official support which could be gained even from a country, such as the United States, where much public sympathy could be mobilised.[34] But it also demonstrated serious flaws in the manner in which the Irish nationalists formulated and executed their foreign policies. To a certain extent this is hardly surprising. Even in established states the ideal of a co-ordinated, informed executive, responsive to public demands and external events, is rarely approached. The Dáil was certainly not in this category, although unlike many revolutionary movements, it was already acting within a parliamentary tradition.[35] But as far as foreign policy was concerned, the characteristics of the decision-making group posed particular problems.

The predominant personality in the group, Eamon de Valera, owed his position partly to the fact that he was the sole surviving senior military leader of the 1916 rising and partly to an undoubted capacity for establishing his personal authority, which had been strikingly manifested since then. However, he had not been one of the political planners of the separatist movement and by 1919 still had only a novice's grasp of the issues confronting him. Unlike the cynics of the IRB, he had placed his faith in winning the support of Woodrow Wilson, but was becoming disillusioned by the time he entered the hot-house of Irish-American politics in June 1919.[36] Apart from Griffith, whose attitudes towards objectives and strategies had been formed over a period of twenty years, few of his cabinet colleagues had more political experience than de Valera. Moreover, he and Griffith represented two as yet indistinct but fundamentally different political temperaments. Some, such as Cathal Brugha, adhered rigidly to Republican doctrine, which implied independence without qualification. But Griffith and Michael Collins, in spite of the latter's ascendancy in the IRB, were not purists and were prepared to consider compromise in the short term. The only member of the group with experience in international politics was Erskine Childers, whose career had given him a close acquaintance with the machinery of British government and an informed awareness of major international issues.[37] A relatively recent convert to the separatist cause, Childers was not a member of the cabinet and, although in 1921 de Valera relied increasingly on his advice, he was regarded by others, particularly Griffith, as an outsider. To a large extent he played the role of well-informed but politically peripheral foreign policy adviser that had been Casement's up to 1914.

This group had to work secretly, with little opportunity to test policy proposals against the reaction of a fugitive and infrequently assembled Dáil. It had to deal primarily with short-term contingencies arising out of a revolutionary war, and to maintain a simply defined objective — independence. It lacked intimate information about its opponents' attitudes and intentions (though local intelligence was effective). These were not the circumstances for long-term planning; means replaced ends as violence acquired its own momentum. On top of that, during the three years from mid-1918 to mid-1921 the group's leader, de Valera, spent some nine months in jail, eighteen months in the United States, and only nine months, not continuously, in Dublin with his colleagues . . . and when he finally did assume effective command in 1921 his deputy Griffith was in jail! It is not surprising that there was 'an astonishing degree of mutual ignorance' in the group.[38]

The consequences of this fragmentation of the group making the political decisions were serious for the conduct of the Dáil's foreign policy. Centralised decision-making was often impossible. A striking example of this occurred in February 1920. De Valera suggested publicly that Britain should 'declare a Monroe Doctrine for the two neighbouring islands', which would, as the Platt Amendment did to Cuba, impose restrictions on Ireland's relations with third parties.[39] This revival of Casement's case for guaranteed neutrality, though in a very different context, was immediately seen as a diminution of the claim to sovereignty. De Valera had been in the United States for over six months but apparently had consulted no one there before making his announcement. His own representative, Patrick McCartan, was privately furious but publicly defended his superior. When sent to Dublin to explain de Valera's action, McCartan found an unhappy cabinet. Divisions over the merits of the policy were only avoided by the efforts of Griffith and Collins to 'shut down the discussion'.[40] McCartan had the impression that most of the cabinet believed de Valera's 'thinking aloud' to be at the very least careless, but since their collective adulation had helped make him the personification of the Republic, they could not repudiate him. Decision-making by a combination of casual *fait accompli* and the postponement of internal debate on the fundamental issues was to reap a sad harvest in the long term.

Relationships between central decision-makers and the Dáil's representatives abroad were also difficult. Some of these representatives, particularly when they were also members of the Dáil, were inclined to take policy matters into their own hands, thereby incurring the wrath of the cabinet.[41] But the representatives were often frustrated by unnecessary delays and a lack of guidance from their superiors. McCartan's efforts to establish relations with the Russian government were a case in point. Although he made encouraging contacts in May 1919, it was not until the following spring that de Valera took them up by meeting the Russian representatives in Washington. On de Valera's instructions, McCartan then negotiated the draft treaty, which was sent to Ireland for discussion. Weeks passed before de Valera responded by asking McCartan to go to Moscow, but without the plenary powers the latter claimed were necessary if the Russians were to take his mission seriously. McCartan complained he had been given no formal consultations on the draft treaty and had received no indication of the Dáil's attitude, though he had asked for it. Another six months passed before de Valera reacted, by sending McCartan to Moscow on what proved to be a futile mission.[42] This outcome may have been what de Valera desired, but even if this were the case, the episode reflected indecision and delay rather than a finely calculated deviousness.

The uncertain, and sometimes chaotic, nature of decision-making in the Irish revolutionary movement was also to be reflected in the negotiations with the British government after the truce in the summer of 1921. The generally poor quality of information which decision-makers had received during the previous three years contributed to their serious failures of perception. There was insufficient grasp of the realistic limits of British concessions, the impregnability of the Ulster unionists, the military situation in Ireland, and, indeed, Irish public opinion.[43] Vital issues were still unresolved; 'Ireland had moved too rapidly to freedom to be unanimous as to where its essence lay.'[44] That there was confusion and ambiguity about the instructions to the delegates and the procedures to be followed was inevitable. This vagueness was seen most acutely in the problem of balancing the composition of the delegation between hardline republicans and the more pragmatic elements, such as Griffith, and in the problem of maintaining lines of communication between the delegation in London and the cabinet in Dublin. These were to be serious handicaps for the

Irish as they tried to persuade the British at last to give them an independent sovereign state.

*   *   *

The final stage in Irish nationalism's struggle for statehood opened with the declaration of a truce on 11 July 1921. It is doubtful whether this development could be attributed to the international influence of the Dáil. Although the prospects of an Anglo-Irish settlement removed a persistent impediment to satisfactory relations between the United Kingdom and the United States, there is little evidence to suggest that it was an essential prerequisite for the success of the strategic settlement between the two powers which was to be concluded in the Washington Naval Agreements of 1921–1922.[45] The truce above all reflected the effect of the military situation in Ireland on British public opinion.

Immediately after the truce, de Valera met the British premier, Lloyd George, in London. Their opening exchanges were supplemented by a correspondence in which they attempted to find a formula which would permit substantive negotiations without unacceptable prior conditions being imposed on either side. This achieved, an Irish delegation was chosen. Its leader was Griffith, for de Valera felt it more important for him to remain in Dublin to ensure the continued unity of the cabinet. On 11 October the delegation met its British counterpart in London, and nearly two months of harrowing negotiations followed before the Anglo-Irish Treaty was signed on 6 December.

The story of this critical period in Irish history has been related elsewhere.[46] Its significance for future Irish foreign policy was twofold. First, it saw the creation of a state which would formulate and conduct foreign policy on the basis of diplomatic orthodoxy; Ireland was no longer to be a transnational actor in international politics. But the period is also important because it saw the emergence of most of the fundamental issue-areas of future foreign policy, with a particular focus on Anglo-Irish relations. For the Irish this was to prove an enlightening but often painful experience; there were few solutions, and the unfolding of many intractable problems to come.

Of these fundamental issue-areas the one which aroused least controversy was that of economic relations between Ireland and

Britain. The Irish delegation was concerned with the settlement of outstanding financial claims, and insisted that Ireland had been overtaxed throughout the nineteenth century. But the major objective was to gain tariff autonomy, which was seen as vital to the development of the Irish economy and especially to industrial growth. The British government conceded the Irish case, though the final concession was held to the end of the negotiations to sweeten what would otherwise have been a very bitter pill. Thus the Irish gained the formal power to control their own economic affairs, but the granting of this power must be seen against British awareness of the underlying realities of the economic relationship between Britain and Ireland. The smaller economy, grossly undeveloped by British standards, depended heavily on trade with its larger neighbour. Both countries' financial and business concerns were closely integrated, and on the Irish side were often controlled by southern unionists. Since the 1917 Convention the latter's readiness to accept political change and the generally conservative nature of Sinn Féin's economic thinking had mollified the British government's fears — in granting economic independence, Britain had little to lose.[47]

It was a different story with Ulster. The Irish delegation aimed to maintain the 'essential unity' of Ireland as a political entity, but well before the negotiations had started the partition of the island was an established fact. Since 1918 British policy towards the demands of Ulster unionism had been made in the absence of direct nationalist pressure, following the withdrawal from the Westminster parliament of both the Irish Party and its successor, Sinn Féin. Thus when Lloyd George attempted to provide a unilateral Home Rule solution to the Irish problem in the Government of Ireland Act of December 1920, the separate identity of the Ulster unionists was recognised in the creation of a parliament and regional government for the six north-eastern counties. This government, under Sir James Craig, had already been in power more than a month before the Anglo-Irish truce began. With its supporters in the British cabinet (and one of the most intransigent, Lord Birkenhead, participating in the treaty negotiations), all it had to do in the face of nationalist demands was to sit tight. But the Dáil leadership never seems to have grasped the implications of this fact. They saw Ulster intransigence mainly as a desirable excuse to break off negotiations, should this prove necessary, because in the eyes of world opinion this would place the ball in Britain's court; thus Ulster became 'a strange abstract factor in tactics'.[48] Yet in the end the Irish delegation was manoeuvred into accepting the existence of Northern Ireland, as the six counties were now called, subject to the findings of a Boundary Commission. They believed, rather than reasoned, that this would further reduce the territory of Northern Ireland and thereby make it economically impracticable.[49]

The third major issue-area in the negotiations was security. Britain's security objectives reflected a continuing sensitivity about her traditional strategic interest in Ireland, hardly surprising in view of her recent experience in World War I, which had seen her supplies threatened by submarine warfare and which, in the rising of 1916, had raised the spectre of fighting a war on two fronts. Thus Britain demanded control of the seas around Ireland, the use of permanent naval facilities in Ireland, as well as facilities for air defence and the control of civil air links. In addition, no Irish naval force would be allowed, and land forces were to be essentially 'territorial' and no larger than those of Britain, relative to the population. Most of these demands were modified to some degree by the end of the negotiations: the absolute British naval monopoly was waived to allow Ireland 'a share' in coastal defence after five years, and her land forces were not to be described merely as 'local'. Yet, in substance the British demands were accepted by the Irish with little demur.

Of course a major change in Britain's security policy had been conceded; there was no longer to be an obvious British military presence in Ireland, in the shape of a large permanent garrison. The naval bases were few, specifically identified and capable of being run by small maintenance parties in times of peace. Moreover, the British interest in naval defence was generally seen by Irish nationalists as a valid one, and the prospect of developing an Irish naval force from nothing was financially daunting. Nevertheless, clauses 6 and 7 of the final Treaty would almost certainly involve Ireland in any future war in which Britain was a belligerent. Coming only three years after such an unhappy experience, the Irish equanimity towards this issue is amazing; only Childers, who was a secretary to the delegation, seems to have grasped its implications. Moreover, these same clauses represented a considerable departure from the Irish delegation's initial objective. This, as contained in Article V of the delegation's principal guideline, 'Draft Treaty A', entailed the status of guaranteed neutrality for Ireland.[50] Casement's legacy again emerged, though the guarantors of Irish neutrality were not to be Germany, but the British Commonwealth. Yet the British flatly rejected this notion. They had no faith in either the ability or willingness of an Irish government to defend neutrality by force of arms, and in any case required not merely the denial of Irish territory to an enemy but the possession of what were regarded as essential bases in Ireland to combat the submarine threat.[51]

However, the argument about Irish neutrality was not only an argument about the technicalities of external defence. Indeed, it exposes a fundamental difference between the Irish and British images of Ireland's future role in international politics in general. The Irish view was that 'they could best realise their destiny as a neutral independent state in political isolation like certain of the small states of Europe'[52]; the British view was that, as far as foreign policy was concerned, Ireland, particularly in the large matters of peace and war, should come under British control as exercised through Imperial or Commonwealth consultation. The divergence of these views was reflected in what proved to be the central issue-area in the negotiations – the nature of the constitutional relationship between Ireland and Britain.

The British government came to the negotiating table with an offer of dominion status for Ireland. This implied a good deal more than domestic autonomy, but precisely how much was not then certain, for the Empire was only just becoming the Commonwealth and the dominions did not always act as sovereign states. It could be argued, however, that the practical developments within the Commonwealth would lead to constitutional reform which would tend to recognise the legal equality of its members. Set against the possibilities contained in this complicated new experiment in international relations was the old and simple doctrine of Irish republicanism, which focused on an absolute rejection of any claim of Britain to act on Ireland's behalf. Allegiance to the Crown was seen as the constitutional basis of dominion status by the British; to Irish republicans, the Crown was the symbol of national betrayal.

De Valera attempted to bridge this gap with his concept of 'external association'. Ireland would not be *within* the Commonwealth, and therefore no allegiance to the Crown would be involved, but she would be an 'external associate' of the states in the Commonwealth, represented in Imperial Conferences where her government would consult with the other participants on specific matters of common concern, particularly the larger strategic and political issues. Originally the idea of guaranteed neutrality was seen as a corollary of external association, the implication being that the consultations on matters of common concern would have a strictly limited outcome in time of war. The British did not yet accept that Commonwealth members had the right to opt out of Commonwealth wars, and in an attempt to keep external association alive the Irish delegates forgot about neutrality.

But there still remained the Crown, the authority which, 'by convention, accredited representatives abroad, signed passports, and generally externalised the state in its dealings with the world at large.'[53] The British were adamant that this convention be maintained — to many, constitutional evolution in the Commonwealth was already alarmingly rapid. Some of the Irish delegation did not think a renewal of war with Britain an appropriate price to pay for rejection of a symbol, and their leader, Griffith, had after all advocated in the past a system of dual monarchy on the lines of the Austro-Hungarian Empire. The delegation and the cabinet were divided and confused about the delegation's obligation to refer any final draft back to Dublin. At last, weary, threatened and bewildered by Lloyd George, the delegation accepted dominion status and signed the Treaty.

After the delegation's return to Dublin the cabinet divided — four for the Treaty to three against, the latter including de Valera. Before and after Christmas there followed a bitter debate in private and public sessions of the Dáil. Little was said about Ulster and only Childers pointed to the diminution of independence contained in the defence clauses. The constitutional issue was all-pervading. The Dáil ratified the Treaty by sixty-four votes to fifty-seven, but mounting opposition mainly within the revolutionary army led to a civil war by the summer of 1922.[54] By the time this had ended a year later, a new generation of political leaders was responsible for the foreign policy of the new state; Griffith, Collins and Childers were dead, and de Valera was in hiding. However, the issues they had to deal with were largely those which had faced their predecessors before the state existed.

PART II

Aspirations and Policies:
The Major Issue Areas

"The time has come", the Walrus said,
"To talk of many things:
Of shoes — and ships — and sealing-wax —
Of cabbages — and kings . . ."

Lewis Carroll

Chapter 4

Independence and Identity

Ireland is a sovereign, independent, democratic state.

Bunreacht na hÉireann, Article 5

*No Republic that can be set up, no monarchy in this world, can
have that absolute independence which haunts [Mr de Valera's]
dreams. It does not exist in this world.*

Hugh A. Law, TD, in the
Dáil, 21 November 1928

The negotiations leading to the Treaty of 6 December 1921 were
expected by the Irish side to be the culmination of the long and
confused search for national independence. With the advantage of
hindsight we can see that they did indeed mark an important stage
on the road to that objective, but at the time a substantial minority
of the nationalist movement dismissed the Treaty as a sham. Civil
war was the immediate outcome of their opposition to the Treaty,
and the bitterness engendered in that conflict served to exacerbate
what was to be for nearly thirty years the most contentious issue-
area in Irish foreign policy — the independence of the Irish state.

Independence is often seen as a characteristic of a government's behaviour, which prevails in varying degrees in particular
issues of foreign policy but can also be important as a general condition in which the state exists or is assumed to exist. It is in this
broader sense that independence was first reflected in Irish political
debate. Its first manifestation was in the form of the legal concept
of sovereignty, whereby all states were held to be autonomous in
their relations with each other and to be equal in international
law. From the perspective of 1921 — so long as the Great War was

regarded as an unrepeatable aberration of international behaviour – an observer of international affairs could point to the evolution of an increasing consensus concerning the rights and duties of sovereign states, enshrined in the basic document of the new international order, the Covenant of the League of Nations, as well as in well-tried diplomatic procedures. Yet such a consensus was never so strong that a more pessimistic view could not plausibly be advanced; here the substance of sovereignty was more important than the claims it made, and the substance of sovereignty depended both on the type of international system that existed and on each state's particular position within that system.[1] In the long view it could be held that the international system of the nineteen-twenties was anything but stable, while the Irish Free State's position in the shadow of a great imperial power made equality seem theoretical indeed.

But such a cold appraisal of the prospects for Irish independence did not come easily to nationalist leaders who had fought that same imperial power to the negotiating table. The challenge to the Treaty came from men and women who saw independence as an absolute condition, just as it was embodied in legal theory; their ideal was the 'isolated republic' and independence was not so much a means of providing Irishmen with good government as of providing them with what was seen as the necessary prerequisite of good government – absolute independence. This challenge struck deep at the conscience of the Treaty's supporters. The latter had been repelled by the probable cost of prolonging the armed struggle against the British and advanced the claim that the Treaty, in Michael Collins's words, gave the Irish Free State 'freedom, not the ultimate freedom that all nations aspire and develop to, but the freedom to achieve it.'[2] In time the claim was to be justified to a large extent, but in the nineteen-twenties it called repeatedly for proof. In so far as the Treaty tied the Irish Free State to Britain, the assertion of a truly distinctive national identity was difficult to make; thus, both supporters and opponents of the Treaty experienced a strong psychological and political need to achieve visible manifestations of the state's independence.

The experience of the Treaty negotiations had shown that in the major substantive issues of Anglo-Irish relations the fruits of independence would be slow to come to maturity, if indeed there were to be fruits at all. Fiscal and financial autonomy had been granted but in practice the economies of the two islands were closely linked. So too was their security from external invasion; in both cases the costs of even a small degree of independence could be high.[3] The negative attitudes of Ulster unionsts towards the very notion of independence were to ensure that there were to be no displays of the Irish Free State's independence on this issue.[4] But, paradoxically, what appeared in the first instance to be the most barren ground for the achievement of Irish independence proved to be the first in which it grew — the constitutional framework of British imperial authority. On this issue Lloyd George had refused to budge in 1921 in spite of de Valera's ingenious attempts to circumvent him; yet in fifteen years de Valera was to have his way, while his predecessors had helped stretch the imperial framework far beyond what had been envisaged then.

It was thus the constitutional dimension of independence which was to be the first great issue in Irish foreign policy, and in various forms it was to hold the centre of the stage up to 1949 when both British and Irish governments accepted what had in most important respects long been an accomplished fact — that Ireland was a republic, outside the British Commonwealth. From a British perspective this issue was a direct continuation of the complex constitutional evolution of the British Empire, from an Irish perspective it was the focus of all the bitterness of a civil war. It was an issue fraught both with obscure legal subtleties and unyielding emotions, which at last provided the rules of the game in Anglo-Irish relations but which left unanswered a good many questions about the relative strengths of the players.

*   *   *

The first attempt to revise the Anglo-Irish Treaty of 1921 was made barely six months after it had been signed. The Provisional Government of the Irish Free State, in an attempt to stave off civil war, produced a draft constitution which was closer to de Valera's concept of external association than to dominion status as it was then understood. The British Crown was no longer the central authority, the oath of allegiance disappeared altogether and the right to make treaties — a significant indicator of diplomatic independence, which dominions did not at that time enjoy — was claimed. But the British government would make no concessions on these lines, demonstrating the weakness of the Irish in direct bilateral bargaining. It would have been small comfort to the latter had they known that in so far as British ministers envisaged a renewal of the use of military force against them, such an armed conflict would have been in British eyes an interstate war and no longer a rebellion.[5]

Yet revision of the Treaty had to remain a continuing and vital preoccupation for W. T. Cosgrave's government, which replaced the Provisional Government in December 1922. Quite apart from the dissatisfaction with the Treaty of members of the government, its opponents, although militarily defeated, soon resumed their political resistance. Eamon de Valera focused his attack on what he saw as the government's fundamental acquiescence in the face of an unjust constitutional settlement: 'There is a vast difference between patiently submitting, when you have to, for a time, and putting your signature to a consent or assent to these conditions.'[6] De Valera represented a significant minority, which won forty-four seats in the first post-civil war election in August 1923. As yet it was a minority which abstained from parliamentary politics, but if domestic political stability was to be established, it had to be encouraged to agitate within constitutional limits and therefore its own brand of constitutional revisionism had to be accommodated to some degree.

The grounds for revision lay in the Treaty's ambiguity regarding Anglo-Irish relations, although this was only part of a broader ambivalence over the role of the dominions. The traditional dominions, in particular Canada, Australia and New Zealand, with populations predominantly British in origin, had gradually emerged to the point where they were political entities of some consequence in international relations; this had been reflected in their participation in the Great War and in their membership of the League of Nations, although they still (often reluctantly) regarded the Westminster government as their mentor in foreign affairs. The Irish Free State had been forced into this uncertain and now rapidly changing position, though in several important respects she was quite unlike the dominion norm (usually represented by Canada). She was not as physically and therefore strategically distant from Britain as other dominions, and her population was emphatically not inclined to view Britain as a natural mother country. Ireland, like South Africa, was a cuckoo in the Commonwealth nest.[7]

Nevertheless the Commonwealth provided the Irish Free State with an invaluable opportunity to press its claim in a multilateral setting, in which it could seek its own particular advantage by forming coalitions with other dominions which sought to improve their position, though motivated by less radical considerations. As an international organisation, the British Commonwealth had many of the characteristics of the Cheshire cat. Apart from the intermittent Imperial Conferences, it was often difficult to discern precisely what relationship existed between the Commonwealth states; indeed, it was British policy to maintain a high degree of ambiguity on this point, while real control could be exerted on a day-to-day basis by co-ordinating activities through the Dominions Office in London in consultation with the dominions' high commissioners. But this very flexibility and ambiguity gave the dominions scope to formulate different and more specific views about dominion status and the Imperial Conference 'in spite of its centralising nuances . . . remained the chief stage upon which the dominions advanced towards full and independent sovereignty.'[8]

At the same time the League of Nations, which the Irish Free State joined in 1923, though without any special regard for British Commonwealth relations, provided, if not the body, at least the tail of the Cheshire cat. Because of its more frequent meetings and the opportunities it provided for its members to act — and to appear to act — as independent states, it enabled the dominions to establish precedents which British governments subsequently found it impossible to repudiate. Further, it enabled the dominions to act to a large extent collectively; it was a natural setting for the formation of coalitions which could make a greater impression on British governments than would have been the case if each dominion had submitted its case individually.

Thus, from the outset of Irish membership of the League, the emphasis in policy was on clarifying the international status of the Irish Free State; in the words of Desmond FitzGerald, Minister for External Affairs from 1922 to 1927, 'every matter that came up we viewed rather from the aspect of narrow nationalism . . . we always watched closely as though we stood for the absolutist national State.'[9] An early and significant illustration of this policy was the registration with the League in 1924 of the Anglo-Irish Treaty of 1921. Registration of international treaties was a formal obligation of League membership, and the British argument that the 1921 Treaty was not a full international treaty, but merely an intra-imperial agreement, proved to be of no avail. The Irish Free State was accepted as an independent state, and subsequently on every issue arising within the League she took pains to establish her own position rather than follow British decisions. Thus in 1926 a hastily prepared but undeniably 'Irish' attempt was made to win a non-permanent seat on the Council of the League. Although unsuccessful it established a precedent for the dominions and in 1930 the Irish Free State became a beneficiary of this precedent.

But it was at the Imperial Conference of 1926 that the central assault in the revisionist strategy was made. Ireland and South Africa pressed hard for a specific and far-reaching definition of dominion status and the Canadian government lent both its respectability and its own brand of isolationism to their claim. It was a classic demonstration of the advantages which can be obtained for a weak and rather suspect state in multilateral negotiations. The Canadian and Irish delegations worked closely together, and proposals that would have been unacceptable, if they had been presented by the Irish alone, met with a more positive response when they appeared in the guise of Canadian policy. The outcome was the famous Balfour declaration of the co-equality of all members of the Commonwealth, which were described as

> . . . autonomous communities within the British Empire, equal in status, in no way subordinate one to another in any aspect of their domestic or external affairs, though united by a common allegiance to the Crown and freely associated as members of the British Commonwealth of Nations.[10]

It was on this basis, after further detailed negotiations in which Irish representatives played an active part, that the next Imperial Conference in 1930 prepared the way for the Statute of Westminster, which became law at the end of 1931.

This statute, confirming the legal status of the dominions as full members of the international community, marks the culmination of the first phase in the revision of the 1921 Treaty. Its most celebrated British critic, Winston Churchill, argued that it gave the dominions such autonomy that the Treaty was a dead letter if the Irish parliament wished it to be so. The Cumann na nGaedheal government of W. T. Cosgrave did not take this view, maintaining that the Treaty could only be altered by mutual agreement. His successor, de Valera, however, inclined to the Churchillian interpretation. Although further amendment of the Treaty was not to be quite as simple as Churchill had feared, it soon became clear that a significant measure of constitutional independence had been won during the first ten years of the Irish Free State's existence.

However, in another sense independence remained an elusive goal. The Cosgrave government's policy had after all been designed not only to encourage recognition from without, but, perhaps more importantly, to make an impact within the state. This it failed to do. That this was so was partly because of the nature of the achievements and the manner in which they had been gained. The substance of the policy was remote, abstract and expressed in highly technical legal language; the diplomacy it entailed was equally far removed from the consciousness of the Irish voter. As one writer has put it: 'The announcement "The Optional Clause has been signed *without reservation*" was important but unlikely to make the rafters ring in Roscommon.'[11]

An even greater political liability was the fact that diplomacy within the Commonwealth was seen as a reversion to the dis-credited Home Rule politics of the pre-independence era. By 1926 the opponents of the Treaty had formed two major political groups. One established a tradition of violent agitation, but the other, under de Valera, came into parliamentary politics in the guise of the Fianna Fáil party. De Valera's attitude towards the achievements of multilateral diplomacy was dismissive; rather he stressed what it had not gained. In particular he emphasised the continued existence of the oath of allegiance — an issue on which he himself was not only extremely sensitive but which had coloured the theatrical entry of Fianna Fáil into the Dáil in 1927. A specific commitment unilaterally to repudiate the oath was a major item in the Fianna Fáil campaign during the general election of 1932, while Cosgrave's government remained silent on the achievements of its strategy. As de Valera's biographers remark, 'Free State membership of the Commonwealth, even a liberated Commonwealth, was not apparently a winning card.'[12]

De Valera's victory in the 1932 election marks the beginning of a new phase in the quest for constitutional independence. He concentrated on unilateral acts rather than on multilateral diplomacy. It is probable that the advantages to be gained from the latter would have been less striking than heretofore, because the Statute of Westminster had satisfied most of the obvious claims of Ireland's dominion allies, but in any case de Valera had never shown any taste for a close relationship with the Commonwealth. There was, however, no overall repudiation of the Treaty. Shortly after obtaining office, de Valera indicated his strategy:

> . . . we yield no willing assent to any form or symbol that is out of keeping with Ireland's right as a sovereign nation. Let us remove these forms one by one, so that this State that we control may be a Republic in fact; and that, when the time comes, the proclaiming of the Republic may involve no more than a ceremony, the formal confirmation of a status already attained.[13]

Nevertheless, caution about the ultimate deadline for the achievement of his goal did not prevent de Valera from making an immediate start in 'dismantling the Treaty'.[14] Within his first year of office he was well on the way to removing the oath of allegiance from the Constitution and to reducing the status of the Crown's representative, the governor-general. After the consolidation of his position in the 1933 general election, further legislation abolished the right of appeal to the Judicial Committee of the Privy Council, while the Irish Nationality and Citizenship Act and the Aliens Act of 1935 underlined the legal distinctiveness of Irish citizenship. Intertwined with this assault on the existing constitutional links with Britain was a conflict, which, while not directly related to the Constitution, had a good deal to do with what de Valera saw as the unjust exploitation of Ireland's dependence on Britain in the nineteen-twenties. This was the dispute over the land annuities arising out of the land purchase schemes at the turn of the century, which the Cosgrave government had agreed to accept as a binding obligation.[15] De Valera's withholding of payments to the British government led to a tariff war which did much to exacerbate the constitutional issues, though, even without the land annuities dispute, it is possible that the British would have resorted to economic pressure.[16] In all of this there was a definite emphasis on unilateral action. The minutes of the second cabinet meeting of the first de Valera government, when considering the preparation of a Bill to remove the oath, record the agreement 'that it was not necessary that any intimation should be made to the British Government preliminary to the introduction of the Bill . . .'[17] Independence was now to be the hallmark of the means as well as the ends of Irish diplomacy.

The British response to this new style of Irish revisionism was confused. An initial flurry of bilateral negotiations in 1932 served only to emphasise the increased mutual suspicions which now characterised Anglo-Irish relations. A British cabinet sub-committee − the Irish situation committee − was established as a means of bringing attention to bear on the Irish problem, but up to 1935 it floundered in a sea of uncertainties relating to general international developments as well as those in the British Isles.[18] By 1935, however, the dust began to settle on both sides of the Irish Sea. The Irish government, having survived the consequences of its initial assault on the Treaty, now entered a more constructive phase. In the Spring of 1935 preparation for the drafting of a new constitution was begun, on the basis of the idea of external association with the Commonwealth, rather than full membership of it. On the British side, a new Secretary of State for Dominion Affairs, Malcolm MacDonald, initiated effective bilateral relations at the ministerial level when in March 1936 he had the first of a series of secret meetings with de Valera, as the latter was passing through London.[19] These meetings did much to reduce the tensions which had been caused both by de Valera's abrasive unilateralism and the British government's reluctance to recognise that the Commonwealth had indeed changed dramatically during the previous ten years.

At the end of 1936 de Valera found an unexpected opportunity to put a major element of his new constitutional system into the statute books, at a time when British attention was diverted by the constitutional crisis occasioned by the abdication of King Edward VIII. In particular, the Executive Authority (External Relations) Act of that year acknowledged the Crown, but only for very limited purposes, such as the accreditation of diplomatic representatives, and on condition that the Irish Free State remained associated with the Commonwealth. This was de Valera's formula of 'external association', but without the more specific obligation to consult with Commonwealth governments on matters of common concern which he had been ready to accept in 1921. When the new Irish Constitution was published less than six months later, in May 1937, external association was incorporated in Article 29; in all other references to international affairs the sovereignty of the state was explicitly expressed. Less than sixteen years after the Irish delegation had reluctantly signed the Anglo-Irish Treaty, the major constitutional question-mark over Irish independence had been removed.

On 30 December 1937 the British government officially accepted the new situation although they expressed reservations concerning the Irish claim to Northern Ireland, made in Articles 2 and 3 of the new Constitution.[20] There were considerable misgivings about the implications of external association but MacDonald argued that it was better to turn a blind eye to these rather than provoke a renewed confrontation with the Irish government. The Irish case was partly helped by the fact that the other dominions offered no objection: in spite of de Valera's indifference towards the Commonwealth throughout the mid-nineteen-thirties, one of the reasons for the success of his unilateralism had been the British government's reluctance to act harshly against one dominion and thereby arouse the antagonism of the others. Adverse reaction from other governments, in particular the United States, was also an important consideration, and the new British prime minister, Neville Chamberlain, took the view that the appeasement of Ireland was a logical and desirable part of a general scheme to meet the claims of revisionist states, principally Germany and Italy, and thereby establish stability in European relations.

The settlement of the constitutional issue in 1937 cleared the way for direct bilateral negotiations concerning substantive issues where differences existed, especially on questions of defence, financial and economic relations and partition, while the increasing prospects of a European war provided a further incentive for both governments to improve their relations. The outcome of these negotiations, which took place between 17 January and 22 April 1938, is examined below[21], but it is worth noting here that the negotiations were the first attempt to define Anglo-Irish relations in the context of normal interstate relations. Although the discussions were in some respects a curious replay of the 1921 negotiations, and despite the fact that de Valera was fearful of being branded a second Redmond, there was no ultimate threat to the Irish of immediate military coercion, legitimated by a superior legal authority.

If the constitutional settlement of 1937 led directly to the agreements of 1938, then the latter formed the basis of the Irish government's policy of neutrality during World War II — arguably the most dramatic and concentrated test of the state's political independence. By conceding its control of the Irish ports which had been enshrined in the Treaty of 1921, the British government admitted that Irish neutrality was permissible, at least in the eyes of international law. They did not, perhaps, recognise that for an Irish government, neutrality was not merely permissible, but desirable, not least because it was a concrete rather than an abstract manifestation of independence, the fulfilment of a clear psychological need.[22] This attitude recalled the 'non-entanglement' of the early years of the United States and foreshadowed the widespread non-alignment of the new states of the nineteen-fifties and sixties.[23] It is also a persistent motif in the history of Irish nationalism, sometimes expressed only in a general way, but on occasion — as in Casement's view of the post-war world and in the basic working document of the Irish delegation in 1921 — finding a precise form.[24] Shortly after entering the Dáil in 1927, de Valera claimed that 'the right of maintaining our neutrality is the proper policy for this country'[25]; neutrality was the right of an independent state, irrespective of the particular diplomatic and strategic circumstances which might prevail.

The first months after the implementation of the policy saw a further normalisation of Anglo-Irish relations, when, for the first time, a British diplomatic representative was sent to Ireland. The absence of what was shortly to prove an indispensable means of intergovernmental communication had been a result of a long-standing battle of symbols, typical of the de Valera phase of constitutional revision, when the British and Irish governments stood firm respectively on the Commonwealth title of 'high commissioner' and the 'normal' diplomatic title of 'ambassador'.[26] But more serious was the failure of the Irish government to obtain from Britain a guarantee of their neutrality, a situation which was to prevail throughout the war.

Indeed the war was only two months old when a prominent member of the British government, Winston Churchill (the First

Lord of the Admiralty), began to urge the reoccupation of the Irish ports. This was but the first of a series of threats to Irish independence from the belligerent powers, usually, though not always, arising out of specific strategic developments[27], and the fact that Irish neutrality remained inviolate was ultimately a reflection of favourable strategic considerations. Nevertheless, the Irish government might well have been persuaded to abandon neutrality prior to such an extreme eventuality as invasion; that it did not do so indicates both the persistence with which de Valera held to his independent position and the skill of his diplomacy.

Two other factors were also important. In the first place the practice of Irish neutrality did allow for what de Valera called 'a certain consideration for Britain'; there was no visible co-operation on major strategic questions such as the ports, but on day-to-day matters the Irish stance was regarded by the British as one of benevolent neutrality.[28] Secondly, up to the entry of the United States into the war at the end of 1941 — a period which saw the most serious *strategic* threat to Irish neutrality — the belligerents, but more especially Britain, were sensitive about the repercussions which a violation of Irish neutrality might have on the greatest uncommitted power, the United States with its potentially significant Irish-American vote. When the United States herself became a belligerent, the situation became more confused; the Roosevelt administration was not well-informed about the true state of Anglo-Irish relations, and the Irish and American governments regarded each other with suspicion.[29] The American Ambassador in Dublin, David Gray, tried to put Irish neutrality firmly 'on the record' in order to neutralise the post-war manipulation of Irish-American groups by an Irish government seeking to play the American card against British support of partition. The result of his intrigues was the final threat to Irish independence during the war — the notorious affair of the 'American Note' of February 1944, demanding that the Irish government expel the Axis and Japanese diplomats in Dublin, ostensibly on the grounds of security prior to the Allies' invasion of France. While de Valera may have over-estimated the seriousness of this as a threat to Irish independence, it was a threat in so far as Gray's intention was to present neutrality in a poor light. This might have had repercussions on de Valera's domestic position and led to a change in Irish policy. In all of this, however, Gray showed his failure to grasp the extent of popular support for the government's policy. His move only further consolidated de Valera's growing reputation in Ireland as the man who saved his country from the horrors of war.[30] It seemed that against the wishes of the world's greatest powers, in a global conflict of unprecedented proportions, independence was complete.

There remained after the war one final chapter in the saga of constitutional independence. External association, originally conceived of as a compromise to win over British constitutional susceptibilities, was now seen as a device to win over northern unionists by maintaining the link with the Crown and the Commonwealth.[31] This rationale lacked conviction, and the fact that external association still necessitated a measure of symbolic subservience to the British monarch — in the accreditation of diplomats — made it the butt of parliamentary opposition from 1945 until the general election of February 1948. Then, after a confused campaign in which republican status was raised by the new Clann na Poblachta party, de Valera was defeated and the succeeding coalition government, in somewhat controversial circumstances, repealed the Executive Authority (External Relations) Act of 1936 and on 18 April 1949 declared Ireland to be a republic. Mr John A. Costello's government made it clear that Ireland was no longer a member of the Commonwealth, though, even at the last, the sympathy of some of the other dominions helped ensure that there was little practical change in Anglo-Irish relations.[32] The declaration of the republic to a large extent merely confirmed the position which had prevailed since 1937.[33]

At the beginning of 1949 also, the Irish government declined an invitation to join the North Atlantic Treaty Organisation, the first great military alliance of the post-war era. This decision was taken on the grounds that partition precluded military co-operation with Britain, a line of reasoning that had recurred frequently during wartime neutrality.[34] But it also reflected the extent to which neutrality was tending to become, in the popular imagination, a doctrine which it was presumptuous to question. At least in part this attitude may be explained by the psychological need for a dramatic manifestation of independence. De Valera's defence of neutrality, made in response to Churchill's criticism in 1945, aroused much emotional public support.[35] Although, at the beginning of the war, de Valera had disclaimed 'adherence to some theoretical, abstract idea of neutrality or anything like that'[36], we have seen that there was indeed a tradition in Irish nationalism which aspired to neutrality in some form or other. This aspiration was now being realised, not merely in policy but in the development of a myth of neutrality as one of the major successes of Ireland's existence as an independent state. Nineteen-forty-nine thus marked the high point of the politics of independence, as the sovereign republic made its own decision to remain isolated from the mainstream of international politics.

But the same year also marked the end of a period when political independence as such was a major issue of foreign policy, demanding a concentration of diplomatic resources and domestic debate. For the next twenty years, in so far as the question of independence arose, it concerned the state's capacity to act autonomously over specific substantive issues, where all too often the degree of real independence was to be seriously reduced by external constraints. But if the reality of independence was often lacking — and sometimes, indeed, precisely because it was lacking — governments could at least try to assert their distinctiveness by the manipulation of symbols and the projection of an image of national identity. This is of course a commonplace activity of all states, whether it be to impress foreign governments or domestic public opinion. For the general public a sense of national identity may be manifested in attitudes towards foreign countries, and politicians take into account what they know, or assume, to be the feelings of the public in this regard. In particular, attitudes towards Britain (seen either as a government or a people) continued to provide an incentive to display the symbols of independence, although the constitutional issue had been resolved.[37]

There are several widely-used means of symbolising independence internationally. It can be seen in the extent of diplomatic representation and in the resources allocated to 'showing the flag' overseas. The Irish exploitation of this particular instrument of prestige has been limited, mainly on account of the expense of permanent representation abroad and the lack of widespread vital interests which could serve as a further justification for its expansion.[38] It can also be seen in the practice of 'cultural diplomacy' — the establishment of cultural institutes overseas, information services and exchange programmes — which is employed by larger states on a grand scale on the grounds that it enhances the general image which foreigners hold of the state in question.[39] Again, in this generally expensive type of activity, where tangible results are difficult if not impossible to quantify, Irish efforts have generally been in a low key. The Department of Foreign Affairs, in conjunction with an advisory committee on cultural relations, sponsors a limited programme of cultural exchange and endeavours to promote the work of Irish artists abroad, but budgetary allocations to this programme are usually among the first to be pruned in times of financial difficulty. The information services of the department — and of the Irish administration as a whole — are also run on modest resources.

For a small state (and one in which the politicians have traditionally and instinctively distrusted the practitioners, both of diplomacy and culture) there is an alternative means of promoting the image of independence — intergovernmental organisation. In the nineteen-twenties two of these, the Commonwealth and the League of Nations, provided the conditions in which constitutional revision could be advanced, but they also provided the setting for more general displays of independence, by virtue of membership itself — the opportunity to advance unsolicited opinions on major world issues, and the opportunity to participate in the leadership of the organisations.

Membership of the Commonwealth had of course been a condition of the 1921 Treaty, and for that very reason was not perceived by many Irishmen as the hallmark of independence. The League of Nations was more satisfactory as an agency of external recognition, though there were often reservations about it — a consequence of the disillusionment when Ireland was rejected by the 'Great Powers' League' in 1919.[40] Membership of the United Nations Organisation was denied Ireland, from the initial application to join in 1946 up to 1955, because of the Soviet Union's opposition, ostensibly on account of Irish neutrality but also explicable in the context of emerging cold war rivalries.

When Ireland was a member of the League and later of the United Nations, Irish delegations established and maintained a tradition of proclaiming their opposition to the policy of automatically following the lead of other states or groups of states in the practice of bloc voting. One of the first instances of this was seen in a rejection of a British-led Commonwealth group in the League, particularly in the unsuccessful candidature for the

League's Council in 1926, though there is irony in the fact that in
1930 the Irish Free State owed her election to the Council of the
League largely to the united support of the other Commonwealth
states! Irish positions on major issues debated in the League were
sometimes distinctive; support for the admission of the Soviet
Union in 1934 and for sanctions against Italy in 1935 were not
what might have been expected from a self-consciously catholic
state.[41] De Valera's later claim that '. . . on each question which
arose, we were taking an independent attitude, that we were not,
so to speak, adopting some "block" (sic) idea'[42] may stand up to
further investigation.

The desirability of adopting an independent stance in intergovernmental organisations subsequently became a major con-
stituent of the litany of Irish foreign policy. When Ireland was at
last admitted to the UN in 1955, the then Minister for External
Affairs, Liam Cosgrave, delcared that 'our aim should be . . . to
avoid becoming associated with particular *blocs* or groups so far
as possible.'[43] From 1957 to 1969 the responsibility for acting in
accordance with this goal fell to de Valera's close colleague, Frank
Aiken. There were clear instances in his first years of office that
Irish positions at the UN were independently formulated, in spite
of strong pressures, especially from the United States. It is note-
worthy that the Irish delegation persisted in a willingness to
discuss the representation of China in the UN at a time when such
a stance ran against the American and 'western' position. But
during the nineteen-sixties this attitude towards the China issue
was modified, and the Irish government was criticised for its non-
committal line on the United States presence in South East Asia.[44]
Perceptions of Irish independence in the UN depended on a selection of 'test cases' such as the China issue; even in the heyday of
the promotion of independence in the UN the voting record on
all cold war issues showed that Ireland voted with the United
States at least three times as often as against her.[45]

A state may also try to assert its independent status by seeking
formal leadership roles within intergovernmental organisations.
Thus the Irish Free State's attempt to win election to the League
Council in 1926, although in itself unsuccessful, established a
precedent from which the Irish delegation benefited in the Council
election of 1930. Ironically it was de Valera who gained most
from this achievement of his domestic opponents, for when he

came to power in 1932 the Irish Free State held the presidency of the Council by virtue of rotation. This gave him an opportunity to establish an international reputation. Later, in 1938, he was elected president of the League's Assembly, while in the interval the appointment of the Irish permanent delegate, Seán Lester, to be the League high commissioner in Danzig was the start of a distinguished careeer in the League secretariat which served to advertise the existence of the Irish state.[46] This pattern was again found during Irish membership of the UN; in 1960 Dr F. H. Boland, head of the Irish permanent delegation, was elected president of the UN General Assembly, and in 1962 Ireland was elected to serve on the UN Security Council.[47]

However, it is within the European Community that formal leadership roles can carry more influence than in the United Nations, yet, at the same time, particularly for a small country, they can impose a heavy cost. It was with some trepidation, therefore, that only two years after joining the Community the Irish government had to undertake the presidency of the Council of Ministers. As it happened, the six-month period of the Irish presidency (January to July 1975) provided opportunities to make certain initiatives in the Community's decision-making procedures and to contribute to the conclusion of negotiations on the Lomé Convention.[48] The handling of the presidency was generally considered to have enhanced the reputations both of the Minister for Foreign Affairs, Dr Garret FitzGerald, and the Irish administration, but the costs incurred brought the minister to the Dáil in search of a supplementary estimate. Here he had to face an opposition looking 'for the positive results of all this activity, zeal and public concern.'[49] Of course, there was no tangible, immediate return on such expenditure, particularly as Ireland has few vital interests in many of the matters dealt with by the presidency. In the long term, however, the diplomatic reputation of the state was at stake; reliability and impartiality during a term of office may well encourage a sympathetic response from foreign governments when difficulties occur in the future.

Of course Irish membership of the European Community requires much more than projecting an independent posture in yet another intergovernmental organisation; indeed, the fundamental question of the state's independence is re-emerging in the form of the issue of 'sovereignty'. There were some signs of this during

the prolonged public debate which preceded the referendum on
Irish membership in May 1972, when sovereignty was an issue
both in terms of constitutional developments and of neutrality.
However, this debate was based on two largely misleading stereo-
types. On the one hand there was the stereotype of a federal
Europe, in which political independence would necessarily not
exist; while this was an element in the ideology of the European
movement, it was claimed by anti-marketeers to be just around
the corner, putting what was to them the worst interpretation on
membership. On the other hand, pro-marketeers sometimes gave
the impression — at any rate for internal consumption — that
membership of the European Community was little more than a
complex economic rearrangement, limited by inviolable constitutional safeguards. In this view, the survival of political independence
in the constitutional sense hardly merited discussion. Nor was the
debate on the implications for that other traditional yardstick of
independence — neutrality — any more enlightening; pro-marketeers
cautiously desanctified it but saw no reason for any change in
policy, while their opponents claimed that neutrality would be an
imminent victim of membership.[50]

Neither of these views bore much relation to the European
Community which was then — and still is — rather more than a
purely economic system and a good deal less than a European
federation. As a political arrangement it typifies the blurring of
the traditional distinction between foreign and domestic policies
in the modernised states in the western, industrialised world;
member-states find themselves involved in a complex system of
interdependencies where their freedom of action, as traditionally
embodied in the concept of external sovereignty, is continuously
being restrained.[51] They remain separate political entities but it
becomes increasingly difficult to establish clearly independent
policies other than those of a negative nature.

But it would be a mistake to see membership of the Community
simply as a return to the situation prevailing in the nineteen-
twenties when the Irish Free State sought independence in the
Commonwealth. The opportunities for multilateral diplomacy
again are to be found, but with much greater intensity and bureaucratic complexity, and encompassing a much broader range of
issues. Irish membership this time is voluntary, and Ireland is faced
not with the predominance of one great power, but rather with

the hesitations of three.

In what sense is it possible to think of political independence in a diplomatic system of this sort? In part, independence can be measured by the extent to which Irish interests are accommodated in Community policies, but in part, too, it must be seen as determined by the nature and possible evolution of the political procedures of the Community. In this respect, since Ireland joined in 1973, the government's position has generally favoured the 'democratisation' of Community institutions and decision-making procedures. At the December 1974 Paris Summit, Ireland proposed that the European Parliament be chosen by direct elections in 1978, and subsequently supported this move and that of increasing the powers of the Parliament despite the vicissitudes it encountered subsequently. Another often vilified institution, the Commission, has again been rehabilitated in Irish policy statements, in which it has been proposed that the Commission should be appointed collectively and thereby enhance its independence of national governments. Finally, within the forum of national governments – the Council of Ministers – the Irish government has supported a return to the idea of increasing the practice of majority voting over a wider range of decisions, and in the closing days of the Irish presidency managed to put this principle into practice.[52]

At first glance this approach has all the appearances of a blithe acceptance of the goal of western European federalism, but such an interpretation should be treated with caution. Ministerial justifications for it are based on the argument that a move towards granting greater powers to the Community institutions is in the interests of the smaller member states in general and Ireland in particular. The strengthening of the Commission is seen as an impediment to the predominance of the larger and stronger governments; the reduction of the veto in the Council of Ministers is proposed because the veto has been frequently used to obstruct redistributive policies, such as the establishment of the Regional Fund, and in any case smaller states are more vulnerable to retaliation if they attempt to use the veto.[53] In all of this, the member-states remain as separate political entities, interdependent in their relationships with each other but retaining room for independent manoeuvre on specific issues, a vision not necessarily all that far removed from that of the European Community's 'political minimalists', such as Denmark.

In any case, the European Community today approximates to the Danish rather than the Irish model. Decision-making is still predominantly a process of intergovernmental bargaining on the basis of national interests, and the political co-operation procedures still leave even the smaller states the scope to take distinctive positions on world issues. Indeed, it has been argued that:

> The Irish experience is indicative [of an enhanced international standing] ; enabling them for the first time to open direct relations with the Arab states, and discovering through their exercise of the Presidency a greater independence of their British neighbour in foreign policy-making than they had ever had before. The costs, both in terms of incurring monetary burdens and in terms of provoking domestic opposition, were minimal.[54]

Independence may have been circumscribed, but it has not been eliminated altogether.

Chapter 5

Security

What was Ireland made for? Were we planted in the Atlantic Ocean to ward off attacks upon Britain for all time . . .?

Patrick F. Baxter, TD,
in the Dáil, 17 February 1927

We are placed there by God in propinquity to the British Islands and the British Islands, if they are in modern strategy defensible at all, are defensible as a unit and it is useless to have people talking mere tripe about defending ourselves in a position of isolation.

Eamonn Coogan, TD,
in the Dáil, 29 January 1947

When Irish independence became an accepted if controversial reality in the early nineteen-twenties, there were hopes, held particularly by supporters of the League of Nations, that the anarchic nature of international politics was being curbed. But subsequent events showed that all states were prepared to turn to violence in the last resort and some, indeed, well before that. Governments still felt the need to equip themselves to counter the threat of force by force; defence policy and foreign policy were to remain inextricably linked as one of their major concerns.

Security against external coercion has become an issue-area of increasing complexity, however. Nuclear technology has created a crude and risky ceiling to the use of military force globally, but in certain circumstances conventional military forces are still an instrument of policy, even if the anti-war ethos of the late twentieth century has cloaked their use in euphemistic terms. The costs of defence, subject to rapid technological changes, have risen beyond the political and economic capacities of all but the largest states. Hence the choice faced by most governments today: in order to maintain the existence of their states, they participate in complex bureaucratic alliance systems which to some extent at least reduce their freedom of movement, or alternatively they ignore such systems and, with a greater or lesser degree of fatalism, hope for the best. The way in which this choice is made — and remade, for often it is not well made — is, however, not usually clear-cut, particularly in peace time when the burden of paying a high premium to insure against a distant future is most keenly felt. The more security a state enjoys, the greater the temptation to neglect the significance of defence as a political issue.

Such has, perhaps, been the case in Ireland, especially since 1945.[1] In more than fifty-five years the state has not suffered invasion and in a highly-armed world is almost, but not quite, unarmed. Irish military forces have not participated in foreign wars, except in peace-keeping operations for the United Nations. This has not been the experience of many peoples, and goes some of the way to explaining the relative lack of concern about defence in Irish public debate during the past thirty years. Nevertheless, security — both external and internal — has at times been among the most serious problems facing Irish governments and there are even today signs of its re-emergence as an important issue-area of foreign policy.

*   *   *

Security was, of course, a major substantive question in the negotiations which led to the Treaty of 1921.[2] The British government insisted on a naval monopoly around the British Isles, reflecting the assumption that the two islands formed one strategic entity. This assumption was accepted by the Irish delegation, but there were different views as to how the defence responsibilities of each state were to be shared. The position after the signing of the Treaty was that the Irish government agreed to grant the British certain specified harbour facilities in peace time, while 'in time of war or of strained relations with a Foreign Power' more general naval co-operation was allowed for.[3] A separate article envisaged some participation in coastal defence by Irish forces, in so far as it allowed for a bilateral review of the British naval monopoly five years later, but there was no indication as to what 'a share in her own coastal defence' was to mean.[4] A third article limited the size of the Irish military establishment, in relation to the population, to that of the British defence forces, in relation to the British population.[5] During the Treaty debates, de Valera, in presenting his alternative 'Document No. 2', accepted the five-year naval monopoly but proposed that, subsequently, control of coastal defence in Irish waters should be the responsibility of the Irish government. Facilities might be offered to Britain in wartime, but only if judged 'reasonable' by the Irish.[6] His close colleague, Erskine Childers, was however the only figure of political significance to point out that the Treaty defence articles made it extremely likely that Ireland would both legally and militarily be pulled into Britain's wars.[7] Childers's point was not substantially diminished by Article 49 of the Irish Free State Constitution, supposed to be consistent with the Treaty, which asserted that except where an actual invasion occurred the Free State was not committed to participating in war without parliamentary consent. Parliaments may legitimate wars, but they do not often decide on them.

Some of the unreality of the Treaty debates on defence matters stems from the fact that Articles 6 and 7 referred to hypothetical military situations which had little relation to the actual military circumstances of Ireland. After all, there was at that time an Irish army — a revolutionary army which had been formed in guerilla warfare against an occupying rather than an invading power. Its field of action lay within Irish territory and it operated on a local rather than a national basis. Its leadership reflected a concern with political issues as much as with professional military questions; indeed it was amongst this leadership that the civil war divisions were most seriously manifesting themselves. In March 1922 ten of the nineteen army commands declared themselves opposed to the Treaty (and one other was later to join them).[8] It was from the remaining eight that the Irish professional military establishment was formed, whose first task was to open the civil war on 28 June 1922 when it shelled the position taken up by its former comrades in the Four Courts in Dublin. This action probably forestalled a British military intervention[9], but that hardly made the birth of the Irish army less traumatic, or its focus on internal rather than external events less marked.

Further problems were encountered after the end of the civil war in 1923. Massive demobilisation of nearly 30,000 officers and men, between August 1923 and March 1924, in addition to some officers' residual aspirations towards political influence, led to the so-called 'army mutiny' of March 1924. This challenge was swiftly met, thus confirming the principle of the supremacy of civilian authority, but it was not until the end of 1925 that the government attempted to rationalise fully the role of the small professional defence force which was left.[10] This policy is worth examining in some detail, since it contains several strands of strategic thinking which recur throughout the history of the state.

The size of the standing army was normally to be from 10,000 to 12,000, and the force was regarded as a cadre that could be rapidly expanded in times of emergency. The army was described as 'an independent national Force capable of assuming responsibility for the defence of the territory of Saorstát Éireann against invasion, or internal disruptive agencies.' The reference to the latter reflects what was to be a continuing preoccupation with internal subversion by extremist nationalist movements, and particularly the Irish Republican Army (IRA), and it was considered that the army should provide an ultimate deterrent in support of the civilian police.[11]

With regard to external defence, the omission of any reference to naval or air forces also laid the grounds of future Irish military policy. The emphasis was clearly on an infantry army designed to resist invasions which had already occurred. That such external attack could occur was taken seriously. At the height of euphoria over the Locarno settlement in western Europe it was the government's opinion that 'the present international situation does not . . . justify the hope that recourse to arms will in future be rendered impossible.' The most likely contingency − indeed the only one to be explicitly referred to in the 1925 policy document − was the possibility of 'some foreign Power' using 'our geographical position either as a base for an offensive against Great Britain or against sea-borne traffic between ports in Saorstát Éireann and other countries.' It was therefore one of the primary aims of defence policy that the Irish army had to be 'so organised, trained and equipped as to render it capable, should the necessity arise, of full and complete co-ordination with the forces of the British Government in the defence of Saorstát territory whether against actual hostilities or against violation of neutrality on the part of a common enemy.'

Such an appreciation of the Free State's strategic dependence on Britain was politically embarrassing, to say the least, at a time when Irish objectives on other questions were being dramatically rejected.[12] Defence policy was not then made the subject of detailed public debate. However, there was hope in the review of Ireland's coastal defence which was due to take place in 1927. The Irish intention was to effect a substantial revision of the 1921 Treaty by offering to take over and maintain the British-controlled harbour facilities at Berehaven, Cobh and Lough Swilly. Legal control of 'the ports', as they were popularly known, would be vested in the Irish government, but the costs of maintenance might continue to be shared by Britain, depending on the Free State's financial resources. There was, however, to be no question of providing an Irish naval force, for this was regarded as beyond the country's means. In the event, this recommendation proved unacceptable to the British government, which had no faith in either the political or economic capacity of the Irish to look after what were still regarded as vital British interests.[13]

In the meantime the implications of Ireland's strategic position were receiving public attention, with the contribution of the leader of the Labour Party, Thomas Johnson, to the debate on the Defence Forces (Temporary Provisions) Bill 1927. By this time British control of her dominions' foreign policy had been conceded in principle, but Articles 6 and 7 of the Treaty were, as we have seen, a matter for bilateral negotiation. In the course of the debate the Minister for External Affairs, Desmond FitzGerald, admitted that in the event of a general attack on the British Isles 'our army must co-operate with the British army' and then went on to maintain that it was 'practically inconceivable that our Army would ever be opposed to the British Army.'[14]

Two alternatives to this unpalatable association with British militarism were given some consideration. It was suggested that the League of Nation's system of collective security would make any national defence policy unnecessary, but, although the government supported the League in general terms (and as a lever in the pursuit of independence), it did not see it, in one minister's words, as more than 'an element of peace'.[15] A backbencher put it more colourfully: 'To trust ourselves solely to the protection of the League of Nations . . . we should be very much in the position of the man who because he had an umbrella divested himself of his clothes.'[16]

The second alternative raised, though somewhat incoherently, was neutrality. Johnson did not use the word, though he argued that 'the more we disentangle our defence forces from those of Great Britain, the less risk of being involved in war we shall run.'[17] FitzGerald, perhaps reflecting the difficulty of the government's position, tried to have it both ways, on the one hand talking about 'the point of view of maintaining our neutrality and freedom' and the Dáil's veto on decisions between peace and war, while on the other arguing that the outcome would depend on an attacker's perception of military advantage.[18] Kevin O'Higgins, Minister for Justice, was coldly realistic; neutrality might well be 'a consummation devoutly to be wished for . . .' but there was 'that geographical propinquity . . . a certain interdependence . . . a certain mutuality of interests between the two countries.'[19] If Britain felt she could not rely on Irish neutrality to protect her security, then neutrality would be meaningless.

This debate did not effect any change in government policy, which remained tied to the exigencies of British naval interests. It nevertheless demonstrated a widespread aspiration towards neutrality in a Dáil which still did not include the opponents of the Treaty. When they did enter the Dáil later in 1927, that aspiration was simply made more bluntly, when de Valera stated that the 'the right of maintaining our neutrality is the proper policy for this country.'[20] Where de Valera diverged most sharply from government thinking on defence was in his equally blunt assertion that the most likely threat of aggression came from 'England . . . one Power that in the past has been interfering with our rights and attacking us.'[21]

Although within five years de Valera was in power, no dramatic changes in defence policy were immediately apparent. The pressing issue in 1932 was the loyalty of the army to a government representing the rebellious faction in the civil war. In the event, the army's professionalism prevailed and the new government's first new development came with the establishment of a volunteer territorial force to supplement the regular army in 1934. The opposition claimed that this was a ploy to arm former anti-Treaty supporters and to some extent this did happen, but it could also be justified as a response to external threat. Again, there was no real attempt to prevent an invasion; rather, the regular army and the volunteer force were designed to ensure that 'the invading force will have a very hot time while amongst us, and that the power that tries to establish its rule here in a permanent way will find it impossible to do so.'[22]

The Minister for Defence, Frank Aiken, referred to the reorganised army being 'sufficient to make even strong neighbours respect a country'[23], and it is probable that his government's defence policy was designed primarily to deal with a British attack. Although there is no conclusive evidence of this, de Valera told the British representative in Dublin, Sir John Maffey, in July 1940, that Irish army staff work had proceeded on that assumption and that only on the outbreak of war in 1939 had similar attention been paid to the possibility of German invasion.[24]

Nevertheless, for the first six years of the de Valera government, Ireland was still bound by Articles 6 and 7 of the Treaty and, while the Treaty was besieged, there were at first no definite moves to revise those particular articles. But the deteriorating state of international relations in Europe in the mid-nineteen-thirties was causing increasing concern to the government. De Valera, although preferring to talk about security in a League rather than in a Commonwealth or Anglo-Irish context, was generally pessimistic about the League's capacity to guarantee security. During the Ethiopian crisis in the Autumn of 1935 he insisted on the need for national defence[25]; indeed at this time the government established a cabinet committee to examine 'the whole question of the Volunteer Force', which was not progressing as planned, as well as two interdepartmental committees to submit proposals for censorship and supplies in wartime.[26] When League sanctions failed the following summer, de Valera's response was, characteristically, to stress the virtues of self-reliance. At the League he said that 'all the small states can do, if the statesmen of the greater states fail in their duty, is resolutely to determine that they will not become the tools of any Great Power, and that they will resist with whatever strength they may possess every attempt to force them into a war against their will'[27]; in the Dáil he drew the conclusion for his own country: 'we want to be neutral'.[28]

The problem was to bridge the gap between the Irish government's wishes and the reality of British policy. But British attitudes also were being revised gradually in the light of the European drift towards violence, and the nature of Anglo-Irish defence relations became a vital consideration in discussions of the Irish situation committee and in the secret talks between de Valera and Malcolm MacDonald.[29] The British sought active defence co-operation, while de Valera argued that Ireland's benevolent neutrality and the consequent friendship of the United States would be of more value to Britain. Once the British government accepted de Valera's constitutional revision in 1937, both sides' urgent need to clarify the defence issue was in itself enough to bring them to the negotiating table at the beginning of 1938.[30]

The result of these negotiations was the achievement of the Irish government's immediate aim, so far as defence was con- cerned – the ports were returned to Irish control. Partly, this was a result of Chamberlain's general desire to improve Anglo-Irish relations, but it was due also to the British chiefs-of-staff's carefully calculated assessment of the strategic situation. The ports would indeed be valuable anti-submarine bases, but it was recognised that the costs of holding or seizing them in the face of Irish hostility (involving perhaps the occupation of the whole country) would far outweigh any such advantage. The Irish delegation, for its part, was somewhat dismayed at the financial burden of maintaining the ports as strategic strongholds, but could hardly refuse the long- coveted prize. At any rate neutrality would now be a more realistic policy to pursue, while the British could still hope that the improved climate of Anglo-Irish relations might bring defence co-operation in the long term.[31]

The developing German threat to Czechoslovakia in the Summer of 1938 made consultation of some sort more urgent, but the Irish attitude towards neutrality as a manifestation of independence now became more obvious. Only at the end of September did de Valera authorise any technical discussions to take place; these did not make much progress, for after the Munich crisis he turned his attention to partition.[32] During the last months of peace in Europe, the government made the implications of its policy known to foreign governments and its own people, but there was a good deal of concern about the outcome, particularly in view of Irish dependence on continued trade links with Britain.[33] Indeed the Irish high commissioner in London, John Dulanty, was reported to be of the opinion that Ireland would be forced into the war within a week, because of German attacks on shipping.[34]

This was not to be, but at several stages during World War II (the 'Emergency' in Irish official terminology), neutrality seemed to the Irish government to be seriously threatened.[35] In October 1939 Winston Churchill, a bitter opponent of the return of the ports and now First Lord of the Admiralty, unsuccessfully urged the British cabinet to press for the ports and if necessary to consider using 'the weapons of coercion.' A more serious crisis came in the Summer of 1940. There was a real possibility that Germany would invade the British Isles, Churchill was now prime minister of a desperate Britain, and Fine Gael support for neutrality wavered at the prospects of invasion. But de Valera held his nerve, in spite of the British attempt to link the Northern Ireland issue with defence co-operation[36], and, since the German Operation Sealion never materialised, the threat to Irish neutrality receded. Over the following winter, however, it became clear that Churchill's attitude towards the ports would continue to colour British policy towards Ireland. The British refused to guarantee neutrality and took economic measures 'to open the eyes of the Irish people to their true situation.'[37] This attitude was generally reflected in the British press which stressed the moral case against neutrality. The sting in the tail of British policy came in May 1941 with the threat of imposing conscription in Northern Ireland. But de Valera argued that such a move would turn his own population decidedly against Britain and encourage IRA activity both in Northern Ireland and England. Churchill did not proceed with his plans.

During all of this period, from the Autumn of 1939 to the Summer of 1941, Irish neutrality was threatened by strategic developments close by, and especially by the Nazi occupation of western Europe and British responses to this situation. But when Germany turned eastwards and the United States entered the war in December 1941, neutrality was threatened less by military developments than by political ones, and less by Britain than by the United States. Partition, rather than security, became the issue at stake.[38] The maintenance of neutrality throughout the war certainly owed much to de Valera's handling of these crises, but more fundamentally it was the result of strategic factors outside the Irish government's control. We can now see, though it was by no means obvious at the time, that Ireland was never of critical strategic value to any of the belligerents. Moreover the costs of intervention always seemed to outweigh any advantage that might be gained. The Germans established tentative links with the IRA, but thoughts of developing these into full-scale military support (in exchange for an invasion of Northern Ireland) were dismissed in the face of overwhelming technical obstacles; Germany simply did not have the naval or air capabilities to sustain support, and any expeditionary force, once in Ireland, would be extremely vulnerable to a British counter-attack.[39]

British military planners also did their sums with regard to an invasion of Ireland: at ten divisions to control the hinterland of the ports, the price was too high.[40] Nor did the strategic value of the ports, so far as military opinion was concerned, match up to Churchill's estimate. In March 1943 the British deputy premier, Clement Attlee, admitted that even if Ireland voluntarily joined the war, Britain had no resources to spare to help her, and that the ports might even be a financial embarrassment.[41] Of course the British did have the use of ports in Northern Ireland and could thus protect the northern convoy route. When the Americans joined the war, their military assessment too played down the value of the ports. The joint chiefs-of-staff concluded in 1943 that Irish air or naval bases would not have any significant effect on German control of the southern route to Britain and that there was no need to press for the establishment of US bases in the twenty-six counties.[42]

Ireland's strategic value may not have been high, but her defence posture was also a factor to be considered by the belligerents when contemplating a military intervention. At the beginning of 1939 there were only about 20,000 men under arms, of whom only 7,000 were regular troops; they were poorly equipped, lacking anti-tank or anti-aircraft weapons and without significant mechanised transport.[43] By 1942 the regular defence forces stood at about 40,000 men and these were supplemented by a Local Defence Force of 98,000 and a Local Security Force of about 100,000 older men in support duties.[44] The naval and air elements were almost negligible, and throughout the war there were persistent difficulties in obtaining even the most basic military supplies; but, nevertheless, this rather old-fashioned infantry army was a deterrent against the more adventurous strategic notions of the belligerents. Its credibility lay primarily in the degree of public support given to neutrality. As early as October 1939, both the German and British representatives in Dublin were reporting to their governments the popularity of neutrality, even among the traditionally pro-British element of the populace.[45] Subsequently the only political figure to oppose neutrality was James Dillon, deputy leader of the main opposition party, Fine Gael. In July 1941 he made his views known but received no significant support and in February 1942 he resigned from the party.[46]

Ironically, Dillon's pro-Allied attitude was reflected in a pro-Allied bias in the day-to-day operation of Irish neutrality. Just before the war, de Valera warned the German envoy in Dublin, Eduard Hempel, that circumstances would compel Ireland to show 'a certain consideration for Britain'.[47] At the time, this was limited to consultation about such matters as censorship and coast-watching, but in May 1940 high-level secret talks took place, between both military and political leaders. This precedent was further developed in the Spring of 1941 and there was effective military liaison throughout the rest of the war. The largest Irish manoeuvres, held both north and south of the border in 1942, were designed to meet the contingency of a German invasion in which there would be a joint Anglo-Irish military response, and disguised observers were exchanged.[48] A more obvious liaison was the maintenance of economic and social relations between Ireland and Britain; about 60,000 Irish volunteers served in the British forces in addition to maybe 100,000 civilian workers.[49]

In the end wartime neutrality did prove to be as successful a security policy as it was a means of manifesting independence. An alliance with the Axis powers would have had little support outside nationalist extremist groups and would have been strategically suicidal. Alliance with Britain alone, in the period up to the end of 1941, would also have left the country in an extremely vulnerable position — wide open to German retaliation from the air, and without the prospect of rapid significant rearmament by Britain or even the United States. From 1942 on, however, the rationale of neutrality as a security policy became less obvious and the government's insistence on independence and its stand on partition came to the fore.

The immediate post-war years were ones of considerable strategic uncertainty, with the introduction of nuclear weapons by the United States and the development of cold war rivalry. The government's defence policy was based on the continuation of neutrality and the maintenance of a standing infantry army of nearly 13,000 men — the same as before the Emergency, but with an increase in the size of the army. Fine Gael spokesmen were critical of the emphasis on the army to the exclusion of naval and air forces[50], and in 1946 the now Independent TD, James Dillon, put the military case for participation in an alliance: 'Were we to marshal the whole of the revenues of the State we could not maintain an effective Air Force in perpetuity in this country.'[51] By 1947, the military arguments against neutrality were being taken up by Dillon's former colleagues in Fine Gael. The party leader, General Richard Mulcahy, claimed that the government was unique in the 'astounding way' in which it insisted on assuming 'complete responsibility' for defence; another Fine Gael deputy Eamonn Coogan, advocated taking part in any western or Commonwealth defence arrangements.[52] Yet in the following year, when Fine Gael were the largest party in the new coalition government, there was no dramatic change in defence policy, apart from a reduction in the size of the standing army by 1,000 men, and in 1949, when a comprehensive western alliance was formed, Ireland refused to join it.

This turnabout in Fine Gael policy, and the consequent confirmation of the defence policy of the ousted Fianna Fáil party, was a striking demonstration of the subordination of strategic (and broad ideological) considerations to the demands of the anti-partition campaign, which was being orchestrated by de Valera both before and after he lost office in the election of 1948.[53] Fine Gael could not afford to be outbid on this issue, and even less so could the Clann na Poblachta party of Seán MacBride, the new Minister for External Affairs. But de Valera had so successfully made neutrality synonymous with an anti-partition stance since 1938 that when the North Atlantic Treaty Organisation was formed in 1949 the Irish government declared that 'as long as Partition lasts, any military alliance or commitment involving joint military action with the State responsible for Partition must be quite out of the question so far as Ireland is concerned.'[54]

It has been suggested that de Valera's obsession with partition can be partly explained by his desire to keep Ireland out of military alliances, but, whatever his motivation, the effect of his actions had been to do just that.[55] It can be argued that in practice Ireland has been a 'consumer' of such security as NATO has been able to produce, but such considerations bear no weight in political discussion. As far as the general public was concerned, for twenty years neutrality took on the appearance of unalterable doctrine or 'a veritable creed'.[56] As early as 1944, the Fine Gael spokesman on defence, T. F. O'Higgins, had complained that 'we are bringing up a generation blissfully unconscious of facts, in imbecile innocence, thinking that in a world war a declaration, plus a comparatively insignificant army, is sufficient to keep a country free from war...'[57] Subsequently, this belief in neutrality was reflected in a complacent indifference towards, or even fatalism about, external security. One result of this 'mood of inattention' was that the defence forces remained frozen in their posture of the late nineteen-forties. Much equipment became increasingly outdated, and although some items, such as small-arms and uniforms, were renewed, this was done without reference to any clear idea of the army's mission. More seriously, oppor-tunities for training were limited and career prospects were restricted. Only in the early nineteen-sixties did large-scale partici-pation in United Nations peace-keeping operations lift professional morale out of the routine rut of state ceremonials, guard duty, civilian emergencies and horse shows.[58]

In August 1969 the outbreak of serious violence in Northern Ireland saw the reappearance of security as a leading political issue-area.[59] This was not of course in the traditional context of a general European or global war, but in the narrower setting of localised and limited guerilla violence, which might arise within the state as well as from outside it. Although Irish security policy has always had this internal dimension, not since the civil war had it posed such problems. The run-down condition of the military machine was soon seen in such mundane matters as coping with civilian refugees and patrolling the border, while the role of some army intelligence officers in the arms crisis of 1970 provoked doubts about civilian-military relations; at the same time the Minister for Defence admitted that the army's capability to protect northern nationalists in a pogrom was doubtful.[60] Gradually increased expenditure and recruiting – even in 1972 a hint of obligatory military training[61] – attested to an *ad hoc* response to the prevailing uncertainties.[62]

In the aftermath of the breakdown of the Sunningdale agree-ment in the Spring of 1974, the Irish army's capabilities again became a public issue when a confidential Labour Party document was leaked to the press.[63] The author of the document, the

Minister for Posts and Telegraphs, Dr Conor Cruise O'Brien, in the course of speculating about the situation which would prevail in the event of a British withdrawal from Northern Ireland, argued that the Irish army did not possess the capability to control events there. It could only hope to hold one border town, such as Newry, and would even be seriously extended in defensive action within the Republic. Although this assessment raised some patriotic and professional military hackles, it was in essence shared by the leader of the Fianna Fáil opposition, Jack Lynch. Thus, although the army by the mid-seventies reached its highest manpower, at nearly 13,000 all ranks, and its highest expenditure for over twenty-five years, it is by no means certain that it is equipped to meet the possible contingencies which might arise as a result of the Northern Ireland problem.

A further uncertainty for Irish security policy also arose in 1969, and this may well prove to have more profound long-term consequences. This was the reactivation of the issue of membership of the European Community, following the resignation of General de Gaulle in the Spring of that year. An earlier attempt to join, blocked by the General in 1963, had seen the Irish government show signs of readiness to abandon neutrality should it be made a condition of membership. Indeed in 1962, the Taoiseach, Seán Lemass, with his former leader, de Valera, safely removed to the presidency, claimed that Ireland was not neutral in its ideological commitment, but simply did not belong to NATO because of a complex quarrel with one of its members. Moreover, in the Dáil on 8 March 1962, he argued that the view that accession to the North Atlantic Treaty implied recognition of partition was perhaps far-fetched. As far as he was concerned, the whole question was 'academic'[64], and with the collapse of EEC negotiations at the beginning of 1963, so it proved to be, though not quite in the sense Lemass had envisaged.

After 1969 a similar devaluation of neutrality was attempted by pro-marketeers. The Minister for External Affairs, Dr Patrick Hillery, advanced the thesis that 'while Ireland remained neutral during World War II we have never adopted a permanent policy of neutrality in the doctrinaire or ideological sense.'[65] If this concept of *'ad hoc* neutrality' was not quite the whole truth, neither was the anti-marketeers' claim that 'we have followed a policy of military neutrality since the foundation of our State which is quite as legitimate and important for us as is their similar long-established policy for the people of Sweden and Switzerland.'[66] The debate proceeded fitfully along these lines — it was always a peripheral issue — with the anti-marketeers claiming that membership of NATO was practically a corollary of membership, while their opponents pointed to the fact that the Treaties of Rome did not cover defence and any such involvement would be in the distant future, and subject to an Irish veto.

After the expanded European Community came into being in 1973, although there were no moves to incorporate defence directly, the Community's 'tangential relevance to military matters'[67] could not be ignored. The procedures of political consultation were developed, with the aim of harmonising foreign policies; although this by no means eliminated the independence of member-states, one of its early successes was the formulation of a common position at the Conference on European Security and Co-operation which opened at Helsinki in 1973.[68] This did not concern the specifically military aspects of European security — apart from procedures for notification of large-scale manoeuvres — but it did establish the broad diplomatic framework in which military policy could develop. The fact that the other eight participants in European Community political consultations are also members of NATO has apparently caused little serious problem to date, except for that of identifying the dividing lines between 'security' and 'defence'.

This dividing line between ends and means may, however, be difficult to sustain in the long run. Proposals to bring defence into the competence of the Community system continue to abound, and it is significant that they do not all imply the evolution of that system into a fully-fledged federation; indeed, some are not much more than a rationalisation of existing alliance systems, with the added element of a more emphatic role for the European states. Developments of the latter sort, such as the evolution of the NATO 'Eurogroup' from 1968, have not yet involved the European Community, but in the context of discussion of the Community's political future — the debate on 'European Union' — this possibility has arisen. In 1975 the reports of the Community's Commission and the European Parliament, and subsequently the Tindemans Report of January 1976, all referred to defence in general terms. Meanwhile more specific suggestions are raised about the possibility of the Community entering the defence field: for example, by way of Community armaments policies, without necessarily implying a revision of the Community's fundamental legal basis.

Irish government reactions to these tentative developments have been slow to arouse public interest. In July 1973 the new Minister for Foreign Affairs, Garret FitzGerald, expressed his distaste for the rigidities and institutionalised rivalry of the military alliance system; in this he was following a traditional justification for Irish neutrality – the idea that a small state could make a greater contribution to peace by staying outside military blocs, rather than by committing negligible resources to one side or the other.[69] Dr FitzGerald had earlier, in his first major policy statement in the Dáil, distinguished between existing alliances such as NATO and the possibility of a future European Community defence organisation. Irish policy was unchanged with regard to the former, which at that time included non-democratic regimes in Portugal and Greece, but was open to reconsideration with regard to the latter.[70] This position was not further clarified until the European Union debate was under way in 1975. The minister was then critical of the Commission's reference to defence, which he regarded as premature. In his view defence should not be considered in the European Community framework until (or unless) there was a significant integration of member-states' foreign policies and a clear move to federal decision-making structures. This stand against a gradual involvement in defence was supplemented by the claim that on occasion Ireland's absence from any military alliance had proved useful to other member-states.[71] The latter possibility had ʰearlier been suggested by FitzGerald and before that by the then French Foreign Minister, Maurice Schumann, on a visit to Dublin on 22 October 1971, but it is not clear to what extent it is appreciated by other governments. In any case Irish reservations about the European Community's role in defence were not critical at this stage. Some NATO members, such as the Netherlands, were equally cautious on account of the implications for the cohesion of NATO and particularly the American commitment; while Denmark and France were reluctant to see the sort of political integration within the European Community which the Irish government would regard as a prerequisite of the abandonment of military neutrality.

The possibility that Ireland would be asked to participate in some form of joint military venture was raised early in 1977, thus reviving the controversy which had taken place prior to accession to the European Community.[72] However, in reply to a question in the Dáil on 2 November 1977 a government spokesman stated, without further comment, that there was no intention to join NATO and there had been no external pressures to do so. The political sensitivity of the issue helps explain official reticence, but unfortunately makes it difficult to assess its military aspects. Although Irish accession to a military alliance (whether in NATO or the European Community) would undoubtedly increase the political cohesion of the alliance. Ireland's strategic value remains unclear. The assumption that the state is strategically altogether irrelevant may be wishful thinking, based on the contingency of an all-out nuclear war and ignoring the preparations continually being made to deter such an eventuality. It could be argued that Ireland's peripheral situation and relative underpopulation make her attractive either as a location for missile bases or as an exemplary target. As for conventional warfare, which is still a significant element in strategic policy, Ireland could provide logistic facilities, such as deep-sea harbourage, or be the location for reserve, training or command units.

At a more general level there is the question of denying any potentially hostile state the room to develop its position on Irish soil or in Irish waters. This is seen most clearly if the traditional assumption that the British Isles form a strategic entity is maintained. In 1972, for example, the British government declared as one of its three major concerns in Northern Ireland 'that Northern Ireland should not offer a base for any external threat to the security of the United Kingdom.'[73] The same principle applies to the whole island from the point of view of the alliance of which Britain is a major member; to some of the more security-conscious groups within NATO countries, even the establishment of a Soviet Embassy in Dublin in 1974 was seen as a security threat.[74] Nevertheless it is a simple historical fact that the western alliance has done without Irish participation for over twenty-five years, sometimes in circumstances a great deal more fraught than those of the late nineteen-sixties and seventies. NATO has required benevolent neutrality from Ireland, and that is what it has received.

But what of Ireland's ability to defend herself, whether inside or outside an alliance? In spite of the increases, both in defence expenditure and military man-power in the nineteen-seventies, as a response to the Northern Ireland conflict, Ireland is still one of the most lightly armed states in Europe, west or east, aligned or neutral. In 1976, Ireland spent 1.6 per cent of GNP on defence. Only Luxembourg (with 1.2 per cent) spent proportionately less among NATO countries, the next lowest being Canada with 1.9 per cent. Of the European neutrals, only Austria and Finland, with 1.1 per cent, gave a lesser share of GNP to defence.[75] The Irish army is still an infantry army, with minimal armour, apparently based on the concept of 'territorial defence' — 'making one's own territory. and people hard to conquer'.[76] The ancillary forces are slight: the air arm contains sixteen combat aircraft, and the naval force, with three fishery protection vessels and three minesweepers, is barely able to cover fishery protection duties within the traditionally limited territorial waters.

It is in fact in the maritime aspect of Irish external security, for so long implicitly abandoned to the British naval umbrella, that the most recent incentive for a revision of defence policy has emerged. With the advent of two hundred mile economic zones, territorial waters are no longer limited and the economic interests associated with them may prove to be vastly more important than hitherto.[77] Instead of protecting a small inshore fishing fleet, the naval and air services will have to ensure the conservation of fish stocks and the protection of oil-rigs scattered over large areas of ocean. This routine, peace-time task could demand a fundamental reallocation of resources within the defence forces and a significant increase in overall expenditure. Alternatively, the policing of Irish waters could be exercised jointly with the navies of other European Community states; however, in this situation, which would probably lead to reciprocal landing rights, Irish military neutrality would become increasingly unreal.[78]

More than fifty years ago the then Minister for Finance, Ernest Blythe, argued that 'a country that will not provide for its own defence according to its capacity is not likely to have its rights protected in a spirit of pure altruism by any other country.'[79] Much has changed in international relations since then but the need Blythe referred to still persists. What is required to fulfil this need, and what the state's capacity to meet this requirement is, are important and difficult political questions which are all too often neglected in Irish public life. At present no convincing

answer has been offered to the question of whether Ireland's
security policy reflects an element of sanity in an absurdly militar-
istic world or the failure to pay an adequate insurance premium.

Chapter 6

Unity

It is perhaps the deepest political passion with this nation that North and South be united into one nation.

Senator William Butler Yeats, 11 June 1925

Ireland, according to the geography I was taught at school, consists of thirty-two counties.

Seán Lemass, TD, 26 March 1930

Both before and since the Government of Ireland Act of 1920 divided Ireland into two regions — 'Southern Ireland', which in the following year was to become politically independent of the United Kingdom, and 'Northern Ireland', which did not — the question of unity has been a central issue-area in Irish politics. Unity, or 'reunification' or 'partition', as it is often referred to, enjoys the leading place in most formal statements of political goals. In the constitution of the largest political party, Fianna Fáil, it has pride of place in the list of the party's aims, the first of these being 'to secure the Unity and Independence of Ireland as a Republic'; the very name of the second largest party, Fine Gael, means 'United Ireland'.[1] In popular terms, the whole question is referred to simply as 'the national aim'.

The emphasis on unity as a goal yet to be achieved marks one of the most notable failures of Irish foreign policy. Independence as such may be unrealisable in absolute terms, yet in the pursuit of constitutional independence and in the manipulation of symbols Irish governments have been able to point to their successes. Security too has been maintained, and not solely because of the fortunes of location. In contrast, the quest for unity has been a demonstration of almost unmitigated failure.

The roots of this failure lie in an image of Irish unity which has more often than not resisted the challenges posed to it by the mere facts of any particular situation.[2] The self-evident nature of unity contained in this image owes a good deal to a view of Ireland as an unambiguously defined geographical entity — one territory. Ireland as a nation is not simply a group of people but is 'a small island nation, whose only boundaries are the seas which demarcate its identity.'[3] In the three articles in the Irish Constitution of 1937 which appear under the sub-head 'The Nation', the only definition given of the nation is in territorial terms: 'The national territory consists of the whole island of Ireland, its islands and the territorial seas.'[4] Such a view is by no means uniquely Irish, being in accordance with the 'doctrine of natural frontiers', which holds 'that the world has been geographically constructed to accommodate nation-states . . .' and which is 'a common nationalist doctrine . . . whenever convenience has suggested its use.'[5]

What of the people on this island? It is a fundamental article of nationalist faith that the Irish nation — in human terms — is indivisible; the one million or so northern unionists thus belong to 'the dissident section of the Irish people.'[6] To admit that this 'dissidence' amounts to a separate identity is heretical, though in practice the Irish nationalist, when talking about 'our people' often does so in a context which excludes the dissidents altogether.[7] If they are included, it is to berate them for their undemocratic failure to abide by the majority decision of those living on the national territory. The power of this image, whatever its ambiguities, has until recent years been an immovable political reality, able to withstand the awkward suggestion that the 'question on Irish unity might be not how or when, but why.'[8]

The question of unity is not conceived of as a 'mere' foreign policy issue; indeed its association with the term 'foreign' policy may be rejected by some doctrinaire nationalists on the grounds that Northern Ireland is not foreign. Nevertheless the fact that in practice it has generally been treated as such, as an issue between governments, follows not merely from the actual situation (where another government exercises jurisdiction over Northern Ireland) but from an important principle of nationalist doctrine. Given the essential, 'natural' Irishness of northern unionists, the fact of partition was seen as the fulfilment of deliberate and skilfully executed British policy.[9] The conclusion is drawn that 'partition can only be ended constitutionally as it began, by an Act of the British Parliament'[10], and the first priority is therefore to persuade the British government to abandon its imperialistic claim. Only when this is done will it be necessary to deal with the problem of Irish 'dissidence' and — the circle closes — this dissidence will disappear, since it depended on British manipulation in any case.

This 'Britain first' strategy has tended to cast the question of unity in a diplomatic mould. It has been seen primarily as the outstanding grievance in Anglo-Irish relations, and as such a proper subject both for bilateral intergovernmental negotiations and the mobilisation of 'world opinion' in whatever multilateral setting is available. Where such pressure fails, the alternative tradition of Anglo-Irish relations, the tradition of anti-imperialist violence, takes over. At cross-purposes with each other, these two traditional onslaughts on the citadel of British sovereignty over Northern Ireland have failed time and again. Only since the last episode in this conflict opened in the late nineteen-sixties have serious doubts been raised as to whether any British government is capable of meeting Irish claims. And, if it is, is the problem of unity in its essence a problem between Dublin and London or a problem to be resolved 'among Irishmen'? But however attitudes change on this still controversial point, in its day-to-day evolution the 'northern crisis' continues to be a major preoccupation of Irish foreign policy.

*   *   *

The Government of Ireland Act of 1920 was designed to allow for intransigent unionist suspicions of Home Rule as exercised from Dublin. It incorporated provision for a consultative Council of Ireland which would include representatives from both the Dublin and Belfast regional parliaments and this, it was hoped, would provide a framework for agreed reunification in the long term. However, only one of the two regional governments — the northern one — was established before the Anglo-Irish Treaty altered the framework in which reunification had been considered. When the Provisional Government of the Irish Free State came into being in January 1922 one of its first major problems was how to respond to the situation in the north, where the large catholic minority was threatened by renewed violence from protestant unionists. The choice lay between supporting the minority with force or attempting to work towards reunification through a mixture of economic boycott, non-recognition of the northern regime and manipulation of the new constitutional framework. Although the Free State government, and especially Michael Collins, did not lose sight of the first option, the non-violent strategy prevailed. Agreements to deal with the immediate threat were reached between Collins and the northern prime minister, Sir James Craig, but possible development beyond this was not then clear. Craig was not happy about the Council of Ireland, but he did propose joint cabinet meetings in its place, while the southern government wanted an all-Ireland constitutional convention.[11]

In order to persuade Craig eventually to accept the latter course the Dublin leaders counted on the findings of the Boundary Commission which Lloyd George had proposed near the end of the Treaty negotiations and which was authorised in Article 12 of the Treaty. This body, consisting of a representative from the northern and southern governments and a chairman appointed by the British government, was to 'determine in accordance with the wishes of the inhabitants, so far as may be compatible with economic and geographic conditions, the boundaries between Northern Ireland and the rest of Ireland.'[12] Its significance lay in the considerable expectations which surround it, particularly when viewed from Dublin. It was not merely that land was to be regained — on a simple majority head-count this might amount to more than two out of the six counties — but rather that the consequences of such a reduction would destroy Northern Ireland as an economic and political unit.

This notion seems to have been very carelessly considered. It reflected some general ideas as to what constituted an economy or a polity — for example, the 'natural' or at least rational relationship between an industrial base and its agricultural hinterland — and it is only fair to point out that such arguments were commonplace in the period during and after World War I. What the Irish government did not see was the fact that their own existence represented the weakness of the argument in practice; before World War I unionists had been 'reassured by the silly but widespread belief that southern Ireland could not survive economically without the north-eastern counties.'[13] Whether the 'natural' economic unit · was the British Isles or Ireland was an open question. The Free State government did not appreciate the extent to which Britain was prepared to make allowances for a geographically isolated and relatively impoverished region, and possibly placed too much faith in the vague assurances of Lloyd George and other British politicians. Hopes that the boundary settlement would lead beyond repartition to the end of partition rested on a flimsy base indeed.

In the event these hopes were to collapse before that base was exposed.[14] Collins had hoped the Boundary Commission would be a reality in the Summer of 1922, but there was a delay of over two years; the southern Irish were distracted by civil war, the British by prolonged government instability, and the northern government's procedural obstruction was merely the icing on the cake. In the interval the latter consolidated its position, while in both Dublin and London nearly all the original architects of the Boundary Commission disappeared from the centre of political power.

When the Commission was finally set up in 1924 the ambiguity of Article 12 concerning the criteria to be used permitted the chairman, Mr Justice Feetham, to take a restrictive view of its role. The Irish representative was a member of the government, Eoin MacNeill, Minister for Education, whose view of his role — as being quasi-judicial rather than political — was held with such integrity that he seems not to have informed his colleagues that their expectations were unlikely to be met. The northern representative, R. J. Fisher, had no such inhibitions. On 7 November 1925 the outcome of the Commission's deliberations were leaked to the British press and it appeared that, although Northern Ireland contained an overall nationalist minority of about one in three, the proposed transfers of territory would be negligible. MacNeill resigned from the Commission (and from the Irish government), and while legally a majority report would have sufficed this move made it politically unenforceable. Hectic trilateral negotiations followed this collapse, leading to an agreement, on 3 December 1925, in which W. T. Cosgrave's government recognised the existing border, and therefore the existence of Northern Ireland. In return the Irish Free State received a favourable readjustment of some of its financial obligations under the 1921 Treaty. It was the last occasion for forty years that the heads of the Dublin and Belfast governments were to meet face to face.

This was an enormous disappointment for the Dublin government, and the fact that it survived was partly due to divisions within the abstentionist part of the opposition, which at that time could agree on little else other than a protest against partition. At a blow the goal of unity had become an aspiration; faced with the obduracy of northern unionists and their influence at Westminster, government policy became a stance of 'neighbourly comradeship'.[15] It was hoped that the boundary settlement would stabilise tensions between unionist and nationalist within Northern Ireland and that nationalists would feel free to play a full part in provincial government.

This conciliatory policy lasted during the next six years, without any noticeable effect on northern attitudes. On the contrary, in 1929 the unionists abolished proportional representation for elections to the provincial parliament at Stormont, thus reducing the effectiveness of a nationalist opposition which had hesitantly come into parliamentary politics in 1926. The alienation of the nationalists was not completed however until 1932, and until then conciliation did not appear an unreasonable line for Dublin to follow. It was, however, a policy which was executed in a passive if not negative way. There was, for example, no serious recourse to the League of Nations, an obvious forum for the grievances of minorities, in spite of the urgings of some political leaders.[16] This may have been seen in Dublin as an instance of restraint, nobly borne, but was hardly likely to arouse interest in Belfast.

In 1932, not only did nationalist frustration in Northern Ireland lead to a walkout from Stormont, but there was a significant change in government in the south. De Valera at first seemed to follow his predecessor's conciliatory line; on 1 March 1933 he declared that 'the only policy for abolishing partition that I can see is for us, in this part of Ireland, to use such freedom as we can secure to get for the people in this part of Ireland such conditions as will make the people in the other part of Ireland wish to belong to this part.'[17] This was in line with de Valera's renunciation of the use of armed force to end partition[18], but beyond this the conciliatory tone was deceptive; in any case the very mention of 'freedom', with its implications for the revision of the 1921 Treaty, was anathema to unionists who saw a certain guarantee of British control over the Free State in that treaty. In fact de Valera was not content to sit back and demonstrate his charms. He continued the policy he had pursued while in opposition of direct involvement — on an abstentionist basis — in northern political life, and in 1933 was himself elected to a seat in South Down.[19] More significant, though, was his opening exchange with the British Dominions Secretary on 5 April 1932 when the issue of partition took what was to be its place for the next twenty years, as the holy grail in a crusade against British wrongs to Ireland.[20]

At first the shape of this crusade did not emerge clearly; the ending of partition was one target among several, and those pertaining to constitutional independence were the first in the line of fire. But as the latter disappeared, so partition came into focus. In the secret Anglo-Irish talks which developed in 1936 it became the stock opening issue in the presentation of the Irish case. But this was no mere ploy. De Valera wrote after a meeting with Malcolm MacDonald in 1937: 'no agreements on other matters could bring about the good relations which he and I desired, so long as partition lasted.'[21] MacDonald appreciated the depth of de Valera's feeling, but not the strategy which the Irish government adopted and which found expression in the new Constitution of 1937.

Article 2 of that document claims the 'whole island of Ireland, its islands and the territorial seas' to be the 'national territory.' This is a direct repudiation of the first Irish Free State government's recognition of the existence of Northern Ireland following the collapse of the Boundary Commission in 1925. Article 3 refers to the *de facto* situation, where, 'pending re-integration of the national territory' and without derogating from Article 2, the effective national jurisdiction is described as that of the Free State.[22] It has been said that fundamental law 'enshrines, elevates, consecrates the interests or ideas it embodies'; such indeed has been the effect of these articles on nationalist opinion, particularly in the party of their origin, Fianna Fáil. But law is also 'a form of policy that changes the stakes and often "escalates" the intensity of political contests'[23], and such has been the effect on unionists, whose leaders henceforth could represent every act of Dublin as being inherently hostile.

De Valera, however, thought that in conjunction with the concept of external association with the Commonwealth and the consequent omission of the word 'republic' in the Constitution, the overall effect of his constitution was conciliatory.[24] North and south could conceivably still be reunited in a Commonwealth context; external association was to be a bridge across which unionists might pass to the promised land. But there was little

either in the Constitution or in the political culture of the south
to entice unionists on to a bridge which in any case was, in terms
of its constitutional structure, a flimsy thing indeed when set
against the certainties of Articles 2 and 3.

The constitutional claim was supplemented by a campaign
against British control over Northern Ireland, in which the instruments of diplomacy and propaganda were used in varying degrees,
but ultimately to little effect. The first occasion during which
diplomatic tactics could be used was the bilateral negotiations
which culminated in the Anglo-Irish agreements of April 1938.[25]
Partition was the one major issue-area where agreement was most
obviously lacking. De Valera tried to make unity a condition of
any defence agreement, but to no avail. He was up against the fact
of majority opinion within Northern Ireland — underlined by a
general election there during the negotiations — in addition to
the northern government's friends at Westminster, in this case
particularly the Home Secretary, Sir Samuel Hoare. Indeed, as the
negotiations progressed not only was de Valera making little
ground in his efforts to make the British take the responsibility
for changing the unionists' position, but the latter were pressing
the British hard to gain trade concessions on their behalf.

Nevertheless, the negotiations did start to expose some weaknesses in the unionist stance. Anti-partition policy was aimed not
only at the question of who controlled Northern Ireland; it was
also concerned with the question of how it was controlled, thus
focusing on unionist repression of the large nationalist minority.
In response to de Valera's raising of this issue the British Home
Office conducted a sketchy and predictably complacent investi-
gation, which was however disputed by the Dominions Office.[26]
In addition, in the context of improved trade relations, southern
and northern civil servants established personal contacts, a process
which apparently was willingly taken up by the Irish Minister for
Industry and Commerce, Seán Lemass.[27]

These were very tentative beginnings, having no immediate
effect on the northern regime and far from either de Valera's
expectations or those he had aroused in others. Thus in the
Autumn of 1938 he returned to direct diplomatic pressure. He
had established some credit with the British government for his
support of Chamberlain's policy during the Munich crisis—support
which was largely based on his 'deep belief in the inherent justice

of the Sudeten case', based on an analogy with northern nation-alists.[28] He saw Chamberlain at the beginning of October and as a result the Home Office was ordered to conduct a fuller investi-gation of minority grievances in Northern Ireland. This was produced at the beginning of November, and again the Dominions Office tended to act as advocate for the Irish case, expressing concern about gerrymandering, the Orange Order and general governmental attitudes towards catholics. The Dominions Secre-tary, Malcolm MacDonald, was in favour of a further inquiry, but by this time the political heat of de Valera's propaganda campaign had caused a lack of sympathy for his position among the rest of the British government.[29]

The slow and gradual process of confidential diplomacy was not generally popular among revisionist statesmen in the late nineteen-thirties, and with regard to partition de Valera was no exception. An important feature of the negotiations at the beginning of 1938 had been his personal involvement with the question of Irish unity; he was 'deeply emotionally susceptible to opinion on partition.'[30] Such opinion was reflected primarily in sustained pressure by delegations of northern nationalists and in the press, especially *The Irish Press,* associated with the Fianna Fáil party.[31] Moreover, de Valera had already warned MacDonald in 1937 that he 'would . . . have to consider a campaign to inform British and world opinion as to the iniquity of the whole position [on partition]'[32], the internationalising of the issue being by now a traditional response for Irish nationalists. Thus what was later to be known as the policy of 'raising the sore thumb' became the predominant characteristic of Dublin's public stance on partition.[33]

Already de Valera had shown some signs of bringing the unity issue before the League of Nations, but this had usually been in a tangential way, either by general reference to the protection of minorities as 'a sacred duty' or in opposing partition elsewhere in the world.[34] During the negotiations which led to the Anglo-Irish agreements of 1938 he solicited the support of the American president, Franklin D. Roosevelt. Although the latter made his interest in a general settlement of Anglo-Irish differences known to the British government, this had no effect on the question of partition.[35] But in the Autumn of 1938 the public advocacy of the unity issue was opened in earnest, with a full declaration of de Valera's policy in the London *Evening Standard* on 17 October.[36]

The solution he offered was the incorporation of Northern Ireland, as a distinct but not separate political entity, into an all-Ireland federal system. For de Valera this was 'not the ideal but a practical solution', which he had advanced before, in May 1921. It also came up during the Treaty negotiations, and was proposed by W. T. Cosgrave in 1923[37]; now it was presented as the ultimate limit to which the Dublin government was prepared to go within the new constitutional framework. If this solution was not accepted de Valera was prepared to call for large-scale transfers of population, in which unionists would be exchanged with Irish catholics living in Britain.[38]

Despite the vague hint of 'a united free Ireland . . . willing to co-operate with Britain to resist a common attack'[39], the reaction of the northern government was predictably one of hostility and that of the British government was intense irritation; further discussion of the issue ceased.[40] The propaganda strategy did not. De Valera planned to visit the United States in May 1939 to secure American support. However, before this the IRA, having been distracted by incursions into left-wing revolutionary politics (including participation in the Spanish civil war), returned to the partition issue. Claiming to replace de Valera's government as the *de jure* Irish government − and effectively rivalling him as a guardian of the national conscience − the IRA delivered an ultimatum to Britain on 12 January 1939 and followed it with a campaign of sporadic bombing in British cities, culminating in four civilian deaths in August 1939.[41] This campaign, though farcical in terms of revolutionary strategy, effectively sabotaged any hopes de Valera had of continuing his diplomatic and propaganda efforts, and compelled him to turn his attention to this internal challenge to his government's authority.

In any case, the outbreak of European war in September 1939 ruled out a propaganda approach; the American visit had been postponed and then cancelled. This did not, however, mean that partition was no longer to be an issue in Anglo-Irish diplomacy during the war years. On the contrary, the old adage of England's difficulty being Ireland's opportunity arose again, in the form of a possible bargain in which Irish unity would be gained at the expense of Irish neutrality. The outlines of this bargain had already emerged during the 1938 negotiations (and the informal discussions preceding them), although it became clear that

'England's difficulty' with regard to security was not felt to such an extent that the British government would seriously consider over-ruling the northern unionists. Nor, as we have seen, had 'Ireland's opportunity' arrived in October 1938, and a year later, although war had been declared and Churchill was pressing for the return of the Irish ports, de Valera's reiteration, in extremely general terms, of the possibilities which might arise following Irish unity failed to elicit any British response.[42]

In May 1940 a very different military situation prevailed, as the German armies swept to the channel. Inevitably the British government pressed for Irish defence co-operation, and just as inevitably de Valera held up partition as an insuperable obstacle. Towards the end of May and throughout June, in an atmosphere of panic, the possibilities of a bargain were explored.[43] The essence of the British proposals was that Ireland would enter the war immediately, while in return the British government would declare that in principle Ireland should be united and establish a joint north-south defence council and a working party on the constitutional implications. De Valera rejected this exchange on the grounds that while Ireland had to make an immediate concession – which would put her largely undefended population at serious risk – the British concession was both vague and distant, and therefore vulnerable to the intransigence of the unionists. There was to be no second Redmond.[44]

De Valera's response has to a large extent been justified by subsequent revelations concerning the British attitudes. The prime minister, Churchill, who the previous Autumn had pressed hard for Irish involvement, now argued that the strategic situation was not so desperate as to put significant pressure on the northern government, and when Lord Craigavon (the former Sir James Craig) did express his 'shock' at the idea, the British cabinet hurriedly reassured him. In any case Craigavon on 30 June made the northern 'veto' public knowledge when he rejected any constitutional discussions, whether Ireland abandoned neutrality or not. Churchill's strategic assessment was correct, for when the German government made *its* bid for Irish support in return for 'the final realisation of [Ireland's] national demands'[45], it was in no position to offer the Irish government anything tangible beyond the prospect of an immediate British invasion.

The possibility of a bargain over unity and neutrality was

again declined, notwithstanding a curious incident after Pearl Harbor. Churchill sent de Valera a cryptic, midnight telegram which the latter at first thought indicated Churchill's intention to link the issues.[46] It was while disabusing de Valera of this impression that the British Dominions Secretary, Lord Cranborne, warned the Irish leader of the long-term repercussions of staying neutral on unionist and British opinion. De Valera accepted that it might delay a solution, but he under-estimated the emotional effect that Northern Ireland's loyalty would have on cementing the British commitment to maintain partition. Thus, although in May 1941 de Valera had demonstrated his claim to speak on an all-Ireland basis when he opposed British conscription in Northern Ireland, his influence on the evolution of the partition issue during the war was essentially negative; it counted little beside 'the six counties [which] by the magnitude and devotion of their war effort, had done more to perpetuate the partition of Ireland than a whole generation of Twelfth of July demonstrations.'[47]

Throughout World War II the position of the United States influenced the evolution of the partition issue. Prior to December 1941 American neutrality was a constraint against British policy towards Ireland. In the Summer of 1940 de Valera had persuaded the State Department to warn the British against an invasion of Ireland[48]; even when the increasingly pro-British administration could not be influenced directly the Irish government could appeal to Irish-American opinion.[49] But when the United States entered the war this inhibition was removed and the full weight of American pressure could be turned against Ireland, with all the confidence of the newly converted. To counter this eventuality, the Irish government laid more stress on partition as a justification for Irish neutrality.[50]

The American representative in Dublin, David Gray, was concerned above all lest 'the Irish question' (now in the form of partition) should intrude into post-war American domestic politics, as it had done with such harmful effects for the Democrats after World War I. In order to prevent this he determined to discredit de Valera's stand on neutrality in American eyes; hence his persistent intrigues to exert allied pressure on Ireland, culminating in the American note of February 1944.[51] Although Gray failed either to bring Ireland into the war or to oust de Valera, it is arguable that he did indeed make it difficult for Irish governments to use the lever of Irish-American opinion on partition after the war. De Valera's first attempt to undertake this ploy in 1946 thus fell quite flat.[52]

Nevertheless, when the war ended the anti-partition crusade was resumed, now as the major outstanding issue of foreign policy. The absence of Ireland from the reality of Commonwealth consultations and the lack of a comprehensive intergovernmental review of Anglo-Irish relations put the emphasis more than ever on the propaganda approach. De Valera was losing interest in the notion of external association as a bridge for unionists to cross the gulf which separated them from the south, and the British government seems to have given him little encouragement that it might work.[53] The greater part of his energies were spent in the discreet encouragement of anti-partition groups, which were being independently formed in Northern Ireland and Britain. When his government was defeated in 1948, however, de Valera threw discretion to the winds and campaigned openly in Britain, the United States and Australia in order to raise general public support for reunification.

In so doing he followed the hallowed path of Irish nationalist propaganda abroad, a path bearing the print of his own earlier efforts, as well as those of earlier nationalist leaders such as Parnell and Redmond. He was the much respected leader of the biggest single political party and it would have taken a strong government to question his treatment of this emotional issue. The first coalition government was not strong, and in order to take partition out of domestic party politics was compelled, willy-nilly, to follow de Valera's lead. If its members thought of defence co-operation as a lever to extract British concessions on Northern Ireland — this time in the context of the formation of NATO at the beginning of 1949 — such a ploy was to be made impossible by de Valera's linking of the partition and neutrality issues.[54]

It was against this background that the coalition government proceeded to tie up the loose ends of constitutional revision by repealing external association.[55] The Taoiseach, John A. Costello, argued that it had not worked as regards unity, but he underestimated the effect its removal would have on future attempts to reunite the island. The British response, in the Ireland Act of 1949, was to increase the legitimacy of the Belfast veto on constitutional change by confirming that Northern Ireland would not be detached from the United Kingdom without the consent of the Stormont parliament.[56] This move in turn provoked the ultimate paroxysms of anti-partitionist fervour in Dublin. De Valera argued that his policy had been based on the assumption that the British government could be compelled to overcome unionist intransigence: 'if you had properly-informed public opinion in Britain and a Parliament and a Government that responded to the fair-minded people in Britain we would have reached the stage when this would be done.'[57] In spite of the evidence that the British government would not act in this fashion, and de Valera's own doubts arising from his lack of success, the Irish government shared this simplistic view of the nature of public opinion. It sponsored an all-party committee to raise funds for the education of the 'fair-minded people in Britain', while the Minister for External Affairs, Seán MacBride, bewildered delegates with his insistence on the iniquities of partition at the only major international forum open to Ireland, the new Council of Europe. By the time de Valera was back in power in 1951, the anti-partition campaign had degenerated into a futile ritual.[58] When de Valera met Churchill in London in 1953 the claim to unity was raised and rejected, and the two old adversaries had a polite lunch.[59] Little effort was subsequently made to pursue the associated question of northern repression of the minority.

The most obvious development of the nineteen-fifties was a renewed IRA campaign on the border, which opened in December 1956 and was not finally wound up by the IRA until 1962.[60] This was a factor in the loss of support for the second coalition government early in 1957, but although in the subsequent general election Sinn Féin, the IRA's political front, won four seats, the return of de Valera to power saw a determined repression of the IRA. Two years later de Valera himself retired from active politics (being elected President in 1959) and was replaced by Seán Lemass, and gradually a new approach to unity policy began to replace the discredited anti-partition crusade.

The Lemass policy was one of rapprochement with northern unionists rather than the traditional assertion of the claim to unity, aimed at British governments; in essence, it implied a return to the possibilities of the stance of neighbourly comradeship of the mid-nineteen-twenties. The obstacles to this policy were formidable; the constitutional claim was sacrosanct, and if indifference towards partition was perhaps becoming a feature of southern opinion, traditional prejudices remained firmly entrenched in the north.[61] Nevertheless, once the IRA had admitted defeat in 1962, and against a background of material prosperity and growing religious ecumenism, Lemass felt able to advance the view that 'from the extension of useful contacts at every level of activity, a new situation would develop . . . The solution of the problem of partition is one to be found in Ireland by Irishmen . . .'[62]

The Lemass policy received its most dramatic expession in his exchange of visits with the northern prime minister, Terence O'Neill, at the beginning of 1965, which symbolised the attempt to normalise north-south relations at the highest level. This was followed by departmental discussions of schemes of functional co-operation, the most notable being in the provision of cross-border electricity links.[63] The final element in the strategy was an attempt to tackle the sensitive question of constitutional revision, by the establishment of a Committee on the Constitution in September 1966, just before Lemass resigned as Taoiseach.

This was a new departure and one which seemed to be widely accepted at first. But sectarian animosities were to undermine O'Neill's position in the north. The long gestation of functional schemes and their technical nature meant that although civil servants on both sides of the border might perceive future mutual benefits, to electricity consumers electricity was simply electricity. On the other hand, to unionist extremists cross-border electricity was the thin end of the wedge, and one of the first victims of a new round of violence in the Spring of 1969 was to be an electricity pylon belonging to the cross-border link. Meanwhile, in the south, constitutional revision did not quite escape the suspicions of traditional nationalists. In December 1967 the Report of the Committee on the Constitution recommended that Article 3 be replaced by an expression of the aspiration that the island be 're-united in harmony and brotherly affection between all Irishmen', and that the state's jurisdiction was limited to the twenty-six counties 'until the achievement of the nation's unity shall otherwise require.'[64] This was too much for the secretary of the Fianna Fáil party, the Minister for Local Government, Kevin Boland. Although he did not succeed in making it a public issue, no action had been taken on the report by the time the question of Northern Ireland became an acute crisis for the Dublin government in 1969.[65]

The Lemass policy towards unity represented a significant change of strategy, but it was cautious if not leisurely in execution. Like the policies of the other two governments concerned, it was now overwhelmed by the unexpected collapse of political authority in Northern Ireland, following the build-up of minority civil rights demonstrations during the nineteen-sixties. This challenge to the legitimised repression by a permanent majority succeeded largely because it at first took place outside the traditional constitutional and intergovernmental framework of Irish nationalism, against a background in which parliamentary governments throughout the world were finding it difficult to use what repressive powers they possessed. But the traditional framework could not be ignored and once the civil rights movement showed signs of success, old patterns of reaction and counter-reaction emerged.[66]

The riots of August 1969 marked an important stage in this process. On the one hand they led to direct British intervention in the initiation of reforms, but on the other hand they were not only sectarian in the most traditional sense, but were followed by a large British military presence, the eventual reactivation of the IRA and the involvement of the Dublin government, now led by Jack Lynch. The latter felt compelled to act because of the vulnerable position of the nationalist minority, a situation which aroused much concern in the south.[67] This was seen in the initial measures – the establishment of field hospitals and refugee camps – but the fundamental question of unity could not be omitted by the leader of de Valera's party.

The important point is that it was still raised as a long-term goal. In his first major statement on the crisis Lynch expressed the hope that a solution would be found firstly by the amelioration of conditions within Northern Ireland and 'eventually by the restoration of the historic unity of our country.'[68] Two years later the attainment of unity was still envisaged as 'a long and arduous process', which must be preceded by the reconciliation of 'the estranged communities' in the north.[69] In conjunction with this theme of reconciliation-before-unity was the rejection of force. By 3 November 1969 the Taoiseach could say that 'it has already been made clear that we have no intention of using our Defence Forces to intervene in the affairs of Northern Ireland', and even after the violent reaction to the introduction of internment in the north he still maintained, on 12 August 1971, that the Irish government 'cannot and will not support any armed activity which will inevitably cause further suffering and death.'[70]

Lynch's overall view of the unity issue was not without its challengers. The IRA, which at the end of 1969 divided into an 'Official IRA' with a left-wing bias and a 'Provisional IRA' representing the traditional violent nationalist approach, agreed neither with the government's means nor its strategy. A more significant influence on the development of Lynch's policy, however, was the reaction within his own party. A cabinet polarisation into 'hawks' and 'doves' resulted in a serious crisis in May 1970 in which the Minister for Finance, Charles Haughey, and the Minister for Agriculture, Neil Blaney, were dismissed on the grounds of an alleged conspiracy to import arms for later use by nationalists in Northern Ireland.[71] Two other ministers resigned, one of them the finally disillusioned Kevin Boland, who started a new party, Aontacht Éireann, in order to promote the traditional republican virtues. This blood-letting did not kill the Fianna Fáil party or the government, but neither did it provide a complete cure; if he was to maintain party support the Taoiseach had somehow to incorporate the claim to unity into his policy.

As a rule this need was reflected in the form of public statements. From the beginning of the crisis Lynch balanced expressions of north-south reconciliation and condemnation of violence with an insistence on the territorial claim expressed in Articles 2 and 3 of the Constitution, and (usually implicitly) denied any contradiction between the two approaches. He also returned to de Valera's emphasis on making explicit demands of the British government. Thus on 11 July 1971, quoting de Valera's assertion of fifty years earlier ('we cannot admit the right of the British Government to mutilate our country'), Lynch called on the British government to 'declare their interest in encouraging the unity of Ireland, by agreement, in independence and in a harmonious relationship between the two islands.'[72] This did not satisfy the departed hawks (though one, Charles Haughey, was later recalled to the nest), but it was a formula which prevented the spread of further dissidence within the Fianna Fáil party.

Such was the domestic base of the Lynch government's northern policy between 1969 and 1971. The major diplomatic objective was to establish the government's position as 'second guarantor' of the Downing Street Declaration of 1969, a programme of reforms agreed by the Belfast and London governments. Though not a party to the Declaration, the Irish government maintained it had a legitimate interest in developments in the north, on the grounds both of the constitutional claim and of the repercussions which northern instability had on the Republic. This position was not readily accepted by the British Labour government of Harold Wilson. It gave a cold reception to the Irish Minister for External Affairs, Patrick Hillery, when the latter asked it to intervene to ban the parades which were to provoke the riot in August 1969. It also opposed Irish attempts to ask for a United Nations peace-keeping force in the Security Council on 20 August 1969, on the grounds that the United Nations had no right to intervene in the internal affairs of a member state.[73] However, the way in which this diplomatic confrontation was handled suggested that some measure of diplomatic consultation would not be ruled out altogether.[74]

By the end of 1970 Anglo-Irish relations were recovering from the shock of August 1969. Both governments were deeply involved in negotiations to join the European Community, and Lynch had demonstrated the limits of his tolerance of hard-line attitudes towards the north. At the beginning of 1971, Irish policy seemed to enter a constructive phase, in two respects. First, the Taoiseach gave a general commitment to reform within the Republic, in order to remove legislation which northern unionists might find offensive in a united Ireland: 'If . . . we must grasp some nettles which sting our pride then we will readily do so.'[75] Mr Lynch did not specify the nettles he would grasp, although it was generally assumed that they would include the recognition of the special position of the Catholic Church in the Constitution (Article 44), amendment of the Constitution with regard to divorce and legislation to allow contraception. The nettle of Articles 2 and 3 was not to be grasped, however, and this general commitment was not followed by urgent legislation.

At the same time, the Dublin government resumed the emphasis on functional co-operation which had been so characteristic of the Lemass strategy. On 20 February 1971 Lynch suggested an extension of preferential tariffs for northern goods, co-operation in cross-border regional development and the availability of information on the current EEC negotiations.[76] This offer was accepted in principle by the new northern prime minister, Brian Faulkner, and detailed talks were initiated at 'senior official level'. For Lynch this was an indicator of 'political confidence that the North is now capable of setting its face on a different kind of future for all its people'[77]; and on 6 August he went further, proposing a joint economic council and suggesting that 'giving representatives both North and South the opportunity of working together in a formal way would expand the scope of their functions.'[78] These proposals reflected the thesis of international functionalism, which maintains that economic and social co-operation can lead to a reduction in political conflict.[79] But on 9 August this line of policy was shelved, when internment without trial was introduced in the north.

The internment crisis of 1971 showed the limited extent to which any of the three governments involved could influence events in Northern Ireland. As a response to rising IRA violence internment was a failure. Conciliatory policies between Belfast and Dublin were suspended, and Anglo-Irish diplomatic relations became noticeably more difficult. The Irish government supported the passive resistance policy of the major minority party in the north, the Social Democratic and Labour Party (SDLP). The British premier, Edward Heath, denounced this as an unacceptable interference in the affairs of the United Kingdom.[80] Summit meetings between Lynch and Heath, the second also including the northern prime minister, had little effect on British policy, and at the end of November the Irish government announced its intention to put the case of ill-treatment of northern internees before the European Court of Human Rights. When, on 30 January 1972, thirteen people were shot by British troops in Derry ('Bloody Sunday'), the Irish ambassador to London was withdrawn and anti-British sentiment in Dublin was shown by the burning of the British Embassy after a protest march.

Prior to internment Lynch had relied on what he called 'quiet diplomacy', based on a level of mutual understanding presumed to exist in a relationship where both sides enjoyed a common language and close trading links and where there still existed sizeable Irish communities in Britain. This was now replaced by the diplomacy of protest, both in the direct contacts with the British government, and indirectly, in a broader campaign to influence other governments. At the very least the British government had to give the appearance of listening to Lynch, for fear that they might otherwise assist in his downfall and replacement by a more radical alternative. To what extent it was subjected to pressure from other governments, acting on Ireland's behalf, is not so clear. Particularly in the aftermath of Bloody Sunday the Irish government made sustained attempts to mobilise such pressure, partly in order to protect the northern minority from further repression and partly to influence the long-rumoured British 'initiative' on the north's constitutional position.[81] At the United Nations Patrick Hillery referred to Britain's 'lunatic policies', and put the Irish case before the American president and West European governments; this diplomatic canvass was backed up by a propaganda campaign which involved the employment of a Swiss public relations agency, Mark Press. Interest was aroused in the United States Congress, the European media and in the Council of Europe, but evidence of governmental pressure being mobilised is lacking. President Nixon, it seems, was determined to keep the Irish problem out of Anglo-American relations.[82]

All of this undoubtedly irritated the British government and damaged Britain's international reputation. But that reputation would have been damaged anyway without the Irish government's pointing finger, for the failure of control through the Belfast government was becoming increasingly obvious. With the all-absorbing business of accession to the European Community out of the way (only eight days before Bloody Sunday), the British government could at last focus its attention on Northern Ireland, and on 25 March 1972 it suspended the Stormont regime and initiated a period of direct rule in which a new form of agreed government was to be prepared.

This measure brought about an immediate improvement in Anglo-Irish relations. For Lynch it was a British admission that partition was unworkable and the basis upon which suggestions for change could again be advanced from Dublin – the repudiation in fact of Britain's insistence that the Northern Ireland conflict was a matter for the United Kingdom alone. He renewed his demand for a positive British commitment to eventual Irish unity, but in the meanwhile indicated his willingness to take up the question of the reform of the Republic's Constitution in the context of a 'new Ireland'.[83] In November 1972 he agreed in principle with the British proposals for political development in the North. Although

Northern Ireland was to remain inside the United Kingdom for as long as a majority so desired it, there was to be an unambiguous, institutionalised 'Irish dimension' approximating the still-born Council of Ireland.[84]

By the time these proposals had been translated into the decision to establish an elected assembly and an executive with minority representation, Jack Lynch's government had been replaced by a Fine Gael-Labour coalition after the general election of March 1973. His successor, the Fine Gael leader, Liam Cosgrave, had already in his first St Patrick's Day message placed the emphasis firmly on reconciliation rather than unity[85], and two leading figures in his cabinet, the Minister for Foreign Affairs, Garret FitzGerald, and the Labour Minister for Posts and Telegraphs, Conor Cruise O'Brien, were well known for their conciliatory views of the northern issue.[86] Cosgrave was not inhibited by as many broody hawks among his backbenchers as Lynch had been, and his own party's background allowed him to take credit for action against the IRA.

After the northern Assembly had managed to produce a power-sharing executive based on the Unionists, SDLP and Alliance Party, all three governmental delegations came together at Sunningdale in December 1973 to work out the basis for north-south relations.[87] It was agreed to establish a Council of Ireland composed of a Council of Ministers and a Consultative Assembly, with both executive and harmonising functions relating mainly to common economic interests, but also with some competence in human rights and policing. The Irish government lacked the confidence to initiate the amendment of Articles 2 and 3 of the Constitution (which would have been subject to the uncertainties of a referendum), but agreed to a declaration that 'there could be no change in the status of Northern Ireland until a majority of the people of Northern Ireland desired a change in that status.'[88] This formal admission that a precondition for unity was the consent of a majority in Northern Ireland was a significant departure for the southern government; for its part the British government agreed to support the wish of any future majority in the north to 'become part of a United Ireland.'[89] Finally, all parties agreed to explore further ways of bringing fugitive terrorists to justice without infringing what seemed to be constitutional commitment to the principle of the non-extradition of political offenders.

But this package was soon ripped apart and the agreement was never ratified. Clause 5 − the declaration of status − aroused rumblings of discontent in the Fianna Fáil opposition, though it was Kevin Boland who questioned its constitutionality in the Supreme Court in Dublin; the government won the case, but in so doing the declaration was made to appear a mere ploy to hide the persistence of the constitutional claim. Then in the British general election of February 1974 the electoral weakness of the northern executive was laid bare and, in spite of ditching much of the Council of Ireland and pushing the agreement through the Assembly, the executive had to face a political strike which effectively brought the province to a standstill. The British government failed to intervene and the executive collapsed on 28 May.[90] Ten days earlier, as if to celebrate the return of the rule of violence (not that it had ever been absent), the Republic had suffered a taste of northern violence in a spate of bombs in Dublin and Monaghan.

The Sunningdale agreement represented the most ambitious attempt to date to place the issue of Irish unity on a less controversial footing. Yet it can clearly be faulted in execution for much of it lacked sufficient preparation and none of the governments concerned put it across effectively nor, above all, with the urgency that the situation demanded. It was a victim, too, of the malevolent 'luck of the Irish' in the form of a disastrous British election. But above all its vulnerability lay in its dependence on reason, on the logic of functional co-operation. The delegations at Sunningdale hoped to represent the Council of Ireland as a body without serious 'political' characteristics (though some hoped it would develop these in the future). To extreme unionists − or loyalists as they were now generally known − it was precisely this possible future that made the Council a critical threat to their fundamental values: as one later said, 'the Sunningdale agreement was designed not to kick us out of the United Kingdom but to change our attitudes, to swing our gaze slowly from the centre of power we have always recognised as London towards Dublin and by slow process to change the attitude of the loyalist people so that one day they might believe the myth of Irish unity which so bedevils many in Northern Ireland.'[91]

The period since the collapse of the Sunningdale agreement has been characterised by drift. Political polarisation was reflected in the failure of the Constitutional Convention of 1975. The IRA truce at the beginning of that year was followed by continued violence and increasing preparations for the use of force by both nationalist and loyalist paramilitary groups. The British government's persistence with direct rule has been accompanied by widespread doubts about its will to remain in Northern Ireland. Devolved government, repartition, independence (negotiated or unilaterally declared), civil war on the grand scale – anything seems possible, but few of the prospects are pleasing.[92]

The coalition government in Dublin tried to rescue what it could of its Sunningdale objectives without provoking any further disasters which might threaten not only Northern Ireland but the Republic itself. Conscious of its own military capabilities[93], it depended on Britain's continuing to take responsibility for security in the north. While this represented a clear accord with British policy (and both governments proceeded with the anti-terrorist legislation promised at Sunningdale), Anglo-Irish diplomacy was clouded by several factors. First, there was a lack of confidence about British intentions, which existed since British acquiescence in the face of the loyalist strike in May 1974; this was accentuated by the British government's readiness to negotiate informally with the Provisional IRA, and, from 1976, its apparent vulnerability to unionist pressure in the Westminster parliament. The second type of difficulty arose out of the sort of demarcation dispute which is inevitable when two sovereign states are faced with a transnational security challenge. Spying – and the publicity which surrounds its disclosure – could cause embarrassment, as occurred in two cases in 1973, the Wyman and Littlejohn affairs; so too could the persistent border incidents arising mainly out of the pursuit of guerillas from north to south.[94] Meanwhile, Ireland's case against the United Kingdom over the treatment of internees proceeded at a measured pace through the legal machinery set up under the European Convention of Human Rights. The Irish government's persistence with the case and the fact there was indeed a case to be answered was a source of intermittent embarrassment for the British.[95]

However, the quest for political solutions depended on the uncertain situation within Northern Ireland. In this respect the coalition government's aim was discreetly to encourage a return to power-sharing, but the institutionalised 'Irish dimension' was abandoned for fear of provoking a loyalist coup.[96] Likewise, the possibility of military intervention was explicitly ruled out, even should a civil war break out in the north.[97] This passivity was also reflected in the dissipation of what had, prior to 1974, seemed to be a will to contemplate changes within the Republic. The leading advocates of such change towards pluralism, Garret FitzGerald and Conor Cruise O'Brien, maintained their advocacy, but this was not reflected in government action. A serious blow to their campaign was Liam Cosgrave's decisive vote against his own government's legislation attempting to liberalise contraception in July 1974. But the principal uncertainty could be seen in attitudes towards the constitutional claim in Articles 2 and 3. The Fine Gael-Labour government stood by its Sunningdale position, but was reluctant to take the risk of the referendum which would be a necessary part of any amendment to the Constitution.

Partly this equivocation was a result of the position of the Fianna Fáil party, which (with the northern SDLP) maintained the argument that to abandon the constitutional claim would either end Ireland's legal right to be involved in the northern issue or diminish her bargaining power in the formulation of any settlement.[98] Indeed, it was at this point that the general bipartisan approach to the north in the Dáil found its limits, with the failure of the Dáil's all-party Committee on Irish Relations.[99] While in opposition, on 29 October 1975, Fianna Fáil policy emphasised the demand that Britain should effect 'an ordered withdrawal from her involvement in the Six Counties', and promised that this demand would be supported 'by diplomatic and political endeavour at the United Nations, through the European institutions and appropriate international bodies.'[100] Although after the party's return to office in July 1977 there were few indications of this aspect of its northern policy, there is little doubt that among political élites unity can still be a divisive goal.[101]

The difference among politicians, and the equivocal behaviour they often induce, are reflected in mass opinion with regard to Northern Ireland. Although political parties associated with violence have consistently failed to make ground in the Republic since 1969 and although the northern conflict is generally perceived as imposing serious costs south of the border[102], the evolution of attitudes towards partition is by no means clear. A pioneering study of opinion in Dublin from August 1972 to April 1973 suggested that, while the majority still subscribed to traditional doctrines on Irish unity, a significant minority (forty-three per cent) did regard nationalists and unionists in the north as ethnically distinct, thus weakening the fundamental assumption of 'one nation'.[103] While there may well be a 'state of attitudinal change'[104], the risks for the politician in misjudging popular support for new initiatives remain high. Thus in electoral politics the issue has been not so much the status of Northern Ireland as the implications of the northern conflict for security in the Republic.

Against this background of uncertainty about both ends and means with regard to the northern problem, functional co-operation remains as one of the few areas where north-south relations are being developed. Politicians tend to see this as the only type of activity where they can initiate policy rather than merely respond to events, and there is overwhelming support from the general public.[105] Functional co-operation has been facilitated by the fact that both parts of Ireland are in the European Community, and by their community of interests, particularly in agricultural and regional policy. On occasion this has allowed the Irish Minister for Foreign Affairs to promote *northern* interests in the Council of Ministers[106]; more substantially it has provided the framework, and the possibility of finance, for specific cross-border development projects under the Regional Fund. Yet progress in this type of policy is by its nature slow; it was September 1976 before the first specific cross-border study was officially launched. Moreover, before it has any impact in the border area concerned, it can be denounced as a foreign intervention by suspicious loyalists, which is perhaps one reason why the British government has not pursued the matter with the urgency shown either by local groups or the Irish government.[107] Functional activity, it has been observed in a more general context, is, 'at least in the short run, more dependent upon the political weather than determinative of the political weather.'[108]

Nevertheless, in spite of its limitations, functional co-operation is an indication of the extent to which Northern Ireland is an international issue. Indeed, the IRA — and occasionally some loyalist extremist groups — have claimed links with revolutionary movements in other countries. Although there is little real ideological or operational co-ordination, the supply of arms by overseas sympathisers has been important. There was a dramatic case of gun-running from Libya in 1973, but the significant source of overseas aid to the IRA has been the United States. The theme of expatriate influence on Irish affairs has been a constant one, both before and since independence. Although Irish-American identity is by no means as pervasive as it was in the nineteenth century, there is still a measure of ethnic support which is significant enough to affect the military capabilities of the IRA.[109]

However, the internationalisation of the northern conflict has tended to work against the IRA at the intergovernmental level.[110] Both the Irish and British governments have continually tried to persuade Irish-Americans not to support the IRA, and in 1977 this policy was explicitly endorsed by prominent Irish-American politicians such as Tip O'Neill, Speaker of the House of Representatives, and Senator Edward Kennedy, and finally by President Carter in his policy statement on Northern Ireland on 30 August 1977. The latter intervention also emphasised the theme of functional co-operation in a general commitment to increase US investment in the north after a political settlement was agreed internally, and recognised that a 'just solution' to the northern problem has to be one which the Irish government, among others, could support.[111] While the 'Carter initiative' offered an outline of an eventual international 'rescue operation' for a debilitated Northern Ireland, its effect on fundamental political divisions is hard to discern. Other suggestions have been made for introducing an element of international support for a solution to the conflict in Northern Ireland, through a United Nations peace-keeping force, for example[112]; but such a move could only be one part of a broader scheme which as yet remains obscure. Meanwhile, for the Irish government, as for the other parties to the dispute, Irish unity remains an intractable problem.

Chapter 7

Prosperity

The Saorstát is now, and will undoubtedly long continue to be, an integral part of the economic system at the head of which stands Great Britain.

Banking Commission, 1926,
First Interim Report on Banking and Currency

We believe Ireland can be made a self-contained unit, providing all the necessities of living in adequate quantities for the people residing in the Island at the moment and probably for a much larger number.

Seán Lemass, TD,
in the Dáil, 22 February 1928

The issue-areas already considered — independence, security and unity — concern matters which are generally accepted as falling under the label 'foreign policy'. They relate to a traditional image of international relations in which the diplomat and the soldier are the decisive figures, representing the interests of autonomous and clearly delineated units, whose relations are seen primarily in the dramatic terms of peace and war. The goal of national prosperity, on the other hand, has not always been granted a leading place in this image; when the diplomatic profession is seen as the last refuge of the aristocrat, and when economic activities are assumed to be best left to the interplay of market forces, economic determinants of foreign policy are often given scant consideration. Such views, typical of nineteenth-century Britain, still exert some influence on our concept of what 'foreign policy' properly encompasses, in spite of drastic changes in the world economy and economics-based theories of international relations which have subsequently emerged.[1] It is thus necessary to confirm the goal of prosperity, or the maximisation of wealth, as one of the fundamental purposes of political organisation, and one moreover which cannot be pursued solely within the boundaries of the state. Economic foreign policy is a fundamental concern of governments.

Nevertheless, the government is often not the only actor concerned and may not in some cases be the most important one. In a state where the economy incorporates a significant degree of free enterprise the pursuit of national prosperity can easily become confused with the pursuit of the prosperity of particular individuals or groups; the fact that a governmental measure, such as the erection of tariff barriers, benefits the state as well, may be incidental. Such objectives have been called 'indirect national goals', as opposed to 'direct national goals', such as independence or security, which 'have no meaning for men as private individuals except as these individuals identify themselves with their nationstate.'[2] The extent to which governments attempt to exert control over economic activity has varied widely, and the means of control over economic foreign policy are in many respects more complex and more uncertain than those in other issue-areas.

Further problems of control arise from the nature of economic interactions between the state and the world outside. The state enjoys the legal right to exert control, but this is a 'negative freedom', which in practice may be severely circumscribed and which does not in itself necessarily lead to prosperity.[3] When the Irish delegation at the Treaty negotiations in 1921 achieved the right to establish tariffs they gained an indispensable attribute of economic sovereignty; this was a prerequisite of Griffith's dream of economic development but it did not of itself translate the dream into reality. Of the one hundred and fifty-odd states in the world, few have achieved either a high degree of self-sufficiency or of prosperity, fewer still of both, and Ireland is manifestly not one of them.

Three closely related characteristics of the Irish economy have influenced the evolution of Irish economic foreign policy — its size, its openness and its dependence on the United Kingdom. The Irish economy is small, both with regard to the population it serves and the level of economic activity that is maintained. Indeed, as far as the latter is concerned, for some economists 'Ireland is most interestingly thought of as a developing country.'[4]

In spite of a level of income *per capita* which is high by world standards, and in spite of the existence of many of the advantages and disadvantages associated with other west European economies, Ireland does in several respects face the sort of problems known by non-European developing economies. The transformation from a predominantly agricultural economy to one with a solid industrial basis has been described as 'spectacular'[5], but it is still incomplete, while structural unemployment remains the major economic problem.[6] The poorest of all the peripheral regions of the British Isles[7], Ireland like other small countries has naturally tended to rely to a large extent on international trade.[8]

The 'openness' of the Irish economy is striking.[9] The importance of foreign trade can be seen in Table 1.

Table 1   Ireland: Foreign Trade Dependence, 1926–1972

	Merchandise Exports	Merchandise Imports	Exports of Goods and Services	Imports of Goods and Services
(As a percentage of GNP at current factor cost)				
1926	26.8	39.8	n.a.	n.a.
1929	29.3	38.0	n.a.	n.a.
1931	24.7	34.4	38.7	37.7
1938	15.1	25.8	27.4	26.2
1950	20.1	44.3	38.1	46.5
1955	22.8	42.7	37.2	44.5
1960	25.9	38.4	39.8	39.9
1965	27.2	43.7	39.7	45.0
1970	32.4	47.0[a]	46.2	50.7[a]
1972	33.8	44.1	44.0	46.9

Sources: Pre-war data are taken from Kieran A. Kennedy, *Productivity and Industrial Growth: The Irish Experience*, Oxford University Press 1971. Post-war data are from official publications *Statistical Abstract of Ireland, National Income and Expenditure*, various issues, and from *Review of 1972 and Outlook for 1973.* Reproduced from T. K. Whitaker, 'Monetary Integration: Reflections on Irish Experience', *Quarterly Bulletin, Central Bank of Ireland*, Winter 1973, p. 69

[a] Distorted by exceptional imports of aircraft.

Only in the nineteen-thirties and during World War II, when international trade in general declined, are exports and imports reduced, both absolutely and in relation to GNP; the overall trend shows an increasing dependence on foreign markets, as well as on raw materials and capital from overseas. Indeed, Ireland has been described as 'one of the most open economies in the world surpassed only by a handful of countries such as Iceland, Norway, Belgium, the Netherlands and, of course, oil-producing countries which are special cases.'[10] This economic characteristic in itself demonstrates the importance of economic issues in Irish foreign policy.

Openness to external economic forces in general has in practice been manifested in dependence on the United Kingdom. Again, the trade figures in Table 2 reveal the extent of this phenomenon.[11] Two points are worth making at this stage; first, the degree of dependence has decreased, but in spite of this it still remains at a high level. Irish economic foreign policy can be seen, therefore, in terms of an asymmetrical relationship with the United Kingdom, punctuated by various attempts to escape from or modify the harmful consequences which this has entailed for the smaller economy.

Table 2   Trade Dependence on the United Kingdom, 1926—73

	1926	1936	1950	1960	1970	1973
Imports						
From United Kingdom	75.7	53.3	52.9	49.6	52.2	50.8
(percentage from Britain)	(65.1)	(51.9)	(51.4)	(46.3)	(47.7)	(47.0)
(percentage from Northern Ireland)	(10.6)	(1.4)	(1.5)	(3.3)	(4.5)	(3.8)
Exports						
Percentage of domestic exports to United Kingdom	96.3	91.5	86.7	73.7	62.3	54.7
(percentage to Britain)	(82.7)	(81.4)	(75.0)	(60.4)	(50.6)	(45.2)
(percentage to Northern Ireland)	(13.6)	(10.1)	(11.7)	(13.3)	(11.7)	(9.5)

Source: D. McAleese, 'The Foreign Sector' in N. Gibson and J. Spencer (eds.), *Economic Activity in Ireland* (Dublin: Gill and Macmillan, 1976), Table 4.1

Before examining the principal stages in the evolution of this relationship it must be stressed that Irish dependence on the United Kingdom is deep-rooted, often immune to short-term governmental action, and the source of much uncertainty. It involves not merely a high degree of trade, as might be found between any two states, but a degree of human and financial interaction which is free of state regulation to an extent not often found in international relations. The two states form a 'free travel area', without passport controls and permitting the movement of Irish labour to the central regions of British industrial activity. In this important respect the patterns of economic and social activity which evolved when the British Isles were a common political jurisdiction have continued, and so too has the high degree of the integration of the capital and money markets.[12] The disruption of such well-established links of business, finance and labour would have considerable short-term political costs (let alone economic costs), for Irish expectations of economic performance and welfare benefits are related to standards attained in the United Kingdom and in this context economic independence is often seen to have a high price indeed.[13]

Yet the closeness of the relationship can be a source of resentment. Labour mobility has softened the short-term effects of unemployment, but in the long term has been a source of uncertainty and high costs for Irish employers. Trade dependence in the long term produces a tendency to 'import' British rates of inflation. Market access for Irish goods has often been at the mercy of policies designed to meet British rather than Irish interests, the most notorious case being that of agricultural produce. Economic dependence thus has often seemed to give the lie to the achievement of statehood; colonialism in the nineteenth century has been replaced by neo-colonialism in the twentieth, and Britain could still be blamed for her economic indifference, if not malevolence, towards Ireland. Such a view has led either to an attitude of fatalism or of counter-dependence, both of which can be seen reflected in Irish economic foreign policy.

*   *   *

The economic situation following independence was hardly encouraging; Ireland had after all just been one of the most depressed regions of the British economy, at a time when central government paid little attention to regional problems.[14] The major industrial area in the island — the north-east — unexpectedly remained British, leaving a predominantly agricultural economy, with over half the work force employed in this sector and two-thirds of the population living in rural areas. Agriculture, though important, was stagnant, characterised by small farmers who 'combined extreme political radicalism, of a rather abstract kind, with social and economic immobility.'[15] Industrial activity was mainly on a small scale, lacking both raw materials and skilled labour. The economy as a whole had been disrupted by the war of independence and was to face little respite before the civil war broke out in the Summer of 1922.

It is true that the new Irish regime also inherited a developed administrative infrastructure, in addition to established business, financial and professional institutions, but this seeming advantage was not fully exploited by a government which leaned heavily on the economic orthodoxy of the day — 'the middle class was on the stage.'[16] Indeed, there was a marked continuity with the pre-independence era in the general economic thinking of the officials in the new Department of Finance, no matter how firm the latter might be where specific interests diverged from those of their former mentors.[17] The role of the state was to ensure that the basic conditions for free enterprise existed, and in the circumstances this meant that economic policy stressed the restoration and continuity of existing patterns of behaviour, in order to reduce the uncertainty over the country's economic picture which prevailed. The few elements of state intervention that did occur, such as the creation of the Electricity Supply Board in 1927, were still exceptions that proved the rule.

As far as economic foreign policy was concerned, this implied an acceptance of established patterns of trade, which now simply came under the heading of international trade. In 1926 no less than 96.3 per cent of Irish exports went to the United Kingdom, the source of 75.7 per cent of imports. The most important element in Irish exports was agricultural produce, and in so far as the government articulated and followed a positive economic strategy it saw agriculture as the 'motor' of the economy. It was hoped that the development of agricultural prosperity would gradually spill over into the industrial sector; the government could hardly provide more than careful book-keeping and civil order.

This approach was a far cry from the traditional doctrine of economic nationalism, so recently advocated by Arthur Griffith, who had envisaged the development of an industrial sector behind tariff barriers, which would provide employment and thereby stem the continuing high rate of emigration. Protection had seemed attractive both because it involved the exercise of political independence and because it seemed to promise long-term economic benefits. However, when the opportunity arose its friends were dispersed. Griffith's death in 1922 represented the silencing of its major advocate, while other supporters of protection were on the anti-Treaty side in the civil war. Moreover, the international economic system in general was hostile to protection, and Ireland's major — almost sole — trading partner was the champion of free trade. Protection on a wide scale in the nineteen-twenties was not a policy to be followed by a government seeking 'to establish the standing of the state in the eyes of the world.'[18]

The government and, in particular, its leading civil service advisers were fearful of the effects of possible retaliation on agricultural exports should industrial protection be introduced, and the few existing large-scale industrial units (brewing, distilling and biscuits) did not want protection either. But neither the aspirations of traditional economic nationalism nor the demands of small industrial interests could be ignored altogether. In 1926 a Tariff Commission was established to review new applications for protection, and a policy of what subsequently became known as 'selective' or 'limited' protection was adopted. It amounted to little in practice, and by 1931 the Irish average tariff level was only nine per cent.[19]

Monetary policy also reflected the sensitivity of the government towards the external constraints it faced.[20] In 1926 a Banking Commission recommended the establishment of a separate Irish currency, but based on parity with sterling. These recommendations were included in the 1927 Currency Act, largely based on prevailing Commonwealth lines, and ensuring that any change in the exchange rate would need legislation. The policy was based on the need to end uncertainty about the future of the financial system and, more important in the long term, Ireland's trade dependence on the United Kingdom. This decision established the basis of Irish external monetary policy up to the nineteen-seventies; exchange rate manipulation was to be eschewed in favour of other instruments for influencing the flow of international payments.[21]

The economic foreign policy of W. T. Cosgrave's government came under sustained domestic criticism when Fianna Fáil entered the Dáil in 1927. De Valera's new party adopted an unambiguous advocacy of economic nationalism.[22] Self-sufficiency was the declared goal of economic foreign policy and it was seen as impinging on other foreign policy goals as well. It was regarded as a basic corollary of political independence, and well before taking office de Valera clearly viewed it as a prerequisite of neutrality.[23] But, for de Valera at least, it was valued for its own sake; the economic and social costs it might imply were not seen as such by the Fianna Fáil leader. He is reported to have said in 1927 that he was 'not satisfied that the standard of living and the mode of life in western Europe is a right or proper one. The industrialized countries have got themselves into a rut and Ireland is asked to hurry along it after them.'[24] Frugality rather than an infinitely expanding prosperity was the key-note of his economic philosophy, though it was nevertheless assumed that self-sufficiency could be maintained at an 'adequate' standard of living, which would be an improvement on that which existed under his political opponents.[25]

Self-sufficiency implied the development of a highly protected industrial sector, strict controls over foreign investment and a reduction in trade dependence both generally and with regard to the United Kingdom. All of this was attempted when Fianna Fáil came into power in 1932, representing the most striking example of a sudden and comprehensive change in Irish economic foreign policy.[26] That it was politically acceptable can largely be explained by two factors – the general economic climate, and the popularity of the new government's revisionist stance in Anglo-Irish relations. By 1932 the world depression, triggered off by the Wall Street crash of 1929, had bitten deep and the free trade ethos of the twenties vanished as one country after another sought refuge in protection. The pressure on any Irish government to follow suit was almost unbearable; indeed, over the winter of 1931–32, the Irish Free State 'was the last surviving example of a predominantly free-trading state left in the world.'[27] Economic nationalism was no longer a radical alternative, rather it was the new, if often mindless, orthodoxy; even had the Cosgrave government remained in power, it would have been compelled to change its economic policy.

In the Irish case economic nationalism was also given added political respectability by de Valera's general onslaught on the Anglo-Irish Treaty of 1921.[28] This included his refusal to continue payment to the British government of annuities arising under the pre-independence Land Acts, on the grounds that his predecessor's commitment to pay was not binding, as it had not been ratified by the Dáil. In June 1932 attempts to negotiate broke down, and the British imposed tariffs in an attempt to recover the money; this was the start of a tariff war in which the Irish Free State was excluded from the Commonwealth preferential tariffs negotiated at the Ottawa conference later in 1932. Irish exports were reduced in value from £43.5 million in 1929 to just under £18 million in 1935; particularly hard-hit was the cattle trade which declined from three-quarters to half a million head of cattle between these dates.[29] Retaliatory tariffs were reduced in the 'coal-cattle pact' of 1935, but the issue was not finally settled until 1938.

This so-called 'economic war' was not in itself a central feature of economic foreign policy, for it was essentially a political dispute fought with economic instruments.[30] But it did influence economic policy in two ways. First, in dramatising the general attitude of economic counter-dependence[31], it enabled the government to erect high tariff barriers almost at will. Protection was implemented in a doctrinaire, politicised manner, in 'a heated atmosphere of retaliation which was hostile to any careful adjustment of aid to need.'[32] This was to create vested interests, some of which had little economic or social justification, but which were to be difficult to abandon in the future. But in the long term the economic war also demonstrated the vulnerability of the Irish economy to economic retaliation from Britain. So long as the consequences of tariff rivalry seemed to be confined to the relatively small number of big cattle-farmers, the despised 'ranchers' in Fianna Fáil demonology, a policy of active counter-dependence could be maintained, but when the economy as a whole appeared to suffer, some accommodation to external forces had to be made.

Protection was not of course the beginning and end of Fianna Fáil's economic foreign policy. Foreign investment in Irish industry was restricted by the Control of Manufactures Act of

1932, a move complemented by the establishment of the Industrial Credit Company in the same year and by the expansion of the state-sponsored companies which had been introduced in such a tentative manner under the Cosgrave government. These moves went some way to fulfilling the government's intention 'to build up the industries of the country with native capital and organisation and to permit outside control of industries only when the possibilities of developing the industries concerned under home control had been exhausted.'[33] Other policy actions were more hesitant. The creation of a Central Bank was recommended in 1934, but the recommendation was not implemented until 1942 and there was no change in the exchange rate policy of parity with sterling. Attempts to diversify trade outlets met with little success. International conditions were unfavourable, to say the least; bilateral trade agreements proved to be limited both in time and scope, offering no real long-term alternative to the long-established links of the British market.

The overall success of the self-sufficiency approach was mixed.[34] Industrial employment rose from 111,000 in 1931 to 166,000 in 1938, marking the beginnings of an expanded industrial sector, and this was to be the basis for real gains in the long-term development of the Irish economy. However, the more immediate effects were less striking – industry was still heavily dependent on imports, with a limited domestic market and high labour costs. As far as agriculture was concerned, 'self-sufficiency became less a policy of economic advance than a vast rescue operation.'[35] Emigration again rose in the late thirties and Irish incomes per head were reduced from sixty-one per cent of the British equivalent in 1931 to forty-nine per cent of the British level in 1939. The original vision of self-sufficiency seemed remote, when the aspirations of the existing population could not be met, and the promised expansion in population had not materialised. Indeed, by late 1937 the persisting deterioration in Ireland's economic situation was an important incentive for de Valera to seek the comprehensive negotiations with the British government which were to result in the agreements of 1938.[36] The negotiations (in which trade with Northern Ireland proved to be one of the most difficult issues) led to improved access to the British market for Irish agriculture in return for a lowering of some industrial tariffs. Thus the average tariff level fell from forty-five per cent in 1936 –

its highest mark — to thirty-five per cent in 1938. The phase of counter-dependence was over, and Ireland was left with the 'very modest measure of national self-sufficiency' which the celebrated British economist, J. M. Keynes, had recommended in 1932.[37]

There is some irony in the fact that only a short time after the limits of voluntary self-sufficiency had been accepted they were exceeded, as an even harsher measure of self-sufficiency was imposed by circumstances quite beyond the Irish government's control — the outbreak of World War II. Tariffs became irrelevant (and were largely suspended) as serious shortages in imports of fuel and natural resources prevented any further industrial development. A drastic switch in agricultural production from grazing to tillage — the acreage under wheat was almost trebled between 1938 and 1944 — at least ensured basic food supplies, though many commodities had to be rationed. To a large extent, the self-sufficiency of the thirties paid off during the 'emergency'; native leather and textile industries existed and turf proved to be a substitute for coal (though not in transport). But gaps in the original policy were also revealed, such as the lack of a viable national shipping line — for a supposedly self-sufficient state mostly surrounded by sea![38]

A curious feature of this period was the rather tentative policy of the British government to exert economic pressure, in the words of the Secretary of State for the Dominions, Lord Cranborne, in order to 'open the eyes of the Irish people to their true situation.'[39] Pressure was easily exerted, through Irish dependence on British supplies and shipping, but the punitive element was blunted by doubts as to the possible political repercussions in Ireland and, at the beginning of the war, in the United States. In fact it was not widely perceived outside the highest levels of the governments concerned as being punitive at all; Irish opinion seemed ready for once to ascribe its deprivations to fate rather than the machinations of Whitehall. In any case, economic links with Britain remained close throughout the war; in particular the development of Britain's war economy absorbed the large numbers who remained unemployed in a not quite self-sufficient and far from prosperous Ireland.

The international economic system which developed after 1945 was characterised by increasing trade liberalisation and expansion in the growth of world trade; it was a system in which most west European states experienced considerable economic growth and when separate national economies became 'more interdependent than ever before.'[40] Twenty years after this system came into being it could be said that Ireland was indeed conforming to these characteristics, yet for the first fifteen of these years they remained elusive: 'it was only in 1960 that the volume of visible exports first exceeded the 1929 or 1930 levels . . . only in 1967 did the ratio of volume of visible exports to GNP surpass the 1929 ratio.'[41] By this time a major feature of Irish economic foreign policy was the dismantling of protection and the encouragement of foreign investment; self-sufficiency was being replaced by an 'outward-looking policy.'[42]

The route to this outcome was by no means even, and was beset by hesitations in policy formulation.[43] Ireland came out of the emergency with large external assets but with serious structural weaknesses, in particular the narrow base of the highly protected manufacturing employment. An initial post-war recovery failed to last beyond 1949. It had been associated with the establishment of a public capital programme, which was one development heralding the beginning of a more positive approach towards the role of the state in economic management. Other institutional developments were initiated in the foreign sector, principally the establishment in 1949 of the Industrial Development Authority (IDA) responsible, *inter alia*, for attracting foreign industries, and the export board, Córas Tráchtála Teo (CTT), was set up in 1952 to promote exports to the dollar area, and later on a global basis. In 1949 Ireland received a loan of £40.8 million and a grant of £6.5 million from Marshall Aid – the only time before the nineteen-sixties that large-scale external borrowing was adopted.

An important condition of Marshall Aid was the obligation to draw up a plan of future import requirements. It is perhaps an exaggeration to describe this as the first attempt at economic planning in Ireland[44], but it is symptomatic of conservative attitudes towards the role of the government in economic management that the responsibility for this Long Term Recovery Programme was given to the Department of External Affairs, rather than the Department of Finance.[45] Positive government intervention was still tentative and uncoordinated, and the predominant attitude towards economic foreign policy was still one of financial conservatism. The officials of the Department of Finance were wary of becoming directly involved in the new international economic system. Although Britain wanted Ireland to join the International Monetary Fund (IMF) and the International Bank for Reconstruction and Development (IBRD), the Irish response was negative.[46] This caution was further seen when the prices of Irish imports were hit by the effects of the devaluation of sterling in 1949 and the Korean War in 1950. After a heated internal debate the government accepted the Department of Finance's fears concerning the balance of payments deficit on current account.[47] It introduced a series of deflationary budgets, which were one cause at least of a period of stagnation in the mid-nineteen-fifties.

The period was marked by an actual decline in real GNP in 1956 and despair at continuing unemployment and emigration, producing a psychological condition throughout Irish society, and particularly in the political system, which has been described as 'a death wish.'[48] Ireland still depended heavily on livestock exports, but this trade was regulated in the interests of Britain's cheap food policy, and market access was the subject of continual concern for Irish governments. Even though the series of post-war negotiations did eventually lead to more satisfactory conditions, Anglo-Irish economic relations were essentially neo-colonial; indeed, in the early fifties an American consultancy firm concluded that 'the country's dependence on Britain was so strong as to be incompatible with the status of political sovereignty.'[49] Moreover, the perennial problem of industrial expansion remained. The benefits of protection had already been realised and further protection would be increasingly unacceptable in an international economic system which was characterised by more and more institutionalised multilateral trading arrangements. Against a background of quite considerable growth in other west European states, Ireland appeared to be not merely standing still but going backwards.

But 1958 marked the bottom of the trough. Recovery from that point had been achieved by 1961 and was sustained until the late nineteen-sixties. During this period°Ireland abandoned the policy of protection, encouraged foreign investment and developed industrial as well as agricultural exports. This significant change in both performance and policy is generally associated with the introduction of comprehensive economic planning, and especially with the First Programme for Economic Expansion in 1958, based on a report ('Economic Development') by the Secretary of the

Department of Finance, T. K. Whitaker. The 'Whitaker revolution' owed a good deal to existing policies and institutions. The IDA and CTT were already in existence and the major source of invisible exports, tourism, was at last being taken in hand by another state-sponsored agency, Bord Fáilte; a scheme for tax relief for export industries had been established in 1956. There is thus a marked continuity between the periods of stagnation and growth, and the First Programme owed much of its impact to the fact that, as well as being a comprehensive synthesis of policy, it provided a psychological boost at a critical time.[50]

Nevertheless it did mark an important change in attitude with regard to economic foreign policy. The existing emphasis on protection and the native ownership of industry reflected not merely vested sectional interests or financial conservatism; it was a manifestation of deeply rooted political values, a particular image of economic nationalism which was closely associated with the party then in power, Fianna Fáil. In fact, Seán Lemass, the principal architect of the old policy of self-sufficiency, now presided over the conversion of his party and his country to the new faith of free trade and foreign investment.[51] Lemass had been in government long enough to reap the harvest of self-sufficiency as well as sow the seeds; he was concerned about the inefficiency protection sometimes produced, and with his participation in OEEC meetings had come to terms with the move towards trade liberalisation. Thus by 1958, as an immensely authoritative Minister for Industry and Commerce chairing the cabinet committee on the First Programme, he was prepared to advocate the dethronement of protection and the replacement of his old Control of Manufactures Act by the Industrial Development (Encouragement of External Investment) Act.[52] Policy was reversed, though not without reservations from those who felt either economically vulnerable or politically betrayed.[53]

Implementation of the new strategy was given added incentive by developments in the international economic system.[54] It had been hoped to phase out protection gradually over a period of twenty-five years, in the context of a broad European free trade area, but when negotiations to form the latter collapsed, Ireland was isolated from the newly formed groupings, the European Economic Community (EEC) and the residual European Free Trade Area (EFTA). The effect of this was to shorten the original timetable

considerably. In 1960 the government decided to join the General
Agreement on Tariffs and Trade (GATT), a decision which was
implemented in 1967, and Ireland became involved in the more
urgent pace of trade liberalisation envisaged in EEC membership
when, along with Britain, Denmark and Norway, an application
to join the EEC was made in 1961.[55] By this stage, then, economic
considerations had become the dominant feature in Irish foreign
policy. Though EEC membership came to nothing in 1963 on
account of Anglo-French differences, Lemass (Taoiseach since
1959) decided on unilateral across-the-board tariff cuts of ten per
cent in 1963 and 1964. These were regarded both as a signal of
intent to foreign governments and as a preparation for common
market conditions. This policy was followed in the creation of
the Anglo-Irish Free Trade Area (AIFTA) which came into operation in July 1966. This allowed for the complete phasing out of
industrial tariffs over a ten year period; Ireland, still in the mid-
sixties one of the most highly protected economies in western
Europe, was to be exposed to the rigours of international competition by the mid-seventies.

Trade liberalisation was accompanied by a determined attempt
to encourage foreign investment, particularly in export-oriented
manufacturing industry.[56] Direct foreign investment accounted
for one-third of the net capital inflow, and traditional governmental inhibitions about foreign borrowing disappeared as public
sector borrowing increased during the sixties.[57] Up to 1970 the
sources of direct foreign investment varied from the United States
(thirty-four per cent of the total), to the United Kingdom (twenty-
nine per cent of the total) and Germany (ten per cent of the
total), with the remaining twenty-seven per cent being supplied
by other countries.[58] The diversity of the sources – this was one
area where dependence on Britain was less marked than usual –
may be one reason for the relative lack of political controversy
surrounding the early stages of this development. Nor did the
squabbles about tax avoidance, so often found in other countries,
arise in Ireland for the simple reason that foreign firms received
considerable tax concessions, and, being export-oriented, did
not come into direct competition with many of the traditional
domestically-owned Irish industries.

Acceptance of the new measures of foreign penetration of the
Irish economy in the nineteen-sixties may also be explained by the

fact that it was associated with a noticeable increase in the overall
level of prosperity. The Irish average annual growth rate, which
from 1949 to 1961 had been well below most west European
economies at 1.9 per cent, reached 4.1 per cent between 1961 and
1968.[59] For the first time for over a century the Irish population
rose slightly, while the structure of the economy showed a shift
from being primarily agricultural to a more even balance between
agriculture and industry. Irish economic performance contrasted
favourably with Britain's, though the battle to close the gap was
by no means won. The sixties boom still left Ireland a long way
behind the standard of living of most OECD countries, and in that
context it seemed no more than a promising but tardy beginning
to the process of catching up.

In the late nineteen-sixties and early seventies, the export-led
boom slackened. Partly this was due to less favourable conditions
in the international economic system in general, especially in the
form of increasing rates of inflation.[60] Manufactured exports held
their own, but there was a marked fall in invisible exports which
can be very largely accounted for by the effects of the continuing
Northern Ireland crisis on tourism[61]; nor were efforts to attract
foreign industrialists helped by the political uncertainties arising
from the crisis. These immediate difficulties were partly offset,
however, by the re-emergence of the issue of EEC membership,
following the Heath-Pompidou rapprochement of 1969. Negotiations opened in the Summer of 1970 and from then until 10 May
1972, when a referendum was held, there was a prolonged public
debate. Although the major issues discussed were economic in
nature, the importance of these developments for foreign policy
as a whole cannot be ignored.

Both major parties, Fianna Fáil and Fine Gael, supported
membership, as indeed they had done in 1961. They were backed
by a well-organised agricultural lobby, the bulk of industrial
interests and nearly all professional economists. At the centre of
their argument was the prospect of an escape for the Irish agricultural sector from the neo-colonial straitjacket of Britain's cheap
food policy. The original estimates of gains to the farming community were over-optimistic, but the probability of some gain
under the Common Agricultural Policy was hard to deny; guaranteed access to a large market, accompanied by price stability at
a high level and participation in policy-making, added up to a

novel environment for Irish agriculture. At the same time pro-marketeers maintained that Irish industry already had had sufficient experience of free trade to show its competitiveness. A diversification of markets was under way, largely in anticipation of EEC membership, while a rise in imports would be matched by an increase in the profitability of Irish exports. The weakest elements in the pro-market case were the implications of the disappearance of national tax incentives for exporters, and the reliance, not merely as a safety net but as an instrument of long-term development, on a Community Regional Policy which barely existed in more than name.[62]

The anti-marketeers naturally stressed these weaknesses, but also laid much emphasis on the probability of a decline in agricultural employment and production after some unevenly distributed initial gains. They deplored the loss of traditional economic policy instruments, arguing that Irish industry still needed some protection and that Ireland was well situated to negotiate favourable trade agreements with states outside the EEC, such as the United States and Japan. On the latter point their case was weak. In particular, during the nineteen-sixties it had proved to be extremely difficult to negotiate satisfactory trade relations with the United States, and even the traditional pattern of emigration across the Atlantic was being altered by American restrictions. The anti-marketeers maintained that agriculture would survive outside the EEC, and eventually prosper following long overdue domestic reforms.[63] This case was put, with varying degrees of enthusiasm, by the Labour Party which, together with the trade unions, stressed the possibility of loss of employment, and by most of the extreme nationalist groups, principally the left-wing 'Official' Sinn Féin.[64] Neither the association of the latter with the violence of the Northern Ireland conflict, nor the economic arguments put forward by the Common Market Defence Campaign, persuaded the voters from their established party allegiance. Moreover, special entry terms had been negotiated which delayed the abolition of export tax incentives and the threat to the motor assembly industry. Finally, with Britain's entry assured (or so it seemed in 1972), 'Ireland's entry into the EEC involved a choice between two utterly changed situations, not one between entry and the *status quo*.'[66] Membership, in these circumstances, was the lesser uncertainty simply because its implications had to a large extent been teased out during the negotiations. In the 1972 referendum slightly more than fifty-eight per cent of the total electorate voted for membership, twenty-nine per cent abstained and only twelve per cent voted against.

The first three years of membership showed that Ireland was indeed a net beneficiary from European Community policies, but this is not to say that expectations were met. The Common Agricultural Policy brought higher dairy prices and in 1973 beef did well too. But the following year a world slump in beef prices exposed the limits of CAP intervention, which did not cover the large Irish stocks of calves and store cattle, and where it did apply it suffered serious time lags because of the weakness of sterling.[66] Diversification of manufactured exports to the continental Community states made some ground as did foreign investment. But a question mark remained over the Community's Regional Policy; although the whole state (indeed the whole island) was designated an under-developed region, the size of the Regional Fund came nowhere near that which any serious redistributive strategy demanded.

By this time the effects of the world recession, following the drastic rises in energy costs at the end of 1973, made survival rather than development the aim of economic foreign policy, and membership of the European Community was judged on the basis of that criterion. Recession, accompanied by unprecedented rates of inflation — in the Summer of 1975 over twenty-five per cent — reduced Irish competitiveness in European and American markets and posed a threat to the balance of payments position for the first time since the nineteen-fifties.[67] The recession also gave rise to a reappraisal of established policies. Exchange rate policy, so long a constant in the form of the unbroken parity with sterling, became a public issue in 1975. The Central Bank Act of 1971 had permitted exchange rate policy-decisions to be made by government order rather than legislation, and the floating of sterling in the Summer of 1972, together with Irish membership of the European Community, made a break with the so-called 'sterling link' a feasible policy option.[68] It is probable that during the sterling crisis in the Autumn of 1976 the government was close to breaking the link, and there is little doubt that such a change of policy could take place if British inflation were to increase. Unfortunately, there is also little doubt that exchange rate policy is only a partial answer to the country's economic problems.[69]

The question of national resources was also given new urgency by the recession of the mid-seventies. Ireland, so long assumed to be without significant mineral resources, was found to have silver, barytes and lead and zinc deposits in the mix-sixties; the largest lead and zinc mine in Europe was put into operation in 1970. In the early seventies offshore exploration was started and a commercial gas-field was discovered off the south-east coast. These developments not merely have possible implications of great consequence for the country's economic future, they pose more immediate problems for Irish diplomacy. The exploitation of mineral resources, typically the field of large multinational companies, can arouse political controversy because they involve finite resources. It is arguable that up to 1973 the country received little return on its mining wealth, and that subsequently revised legislation was still over-generous to the mainly foreign firms engaged in the industry.[70] As yet criticisms of government policy in this field have been intermittent, but the existence of a strong critical lobby could cause difficulty in the general area of foreign investment.[71]

Offshore exploration expanded at a time when the concept of the two hundred mile economic zone was being strongly promoted by maritime states, particularly in the International Law of the Sea Conference which started in 1974 in Caracas. Quite apart from the possibility of a dramatic improvement in the country's energy resources, the acquisition of a vast new ocean territory makes Ireland an important coastal state.[72] The implications of such a development for security policy have already been referred to[73]; for economic prosperity in general the long-term consequences can only be guessed at.

However, in the short term, Ireland's maritime interests are embroiled in several international disputes. In the Autumn of 1976 the need to agree on an external fishery policy for the European Community led to disagreements among the member-states concerning the revision of national fishery limits. Although the Irish fishery industry is small and neglected, it proved to be an active interest group, encouraging the government to press for an exclusive fifty mile fishery limit. This stance was maintained during confused and sometimes acrimonious bargaining at Brussels throughout the Winter and Spring of 1976-77. In July 1977 the Irish government agreed to interim measures which fell far short of their original demands, but reserved the right to return to the fray with the fifty mile claim.[74] At the same time Ireland and Britain were disputing jurisdiction over the Rockall plateau of the continental shelf — a further reminder that the ground rules of maritime exploitation have yet to be established.[75]

Disputes of this kind are now part of an economic relationship with Britain that has changed considerably since the tensions of the nineteen-thirties. Table 3 shows the reduced importance of the United Kingdom as a market for Irish exports, with a marked diversification of trade mainly to the continental European Community countries, but also to North America.

Table 3   Irish Trade by Area, 1959–73

Exports percentage distribution		Area	Imports percentage distribution	
1959-60	1972-73		1959-60	1972-73
73.8	57.8	United Kingdom	50.6	50.8
5.9	19.1	Other EEC	13.4	19.7
8.3	11.4	USA and Canada	9.8	8.4
1.1	2.7	EFTA	4.2	6.0
10.9	9.0	All other areas	22.0	15.1

Source: D. McAleese, 'The Foreign Sector' in N. Gibson and J. Spencer (eds.), *Economic Activity in Ireland* (Dublin: Gill and Macmillan, 1976), Table 4.3

Although the British market is still by far the largest, the assumption that this fact must in the long term determine Irish economic foreign policy no longer has the force it used to have. This was demonstrated when British membership of the European Community became the issue of a British referendum in 1975. Had Britain withdrawn, the Irish government would have been faced with the choice of a return to the *status quo ante* — a British Isles economic system — or remaining in a Community without Britain, a course involving considerable disruption. In the event the question did not arise, but the choice was in effect made — to stay in the

European Community, whatever the consequences for Anglo-Irish economic relations.[76]

Of course a decline in dependence on Britain, both in terms of economic interactions and in attitudes, does not amount to economic independence. The Irish economy has become increasingly open since 1921, and among its European Community partners it is one of the economies most dependent on foreign trade, and in particular on trade within the European Community itself; this is clearly seen in Table 4. The important point about this new pattern of dependence is that it represents a change from a bilateral to a multilateral relationship. This offers regular, formal participation in decision-making, with the possibility of compensating for inherent discrepancies in power by the mobilisation of diplomatic coalitions, and the right of appeal to a quasi-constitutional authority in the form of the Community's treaties, backed by the courts. This is not to say that Irish interests necessarily prevail, but it does represent a type of negotiation which offers more scope for manoeuvre than the notoriously unbalanced Anglo-Irish diplomatic relationship.

Table 4   Trade Dependence in the EEC, 1971

	Exports as % of GNP	Intra-EEC Exports as % of GNP	Intra-EEC Exports as % of total export
Belgium/Luxembourg	41	30	73
Denmark	21	9	42
France	13	7	55
Germany	18	9	49
Italy	15	7	49
Netherlands	38	27	73
U.K.	16	5	29
Ireland	29	22	75

Source: T. K. Whitaker, 'Monetary Integration: Reflections on Irish Experience', *Quarterly Bulletin, Central Bank of Ireland*, Winter 1973, p.77.

To date, because the Irish government sees the European Community as the framework for Irish economic foreign policy and because Ireland is a net beneficiary from the Community, a generally constructive, *'communautaire'*, strategy has been adopted to the development of Community policies.[77] Nevertheless, Irish vulnerability to external economic forces can lead to domestic demands for a more overtly self-centred approach — in this respect the fishery dispute could be a pointer. The future of the Common Agricultural Policy and of Regional Policy are areas of obvious sensitivity, particularly in view of the prospect of their further dilution following any additional membership of the Community.[78]

The fact that the European Community has little impact on the pressing problems of inflation and unemployment — these are still primarily Anglo-Irish problems — has also led to a reappraisal of Irish economic foreign policy as a whole. It has been argued that economic development through the 'neo-mercantilist export-led strategy', with its consequent openness and vulnerability of the economy, has been over-emphasised and should be replaced by economic policy which would reduce the importance of exports, employ selective protection and require that 'the Irish State accept and exercise its responsibility and authority over the economy.'[79] As yet this view has little obvious political support, but, should the system of regional interdependence through the European Community fail to protect the economy, a swing to a form of economic isolationism could again be possible.

Chapter 8

The International Milieu: Order

The basis of all moves to security and economic progress for Ireland as for the whole world is the maintenance of peace and the reduction of suspicion and tension between all states. Failure in this sphere entails failure in all others; there may be no other problems to resolve if world peace is not maintained and nuclear war breaks out.

Garret FitzGerald, TD,
Minister for Foreign Affairs,
in the Dáil, 9 May 1973

The Anglo-Irish negotiations of 1921 saw the crystallisation of issues related to the central concerns of any state in the contemporary international system. The definition of Ireland's status and of her territorial and human composition were fundamental to the very existence of the state; security and prosperity were goals no less vital for survival in 'the framework of anarchy' which international relations so often seems to be.[1] Foreign policy goals of this type have been described as 'possession goals' by an American writer, Arnold Wolfers, who pointed to the characteristics they held in common:

In directing its foreign policy toward the attainment of its possession goals, a nation is aiming at the enhancement or the preservation of one or more of the things to which it attaches value. The aim may apply to such values as a stretch of territory, membership in the Security Council of the United Nations, or tariff preferences. Here a nation finds itself competing with others for a share of values in limited supply; it is demanding that its share be left intact or increased. Because of the possessive nature of these goals, they are apt to be praised by some for being truly in the national interest, while condemned by others as indicating a reprehensible spirit of national selfishness or acquisitiveness.[2]

However, foreign policy cannot be seen exclusively in terms of issue-areas arising from the pursuit of possession goals. Wolfers identified another contrasting type of goal, relating to the international environment or 'milieu':

> Milieu goals are of a different character. Nations pursuing them are out not to defend or increase possessions they hold to the exclusion of others, but aim instead at shaping conditions beyond their national boundaries. If it were not for the existence of such goals, peace could never become an objective of national policy. By its very nature, peace cannot be the possession of any one nation; it takes at least two to make and have peace. Similarly, efforts to promote international law or to establish international organisations, undertaken consistently by many nations, are addressed to the milieu in which nations operate and indeed such efforts make sense only if nations have reason to concern themselves with things other than their own possessions.[3]

The distinction between possession and milieu goals is one between the primarily competitive aspects of foreign policy and those which are primarily co-operative. The first type emphasises the sovereignty and the power of the state, while milieu goals suggest the interdependence of the international community.[4] Nevertheless, it would be a mistake to ignore the connection between the two categories. Although milieu goals may be to some degree altruistic, they are nonetheless in the national interest in so far as a benevolent and predictable environment is preferable to threats and uncertainties. When a statesman shows concern for the international milieu, he is, to some degree at least, displaying an enlightened self-interest, a concern for the long-term development of his state's position, as well as the immediate and more obviously pressing issues generally associated with the pursuit of possession goals. Often, too, what appears to be concern for the international milieu may be little more than a means of advancing the narrow interests of the state or even of the statesman concerned.

It is easy to neglect milieu goals and the issue-areas associated with them. Where they involve technical, undramatic policies, as in much of the work of the United Nations specialised agencies, for example, they make poor copy in the media beside the recurring and often violent conflicts of international politics. On the other hand, the ambiguous nature and sheer ambition of such goals as 'international justice' or 'disarmament' can lead to a fatalistic and apathetic attitude. Not only do they seem attainable, if at all, in a very distant future, but they seem more difficult to deal with because they depend not upon the will of one state, but of many others.[5] The cynical observer in a powerful state will see his government's pursuit of milieu goals either as an alternative means of exerting national influence or as a waste of public money. The latter reaction can also arise in a small state, where any contribution it might make to its international environment seems so marginal as to be worthless.

Nonetheless, milieu goals have been a persistent feature of Irish foreign policy, although public interest in them has varied greatly according to domestic or external circumstances. The first section in Article 29 of the Constitution, which deals with international relations, states that 'Ireland affirms its devotion to the ideal of peace and friendly co-operation amongst nations founded on international justice and morality.'[6] This image of the ideal international environment contains two broad values, which in practice are often interpreted in such a way as to come into conflict with each other. 'Peace and friendly co-operation' suggests order, that is to say, predictability and restraint in behaviour, which is based on a particular *status quo* among the actors concerned; 'international justice and morality', on the other hand, may imply change, uncertainty and in some degree a disruption of existing order.[7] This dilemma underlies the two issue-areas relating to the international milieu, which may be called 'international order' and 'international justice'.

While by no means innocent of what are often strongly held notions about international justice[8], Irish foreign policy on the whole has demonstrated an overriding concern for international order. Sometimes this is implied in government action (or inaction), sometimes a potential conflict between order and justice is coped with simply by refusing to admit that in the long run it exists. What is meant by order? At first glance it would seem a precarious quality in the near-anarchy of international politics, but it can be argued that there is in fact a rudimentary international society of sovereign states. Thus international order may be described as 'a pattern of activity that sustains the elementary or primary goals of the society of states.'[9] Order in this sense consists of rules which are often crude, uncodified, often honoured in the breach rather than the practice, but in the long term nonetheless essential to the survival of the rudimentary society of states. These basic rules 'may have the status of international law, of moral rules, of custom or established practice, or they may be merely operational rules or "rules of the game", worked out without formal agreement or even without verbal communication.'[10] Whatever means are employed to maintain international order, certain fundamental goals are sought. These include the preservation of the system and society of sovereign states, with all that that implies; they also include the goal of peace, and, in a world where the technology of violence promises global destruction, the limitation of violence. This does not necessarily mean 'peace with justice', rather it is the much more modest aim of 'peace as the absence of war', wherever possible.[11]

*   *   *

International order, seen in this way, may take several forms.[12] It may be the creation of a great power establishing its hegemony over a group of less powerful states, or it may be a result of the maintenance of a balance of power by the leading states in the international system. It can be seen in the agreement of the mutually antagonistic superpowers to limit the extent of their rivalry, often at the expense of other states. Although international order may be equated with peace, it is a peace often dependent on limited violence and on the underlying threat of coercion.

What can a small state like Ireland contribute to this bleak concept of civilised behaviour? It will only rarely seek its own hegemony, and will try to avoid that of other states as far as possible. On the other hand, the small state, too, has an interest in the preservation of all types of international communication, and can seek international order through the exercise of diplomacy, mediation, peace-keeping operations or the promotion of disarmament. To counter its weakness, it is usual for the small state to attempt to promote international order through the medium of international organisations, where at least its voice is formally accepted as being equal to those of vastly more powerful states. It will also stress the role to be played by international law. Indeed, the Irish Constitution explicitly refers to Ireland's 'adherence to the principle of the pacific settlement of international disputes by international arbitration or judicial determination', and this is followed by the declaration that 'Ireland accepts the generally recognised principles of international law as its rule of conduct in its relations with other states.'[13]

Thus, international order as an issue-area in Irish foreign policy has evolved mainly in the context of the 'universal' international organisations, first in the League of Nations, from 1923 to 1946, and then in the United Nations Organisation from 1955 to the present. Although in the nineteen-twenties Irish membership of the League was marked by the pursuit of possession goals, such as independent status[14], the more general role of the League did not go unnoticed. Ernest Blythe, the Minister for Finance, who was a member of the Irish delegation in Geneva in 1926, reported back to his government:

> I feel satisfied that the general work of the League may be of enormous value to the world at large, and, indirectly to this country. Small nations like ours will gain more by the prevention of war than the great nations because, whether or not the small nation is on the victorious side, its rights are liable to be disregarded and its interests prejudiced.[15]

This view had also been expressed four years earlier, by George Gavan Duffy, a member of the Treaty delegation and briefly Minister for Foreign Affairs in the Provisional Government. Duffy, too, had pointed to the possibility of the League's Covenant providing an environment in which small states might be secure[16], but in the interval it seems that little had been done to contribute in a positive way to the 'general work' of the League, for Blythe's report is explicit about the lack of preparation the 1926 delegation had received, and in particular the lack of any instructions from the cabinet.

This inactivity was understandable in a small state which was compelled to define its international status in the face of British obstruction and domestic criticism. It also, however, reflected a certain scepticism about the League of Nations as an instrument of international order. Obligations towards the League's system of collective security, which in theory involved great power agreement and considerable use of coercive powers, were qualified by explicit expressions of national sovereignty. Thus while Kevin O'Higgins, Minister for Justice, claimed the Irish Free State would

'not fail to afford every assistance within our power and competence' to the League's efforts to maintain peace, he also pointed
out that the decision to participate in any way, including a League
war, required parliamentary assent under Article 49 of the Constitution of 1922.[17] Moreover, although the League's supporters
insisted that 'peace was indivisible', the Irish government did not
assume that a threat to Irish security would necessarily lead to
League action on Ireland's behalf; in the last resort, the state
depended on national security rather than collective security.[18]

Public attitudes towards the League were mixed. The general
hope that prevailed in many countries, that it would prove to be
the basis of a new and civilised era in international relations, was
reflected in the creation of an Irish League of Nations Society in
1923. But in spite of participation by members of the government
and the publication of a periodical, membership was never high;
an early target of two thousand was not reached.[19] Support in the
media consisted of generalised editorial sympathy, but little
attempt to inform the Irish public either about the League's
policies or its own government's participation. A small group of
supporters in the Dáil included the leader of the Labour Party,
Thomas Johnson, but this was offset by the scepticism of others,
a scepticism largely based on a mistrust of the great powers: 'There
does not seem to be any sincerity in the protestations of the great
States within the League . . . just as it suits them, and when they
can effect alliances, they will drop the League and disobey its
instructions.'[20]

Such views became more pronounced after Fianna Fáil entered
the Dáil in 1927. For de Valera's followers, the League was associated above all with the infamous peace conference of 1919, at
which the case for Irish independence had not even been granted
a hearing. Subsequent events had compounded the error. Thus in
February 1929 Fianna Fáil opposed ratification of the Kellogg-
Briand Pact for the renunciation of war, on the grounds that the
pact, in conjunction with Article X of the League's Covenant
(which guaranteed the territorial integrity of League states), would
prevent revision of territorial boundaries. Ireland, like Germany,
Italy and Japan, was after all a revisionist state. On the other hand,
for the Minister for External Affairs, Patrick McGilligan, whatever
the deficiencies of either League or Pact, it was 'time that we
should play our part in promoting the idea of peace and not refuse

by any action to promote the main and simple idea of this Pact which is to try and have disputes between nations settled otherwise than by warlike means.'[21]

Fianna Fáil's attitude towards the League softened somewhat in the early nineteen-thirties, but was still equivocal. On 26 June 1931 Seán T. O'Kelly supported the General Act for the Settlement of International Disputes, but on 1 July Seán Lemass declared that the League 'and everything in relation to it was wrapped in utter futility.'[22] De Valera himself remained aloof from the issue while in opposition; when he came to power less than a year later, he found himself acting as president of the League's Council at a time when collective security was facing its first major challenge, the Japanese annexation of Manchuria. De Valera's speech to the League Assembly on 26 September 1932 was an austere exhortation to the League's members to support collective security; he made an impression on his audience, though his speech contained little in substance to distinguish it from speeches made at Geneva by his predecessors.[23] This declaration of intent was, however, backed by sustained Irish efforts over the winter of 1932–33 to press for an unambiguous condemnation of Japan. In particular Ireland's permanent delegate, Seán Lester, took a leading role in an attempt by the smaller states to stiffen the resolve of the great powers.[24] As representative of a Council member, Lester was also deeply involved in presiding over the small committees which were responsible for League intervention in two South American disputes, the Chaco war between Bolivia and Paraguay and the Leticia dispute between Peru and Colombia.[25]

By the mid-thirties, however, the Irish Free State was no longer in the League's Council and Lester's increasing diplomatic reputation had resulted in his appointment as the League high commissioner in Danzig. His former colleagues in the Department of External Affairs were not always as enthusiastic as he was about the League, while the cabinet's attitude – or rather, de Valera's attitude – was marked by a qualified pessimism. De Valera ruled out the prospects for effective League sanctions, or for a 'federation of the States of Europe, for a specific purpose at any rate'; all that could be done was to create a favourable public opinion. Meanwhile Ireland was still 'only too happy to assist anything that can be done to make the League of Nations a more effective instrument in the maintenance of world peace.'[27] On these grounds

de Valera supported the admission of the Soviet Union to the
League in 1934, in spite of reservations concerning the morality
of the Russian regime.[28] With regard to domestic politics this
policy showed some courage, but as far as international politics
were concerned even the introduction of one of the 'great
absentees' from the League system was to prove too late to save it.

Late in 1934 Italian territorial ambitions in Ethiopia became an
issue which the great powers in the League could no longer ignore
indefinitely, in spite of their best efforts to do so. Mussolini's
invasion of Ethiopia in October 1935 led to the imposition of
economic sanctions against Italy, a move fully supported by the
Irish government, though de Valera was by no means complacent
about the League's viability as an instrument of world order.[29]
Nor was his policy on sanctions universally approved at home.
Extreme nationalists, in the best tradition of 'England's difficulty
being Ireland's opportunity', opposed Irish participation.[30] The
Fine Gael opposition suggested that Irish support for the British-
led League policy should be conditional on British concessions in
the Anglo-Irish 'economic war', a policy which led to the resignation of one of the new party's leaders, Frank MacDermot.
Finally, the issue was seen by some deputies as one in which
'Christian Italy' faced the forces of darkness; for them the issue
was one of international justice rather than international order.[31]

There was in any case a point beyond which de Valera was not
prepared to go; he was not prepared to support military sanctions
should economic sanctions fail.[32] Nor, as it happened, were the
governments of most other League members, and when the Anglo-
French proposal to buy off Italy at Ethiopia's expense − the
Hoare-Laval pact − emerged at the beginning of December 1935
the campaign of economic sanctions lost credibility. It failed to
prevent the Italian conquest in May 1936, an event which sealed
the fate of collective security, and on 18 June 1936 de Valera
made no bones about admitting the fact: 'it [the League] does not
command our confidence.'[33]

The conclusion drawn from the collapse of collective security
was that Ireland must be neutral, and in a sense neutrality − as
ever the all-purpose policy − can be explained partly as a response
to the breakdown of the political role of the League, as well as
a means of achieving aspirations with regard to Irish independence,
security and unity. This was demonstrated almost immediately

when, after the outbreak of the Spanish civil war, the Irish government adhered to the non-intervention line promoted by Britain
and France, on the grounds that this position prevented a further
internationalisation of the Spanish conflict. As was the case with
the Ethiopian issue, this concern for international order had its
vocal Irish critics, but government policy was not significantly
deflected.[34]

In September 1938 came the final opportunity for the Irish
government to act in the interests of world peace before general
war broke out in Europe. During the Czechoslovakian crisis it
seems that de Valera considered appealing to Hitler and Mussolini,
not in his capacity as president of the League of Nations Assembly
(which office he then held), but as Irish head of government.[35]
The British prime minister's readiness to travel pre-empted the
possibility of Irish mediation on the banks of the Rhine, but when
asked by de Valera whether Ireland could help, Chamberlain
suggested that de Valera might mobilise opinion in the League
Assembly. The Assembly's president then ensured that a unanimous resolution of 'concern' was passed on 29 September.

With the value of hindsight it might be observed that a unanimous
resolution by the League Assembly in 1938 was worth something
less than a Czech border guard. Indeed in 1936 de Valera himself
had recommended a reform of the League, not in order to acquire
more authority, but in order to set itself 'an humbler task'.[36] But
even after the Munich settlement he was reluctant to ignore it
altogether; on 2 May 1939 he described it as 'a certain element
of support . . . for small nations and for things for which small
nations stand.'[37] Although later that year he bitterly described the
League as 'debris'[38], two considerations seem to have weighed with
the Irish government for continuing membership right through
World War II, until the League was wound up on 19 April 1946.
In the first place the 'reformed' League was starting to develop a
more serious interest in international co-operation in the fields of
economic and social policy; in addition, the preservation of even
the slightest shadow of the League would be an element of continuity with the post-war world and possibly the basis of a new
international organisation. Thus the Dáil still voted public money
to maintain the League in existence at a time when it had been
abandoned by many other governments. Although the sums were
small, they represent a striking example of a government's concern

with the world beyond its immediate and obvious interests.[39]

Such altruism received scant reward after World War II. Neither of the two emerging superpowers had any use for the existing League of Nations; to Americans it had always been the subject of political controversy, while the Soviet Union had suffered the indignity of expulsion, for invading Finland, as recently as 1939. The United Nations Organisation was nonetheless created very much in the image of its predecessor — but neutral states had to apply for membership as if the latter had never existed. In this way Ireland's application was rejected by the Soviet Union, largely because of hardening cold war rivalries. It was not until 1955 that this deadlock was broken and Ireland once again had an opportunity to develop policy towards the maintenance of international order.

By this time the over-ambitious strategy of collective security had been replaced by peace-keeping operations, involving 'UN political-military control of local conflict by politically impartial, essentially non-coercive methods.'[40] The relatively modest aim of such activities is to prevent conflicts with a limited geographical basis from becoming directly involved in cold war confrontations between the superpowers. Most cases arose from disputes associated with the drawn-out process of decolonisation, a process which was approaching its most active phase when Ireland was admitted to the UN. Ireland's own colonial past and her detachment from cold war alliances made her an attractive candidate for UN peace-keeping operations. She was what is sometimes referred to as a 'middle power', a description given by one authority to 'countries occupying a political "middle" on given issues, to those that appeared frequently as interlocutors in the UN's parliamentary diplomacy, or to those that often performed various mediatory and third-party functions in dispute-settlement efforts.' The writer goes on to acknowledge that 'Ireland has repeatedly acted out the middle power role on a range of problems.'[41]

In fact peace-keeping became a central feature of Irish foreign policy in the nineteen-sixties. Out of the twelve UN peace-keeping missions analysed by Fabian up to the end of 1970, Ireland participated in seven, on a par with Norway and Finland, and behind only Sweden, Canada and Denmark with ten, nine and eight missions to their credit respectively.[42] Although this participation, in so far as it demonstrated national independence, was by no means solely motivated by a concern for the international environment, the extent of the Irish commitment does not suggest an attempt to gain national prestige on the cheap. It has been summarised in the following terms in Fabian's comparative study:

> In addition to providing over 100 observers to five missions, the Irish by 1967 had supplied ONUC manning tables with 5,300 men and UNFICYP ones with nearly 5,000. These are weighty figures for an army establishment generally several thousand men below its authorized strength of 12,000. Ireland has made enormous contributions even in absolute terms, ranking seventh, for example, in ONUC manpower. In 1964, counting a large early unit in Cyprus topped only by those of Britain and Canada, fully one-sixth of Ireland's standing, all-volunteer army was on peacekeeping duty.[43]

This development had relatively small beginnings in the late nineteen-fifties with the secondment of officers to UN observer missions in the Middle East, but participation in the UN operation in the Congo from 1961 to 1964 was the first major involvement, which required a change in domestic legislation to allow Irish army contingents to serve abroad.[44] It proved to be a new departure for an army which had never served overseas and was without combat experience, and was the only peace-keeping mission amongst which significant casualties were suffered, twenty-six soldiers losing their lives. An Irish general, Seán MacEoin, was for a time Commander-in-Chief of the UN force, and the Secretary General's representative in Katanga was a seconded Irish diplomat, Dr Conor Cruise O'Brien.[45]

In 1964, when 350 Irish troops were still in the Congo, Ireland was asked to contribute to the Cyprus operation, and an Irish contingent remained on the island for the next nine years. The original contingent of 500 men was gradually reduced to about 150, though by regular rotation of units overseas experience percolated through the army. In the early nineteen-seventies security problems on the border with Northern Ireland began to cast their shadow over the peace-keeping effort, though this did not prevent the commitment of 275 men to the United Nations Emergency Force (UNEF) in Sinai in the aftermath of the Arab-Israeli war of October 1973. Half of these were simply transferred from Cyprus, but their tour of duty proved to be brief. In May 1974, after serious car-bomb attacks in Dublin and Monaghan, the

Irish contingent was abruptly recalled. This decision may have been partly motivated by a desire to produce a visible response to a situation of considerable public anxiety; partly it was due to the need for experienced personnel at home.[46] By July 1976 Ireland's peace-keeping contribution had been reduced to twenty-six officers, five in Cyprus and the rest in the Middle East; but the following year authorisation was given for the return of 300 troops to Cyprus.

Besides actually contributing towards peace-keeping operations, the Irish delegation at the UN has been involved in a continuous battle over the question of financing peace-keeping. The issue was not a financial one (for in the long term costs incurred could be offset against training and experience gained), but concerned the unwillingness of some states to accept a general responsibility for peace-keeping operations. In the mid-sixties, during the so-called 'financial crisis' in the UN, this led to an Irish proposal that seventy per cent of the costs of any operation should be paid by those permanent members of the Security Council which approved of specific operations, twenty-five per cent by other 'wealthy' states and five per cent by 'poor' states. When this was rejected 'Ireland's criticism of inequitable and unenforceable cost-sharing found an outlet in taking a stand that was concrete, demonstrative, principled, and self-sacrificing' — she paid her own costs of the Cyprus contingent.[47] This stand, largely the initiative of the Minister for External Affairs, Frank Aiken, had to be abandoned in June 1965, following pressure from the Department of Finance, by which time it was estimated to have cost nearly two million dollars.[48]

The hand-to-mouth method of financing the Cyprus operation continued to be a theme of Irish policy in the UN under Aiken's successors[49], and may help explain the government's gradual rundown of the forces there and its readiness to transfer them to UNEF in 1973. The Security Council resolution which established the latter provided that costs should be borne by member-states in accordance with their general obligations under the Charter. This was a step forward in principle but by the time troops were recalled in 1974 it did not appear to be accepted as a precedent for future operations, and Ireland, with a share of the costs reduced to seventy-five thousand pounds in 1974–75, was no longer in a position to promote the issue with as much conviction as before.

In very general terms participation in UN peace-keeping operations has been regarded as a valuable activity by the Irish public.
It has been presented by governments as being both a contribution
to international order and to Ireland's national interests, whether
indirectly, because Ireland was a beneficiary of this type of order,
or directly, because it was a manifestation of national prestige. Yet
behind the satisfaction derived from duty performed or from the
'glamour' of performing, public support cannot be taken for
granted. The casualties suffered in the Congo made a deep impression on a public which was not then used to the idea that Irishmen
could die as a result of military action. The political development
of the Congo operation also provoked reservations about Irish
participation. Initially, support had been based on the theoretical
impartiality of the UN, but in the case of the Congo UN intervention was tacitly assumed by the western powers to be a means
of keeping the Soviet Union out of Africa.[50] This led to the
early opposition of two Dáil deputies, Dr Noel Browne and Jack
McQuillan, though it was a matter of some comfort for the main
opposition leader, James Dillon. The latter was less than happy,
however, when the UN action in Katanga, in which the Irish
presence was particularly marked in the person of Conor Cruise
O'Brien, incurred the wrath of Britain, France and Belgium. Ireland
had, since July 1961, applied to join the EEC, and for Dillon it
was 'there our vital interest lies.'[51] Although such reservations did
not lead to a withdrawal of the Irish commitment, it was noticeable
that subsequent peace-keeping commitments were undertaken
with a close look at the small print of the UN mandates concerned.

Peace-keeping proved to be Ireland's major contribution to
international order during the state's first twenty years in the
United Nations, but it was by no means the only activity to be
found in this issue-area. Disarmament was an objective which was
closely associated with Frank Aiken's long tenure of office as
Minister for External Affairs, from 1957 to 1969, and which was
also pursued, though with rather less emphasis, before and since
that time. Strictly speaking, disarmament implies the quantitative
or qualitative reduction of the weaponry at the disposal of
military establishments, but in general usage it also refers to
methods of arms control and agreement not to increase arms
production. It has long been the concern of individuals and organisations interested in creating conditions of international peace,

yet has always been beset by apparently insurmountable problems both of a political and technical nature.[52] The role of international organisations has proved to be a limited one; in particular the attempts of the League of Nations, in which high expectations had been placed, culminated only in the fiasco of the Disarmament Conference of 1932.

Preparations for this conference nonetheless provided the occasion of the beginning of Irish interest in disarmament questions. In 1929 the Minister for External Affairs, Patrick McGilligan, devoted a good deal of attention to disarmament in his speech to the League Assembly, and produced figures to show that Irish expenditure on armaments had been reduced from nearly three million pounds in 1924 to half that amount.[53] This was not of course a consequence of the government's concern for international order, but rather a reflection of its success in achieving order at home after the civil war of 1922–23, and it was also true that Irish armaments were in any case limited by Article 8 of the Anglo-Irish Treaty of 1921. However, finding a virtue in necessity, the Irish government continued to press for disarmament through 1930 and 1931. On 1 July 1931 McGilligan maintained that 'delegates from this country will be instructed to support everything that has for its object disarmament and to make everything proposed for that purpose or end as comprehensive as possible.'[54] In October the Irish Free State duly adhered to the twelve months 'arms truce' which heralded the Disarmament Conference, but by this time domestic preoccupations had accounted for a decline in the level of government interest.[55] With the change of government early in 1932 international disarmament became a peripheral concern for the Department of External Affairs, while the following year the Disarmament Conference itself collapsed.

Twenty-five years elapsed before disarmanent again became an explicit objective of Irish foreign policy. In the nuclear age disarmament questions were even more acute, but were discussed in technical language of increasing complexity. The contribution to be made by a small state, with negligible interest as either a producer or consumer of arms, was strictly limited. Nevertheless, this degree of 'innocence' permitted the adoption of a role in assisting in the tedious negotiations of great military powers, by formulating and promoting initiatives which would be viewed with suspicion coming from the more directly interested parties. Frank Aiken seized on this role and pursued it with great tenacity. In 1958 the Irish delegation proposed a draft resolution to prevent the spread of nuclear weapons, and this was followed in 1961 by the so-called 'Irish Resolution' – Resolution 1665 (XVI) – which was adopted by the UN General Assembly, the first such resolution concerned with the problem of the proliferation of nuclear weapons. This resolution was followed by a long sequence of committees and negotiations leading up to the signing of the Nuclear Proliferation Treaty in 1968, which was agreed by the two superpowers, though not by France and China. Aiken's contribution was recognised in the treaty signing ceremony; his was the first signature on the version signed in Moscow.

It is difficult to assess the overall significance of this type of activity, and even more difficult to assess the role of a small state delegation such as Ireland's.[56] There are few, if any, electoral plaudits to be gained from a domestic opinion remote from the intricacies of nuclear technology. But this did not deter the Irish delegation from continuing Aiken's interest in disarmament after his retirement in the Summer of 1969. Later that year it co-sponsored five resolutions relating to nuclear weapons, following this with six in 1970. In 1971 the Irish delegate to the UN First Committee, Seán Ronan, complained that while 'the pace of disarmament negotiations is poised between torpor and glacial advance . . . the rate of advance of nuclear technology is anything but glacial.'[57] By this time the main forum for arms control measures was the Strategic Arms Limitations Talks (SALT) between the United States and the Soviet Union, and this was reflected in a lack of movement in the United Nations. However, a new urgency was to be seen when India 'went nuclear' in 1974, and a Nuclear Proliferation Treaty Review Conference was held under UN auspices in 1975. Ireland's participation here broke no new ground, apart from an emphasis on controlling the sources of nuclear technology.

Since 1968 the single-mindedness and sense of achievement associated with Irish involvement in disarmament has become less apparent. This can be partly explained by developments at the international level referred to above, but it may also be a consequence of the limited resources which Ireland can utilise. Unlike some of the Scandinavian countries, for example, Ireland does not have a separate Ministry for Disarmament, nor any governmental or privately sponsored research into this most esoteric aspect of international relations. Although in 1971 Ireland co-sponsored a draft resolution which recommended, *inter alia,* 'continuing courses and seminars to study problems of the arms race' in member-states' universities, nothing of the kind either existed or has to date been established at home.[58] The UN delegation's resources, therefore, are limited to the handful of officials it possesses, who are required to master a much more comprehensive brief than that of disarmament alone. One means of compensating for this deficiency has been consultation with like-minded delegations from other states, and indeed this is an inherent part of the United Nations political process, but it may imply a temptation to follow rather than to lead. Ireland's membership of the European Community from 1973 thus poses the question whether Irish policy on disarmament – as on other issues relating to the international milieu – was being dissipated in Community consultations and submerged by a common Community policy.

Before examining this question, however, reference must be made to another aspect of international order which is so pervasive that it is often taken for granted. This is the amalgam of institutions, procedures and activities which are sometimes referred to as 'functional'. They include 'economic, social, technical, and humanitarian matters – that is, . . . problems which may be tentatively described as non-political.'[59] International functionalism is a term which at the same time encompasses many diverse activities at all levels of international interaction and suggests a broad analogy with rather similar activities pursued domestically in the welfare state. However convenient a term it may be, neither the assumptions on which it is based nor its supposed consequences are beyond argument. While maintaining that this type of co-operation is 'non-political', functionalist writers nevertheless see it as being an important – sometimes the primary – means of achieving a lasting peace. Thus the international network of functional activity is seen as an essential component of order among the society of states. The lessons of the last hundred years or so, however, suggest cautious conclusions. Functional activity has undoubtedly expanded, but the hoped-for benefits, with regard to international order, have often proved to be elusive, the links of commerce being no more than 'cobwebs across the mouth of a cannon.'[60]

The hard core of international functionalism is the international economic system. Since World War II this has become increasingly institutionalised and regulated, the purpose of bodies such as the International Monetary Fund (IMF) and the General Agreement on Trade and Tariffs (GATT) being to provide a forum of continuous negotiation about international economic interactions. In the case of Ireland, the organisation with most continuous practical relevance has been the Organisation for European Economic Co-operation (OEEC), of which she was a founder member in 1948 and which was transformed into the Organisation for Economic Co-operation and Development (OECD) in 1960. But given the degree of Irish economic dependence in both trade and finance, it is not surprising that Ireland has no tradition of innovation in this field, and indeed governments in the first decade after World War II were sometimes wary of direct participation.[61] Nevertheless, given the economy's 'openness', particularly since the abandonment of protection during the nineteen-sixties, it is not surprising either that government spokesmen point to Ireland's interest in maintaining an international economic order created by other states:

> We cannot trade with benefit in a world which does not have a substantial degree of order and equity in trade relations. We cannot deal with advantage in other economic exchanges in a world where each nation adopts narrow and unfairly restrictive policies.[62]

The Irish concern for international economic order is therefore very directly related to the state's material interests and less directly to the maintenance of a general condition of peace.

However, in adapting to the development of international economic order Ireland, by joining the European Community, altered the diplomatic setting in which international order, in its broader sense, was to be pursued. The emphasis was now to be on dealing with issues of international order within a regional organisation as well as through a universal organisation. 'Region' is a term used to describe particular groups of states which usually, but not always, have a geographical basis. One which does not is the Commonwealth, of which of course Ireland was a member up to 1949, but Irish governments never sought in any significant way to focus their policy on this region. In 1948 the west European region became a feature of Irish diplomacy when Ireland joined the OEEC. In 1949 Ireland joined another regional institution, the Council of Europe; this organisation has had only a marginal influence on the immediate, politico-strategic aspects of international order, but it has been important in the formation of a legal framework for human rights.[63] Nevertheless, up to 1973, the universal organisation — the United Nations — was the major stage for Irish efforts to make a contribution towards international order.

It is often argued that there is no inherent conflict between regional and universal organisations, though on specific matters interests may diverge.[64] Where the search for peace is concerned, the regional organisation can just as well supplement the effects of the universal organisation as provide a rival to it. Even Frank Aiken, a champion of the universal organisation, had promoted the idea 'that groups of smaller States should be encouraged to organise themselves into . . . "zones of peace", "regions of neutrality" or "areas of law and limited armaments", so that they could devote all their energy and resources to economic and social development and eliminate the possibility of armed conflict.'[65] However, international regions tend to develop for more complex, and often less well-intentioned, reasons than these, and since 1973 it is the interaction between Irish foreign policy in the European Community and in the United Nations that must be considered.

As we have seen, Ireland's UN policy has been based essentially on her role as a 'middle power', and this in turn depends on the state's ability to remain, in the eyes of most members of the organisation, relatively independent and impartial. What Ireland is seen to do can matter as much as what Ireland does. Consequently, it is important for an Irish government which wishes to maintain its credibility in the UN to demonstrate that it will pursue broadly similar objectives within the regional context; the crux of the matter is the maintenance of consistency in each organisation with regard to key objectives which identify 'the middle power'.

Within the European Community system the major forum for establishing positions on these matters is the consultative procedure known as 'political co-operation', which evolved with a maximum of pragmatism and a minimum of publicity, after the Hague summit of 1969.[66] The practice of trying to arrive at common positions on particular issues has developed gradually and tentatively. The most striking example to date of common policy – and of a common expression of that policy – was during the Conference on Security and Co-operation in Europe which opened in July 1973 and culminated in the Helsinki Declaration of 1975. Whether the policy was seen as a recognition of the existing political order in Europe as a whole or as the basis for a greater degree of certainty and a lesser degree of suspicion in east-west relations, the Irish government had little difficulty in agreeing with its European Community counterparts; in the late nineteen-fifties, after all, Aiken had proposed much more ambitious, and at that time much more controversial, schemes for mutual disengagement in Europe.[67] The major Irish contribution to this exercise in détente was to insist, along with West Germany and Spain, that frontiers should be described as 'inviolable', but not as 'immutable'.[68] The fact that all three states had unresolved territorial claims is an indication of the close connection which exists between a government's view of international order and the possession goals it pursues.

The Helsinki Declaration was not seen as conflicting with the UN Charter – the conference was even legitimised by the presence of the UN Secretary-General. But political co-operation in the European Community has not been restricted to détente in Europe, for one of the aims of the consultations was to co-operate within the UN General Assembly. After an uncertain start, there developed by 1974–75 'a relatively cohesive West European "bloc", successful in voting together with increasing frequency, in capturing the attention of other states and groups of states, and in promoting Gaston Thorn as candidate for President of the 1975 General Assembly.'[69] Blocs are anathema to the hallowed traditions of Irish foreign policy; does this development mark a fundamental change?

Should political integration within the European Community advance, the answer would clearly be yes, but given the tentative nature of the Community as a political entity the answer is not so obvious. The extent to which the Nine do form a bloc in the UN can be seen in the fact that they voted together in forty-three per cent of contested votes in 1973, in sixty-one per cent in 1974 and in sixty-five per cent in 1975.[70] Whether this percentage increases, remains to be seen, but there can be no dispute over the fact that the Community states have not voted together on several of the more important issues before the General Assembly. With regard to traditional Irish positions on issues of international order, it is worth noting that there is no European Community bloc so far as peace-keeping or disarmament is concerned. The Nine are split on the question of mandatory financing of peace-keeping operations, and of course Ireland has – since joining the Community – been found acceptable for participation in UNEF. As far as disarmament issues go, Ireland takes a line quite similar to Denmark and the Netherlands but at the opposite extreme to France, which still remains outside the Nuclear Proliferation Treaty.

Participation in political co-operation has also resulted in new opportunities for Ireland to play a mediatory role within the Community framework, a role which can be quite significant during the government's term in the presidency of the Council of Ministers. Thus, the Euro-Arab dialogue may have been facilitated in 1975 because the Community was represented by a state which had no history of partiality in the Middle East. Ireland's 'middle power' identity is further reinforced by the fact that, alone of the Nine, Ireland does not belong to a military alliance. Although alliance membership does not preclude a state from playing such a role – Canada, Denmark and Norway are in NATO – it is not an obvious qualification.

Ireland's military neutrality has generally been justified on self-regarding grounds, such as independence, security, and unity, but it is possible that it could be turned to the advantage not merely of Ireland but of the European Community as a whole.[71] In a general way the persistence of the anomaly signals the non-militaristic intentions of the Brussels system, while on specific issues it may make Irish diplomats more acceptable spokesmen than those from other Community states. This was certainly the view of the government shortly after joining the Community[72], while the then Minister for Foreign Affairs, Garret FitzGerald, is reported to have claimed that military neutrality had proved useful during the Irish presidency of the Council of Ministers in 1975.[73] Whether this will prove to be an acceptable reason for its retention in the long term is another matter.

During Ireland's first year in the European Community the Minister for Foreign Affairs announced his intention of following a middle power role in the UN.[74] More than two years later he argued that political co-operation in the European Community was compatible with this strategy, and that it should 'take the form of a gradual movement of the more "conservative" countries towards the more "progressive" positions adopted by Ireland, the Netherlands and Denmark – rather than any reversal of the positions hitherto adopted by Ireland and like-thinking member-States.'[75] The recognition that some states are 'conservative' and others 'progressive' underlines the fact that attitudes and policy towards the international environment do not reflect merely the search for a minimal level of international order and the reduction of violence. They are also concerned with closely related, and sometimes conflicting, notions of international justice, and these are examined in the next chapter.

Chapter 9

The International Milieu: Justice

Ireland is believed to stand for democratic principles, against Imperialism and upon the side of liberty throughout the World.
George Gavan Duffy, TD,
Minister for Foreign Affairs,
20 June 1922

I am not suggesting that we are a more highly ethical people than other people . . . but it does happen that so far our interests and the interests of the Ten Commandments are identical.
Desmond FitzGerald, TD,
Minister for External Affairs,
5 February 1926

In a political arena lacking central authority and risking self-destruction, the interest of a state in international order is closely related to security. Yet even where this interest is manifested in terms of support for peace-keeping and disarmament, the nature of the order thereby achieved, no matter how precarious, is open to the criticism that it is unjust: 'the institutions and mechanisms which sustain international order, even when they are working properly, indeed especially when they are working properly, or fulfilling their functions, . . . necessarily violate ordinary notions of justice.'[1]

The notion of justice in the international environment is both subjective and complex. A distinction must be made between 'commutative' or reciprocal justice and 'distributive' justice.[2] The former concerns the recognition of rights and duties, a code of fair treatment, in the normal intercourse between states. It does not, however, emphasise the overall outcome of inter-state behaviour, as does distributive justice with its underlying concern with the 'common good' or common interest of society as a whole. It is in this latter sense that the term 'international justice' is used here, to embrace more or less clearly defined ideas of what the common good entails in international relations.

The foreign policies of most countries generally incorporate a view of the common good. Sometimes they are even based on an intention to achieve it, ostensibly transcending the self-interest of the state; a world safe for socialism or for free enterprise may be declared as the ultimate objective of Soviet or American policy. But more modest states also attempt to promote externally the values which are held within their boundaries. The idea that nations have a moral purpose in the world at large, and that this sense of mission should be reflected in state policy, is a pervasive one: 'Ireland has this responsibility of taking her place in the world.'[3]

Quite what moral purpose should be pursued, and quite what interpretation is put on the common good, may be a matter of internal debate. Even if consensus is reached, the extent to which international justice becomes a goal of foreign policy depends on the state's capabilities and the claims of other issue-areas. This is notoriously a corner of the foreign policy field where declaratory policy replaces action, where attitudes are sufficient and where hypocrisy and self-delusion abound. Nevertheless, there is always the possibility that such attitudes do influence policy. In the case of Ireland this can be seen, in varying degrees, in four areas of concern. Two of these, the promotion of political anti-imperialism and the preservation of Christian values, are long-established elements in Irish political culture. In recent years they have been supplemented by an interest in the reduction of economic injustice and a commitment to human rights. In all four areas the sometimes contradictory values of Irish society have been reflected in policy and even in action.

*　　*　　*

Nationalism is a set of values, or ideology, which is often reflected in the desire to create what its advocates in any particular situation perceive as a just international system. Irish nationalists, in seeking independence for themselves, based their case on the general principle of self-determination; independence was seen to transcend Ireland's self-interest and the common good therefore demanded opposition to forces which denied self-determination. Thus Irish nationalists could see themselves as opposed not only to British domination over Ireland, but to British imperialism wherever it was found, and beyond that to imperialism in general. Not all nationalists did in fact share this view, and it has been argued that a basic division in Irish political life from the outbreak of World War I to the civil war nearly ten years later was on the question of anti-imperialism.[4] But after independence was achieved, and largely because of the ambiguity which surrounded it, anti-imperialism was an undisputed and wholly respectable attitude in the nationalist ethos.

It was also becoming respectable in the world as a whole, where the 'rights of small states' were sometimes seen as the moral basis for curbing the increasingly obvious abuses of power.[5] An instinctive sympathy for other 'small states' — occasionally amounting to a belief that 'smallness' (usually undefined) is a guarantee of virtue — can be found in many public policy debates through the history of the state. The fact that Ireland was a revisionist small state, both in respect of the constitutional relationship with Britain and of partition, gave added edge to the Irish attitude of anti-imperialism in the nineteen-twenties and thirties.

Yet revisionism also served to narrow the focus of anti-imperialism; enmeshed in a struggle with a particular imperialist power, Irish governments had little time left over for a universal fight against imperialism. So far as policy was concerned, the international environment was a good deal less important than the position of Ireland.[6] At the same time, after both the major parties which had been created in the civil war had enjoyed some years in government, it became apparent that the imperialism to which most exception was taken was that of a narrowly defined political, rather than economic, domination. These political anti-imperialist attitudes coloured debate on foreign policy. W. T. Cosgrave's government always had to keep its public distance from that group of states which it was itself helping to transform from the British Empire into the Commonwealth. For example, the suggestion that the Irish Free State might belong to the Commonwealth group (as 'blocs' were then called) in the League of Nations was taboo. The League itself was viewed with varying degrees of suspicion as an instrument of its imperialist 'leaders', Britain and

France, particularly while Fianna Fáil was in opposition from 1927 to 1932. And when a Dáil deputy suggested in 1925 that Ireland should try to 'get a slice of Africa', to absorb emigration and help Irish exports, he was told by the Minister for External Affairs, Desmond FitzGerald, that Ireland had no colonial interests, and if she ever did, there should be 'some consideration for the people to whom the country belonged for the last thousand years.'[7]

The anti-imperialist instinct was thus clearly evident before World War II, and support for neutrality during that war may in some quarters have owed not a little to the view that the war was merely a repeat performance of the despicable imperialist antics of 1914 to 1918. But it was not until Ireland was admitted to the United Nations in 1955 that there was a real opportunity to translate attitudes into policies. The then Minister for External Affairs, Liam Cosgrave, recognised that 'what is involved is nothing less than the basic principle on which our policy towards the outside world and its problems is to be based.' He announced three principles, the second of which was that Ireland should 'try to maintain a position of independence, judging the various questions on which we have to adopt an attitude or cast a vote strictly on their merits'; in conjunction with a reference to Ireland's natural sympathy with emergent nations this reflected – albeit in the most general terms – a nod towards the anti-imperialist tradition. But Cosgrave's third principle, the support of the 'free world', might, he admitted, conflict with this.[8]

In the event from 1957 it was Frank Aiken who was the Minister responsible for developing UN policy and he was a good deal less equivocal in his support for an anti-imperialist stance. Addressing the UN General Assembly on 6 October 1960, a time when anti-imperialism was more generally equated with political decolonisation than with the economic ties of neo-colonialism, he emphasised Ireland's support for the dismantling of the European maritime empires:

> We know what imperialism is and what resistance to it involves. We do not hear with indifference the voices of those spokesmen of African and Asian countries who passionately champion the right to independence of the millions who are still, unfortunately, under foreign rule. On the contrary, those voices strike an answering chord in every Irish

heart. More than eighty years ago the then leader of the Irish nation, Charles Stewart Parnell, proclaimed the principle that "the cause of nationality is sacred, in Asia and Africa as in Ireland". That is still a basic principle of our political thinking in Ireland today, as it was with those of my generation who felt impelled to assert in arms the right of our country to self-determination and independence.[9]

Between 1957 and 1961 Irish policy in the UN General Assembly reflected this position. Although it was becoming an increasingly accepted position — Aiken's speech in 1960 also includes a tribute to British acquiescence in the matter — the support of particular cases did expose Ireland to the wrath of imperialist powers. The Irish attitude towards Tibetan independence made no concessions to the Soviet Union (speaking on behalf of communist China), nor did views on the war in Algeria help Irish-French relations.[10] But what has subsequently been regarded as the test case of Ireland's 'independence' at the UN, that is to say the extent to which she was prepared to translate anti-imperialist attitudes into votes, was the issue of the admission of communist China.

Between 1957 and 1961 the Irish delegation stood out against American and domestic pressure to accede to the American strategy for excluding the Peking government, but in 1961, when the strategy (though not the objective) was altered, Ireland's alignment with the United States effectively blurred her anti-imperialist image.[11] But even without this well-publicised controversy the limits of an anti-imperialist policy in the UN were being perceived, and in some cases reached, by the early nineteen-sixties. Ireland had always held back from the anti-imperialist collective of the nineteen-fifties, the group of non-aligned states which held periodic conferences, starting in Bandung in 1955; neutrality had not quite been converted into neutralism, and Ireland's credentials with the new Afro-Asian states, though good, were not impeccable.[12]

This is not to say, however, that anti-imperialist values were no longer pursued. After the climax of decolonisation in the early nineteen-sixties the focus of attention was the hard core of remaining imperialist regimes in southern Africa. Irish diplomatic links with the new African states were limited to Nigeria, but other contacts, particularly through missionary orders, were long established and quite widespread among the anglophone states.[13] In 1964 a well-organised anti-apartheid movement was founded. Apart from engaging in educational activities it sought to mobilise opinion against southern African goods and visiting sportsmen, being particularly successful on the occasion of the 1969-70 South African rugby tour.[14] Meanwhile the Irish delegation at the UN tended to support General Assembly resolutions condemning the racialist regimes in southern Africa. In 1970, for example, it voted for six resolutions against South Africa, and four in 1971. The UN boycott of Rhodesia was adhered to, and in 1970 the state export board, Córas Tráchtála, was not allowed to send a proposed trade mission to South Africa. Ireland subscribed to the Trust Fund for South Africa and the South African Education and Training Fund.[15]

However, Ireland has not been prepared to make the pace on anti-imperialist issues, and government spokesmen have been critical of the strategy employed by some other governments. Seán Lemass, Taoiseach from 1959 to 1966, deplored 'the practice of the new Afro-Asian States, concerned with the subject of colonialism, in proposing unrealistic resolutions calling for types of action which the General Assembly could not possibly implement . . . and [which] tend only to erode and weaken the authority of the Assembly itself.' [16] The same theme was pursued in 1972 by the Minister for Foreign Affairs, Patrick Hillery, when he maintained that the most effective states in the UN were 'not those who speak most often about international morality or those who vote most strongly on resolutions on colonialism', but rather those states which were prepared to follow words with deeds.[17] A year later his successor, Garret FitzGerald, made it clear that deeds involving violence, in particular guerilla activities, would not have Irish support.[18] He also declared that Ireland would continue to oppose resolutions aimed at rejecting the UN credentials of South Africa, on the grounds that the South African government should 'continue to be directly exposed to the pressure of world opinion in the United Nations forum.'[19] A further reservation appeared in 1976. Ireland abstained from a General Assembly resolution calling for an arms embargo on South Africa, because the preamble made 'unsubstantiated allegations' about 'a friendly country', thus provoking the accusation that the government was bowing to pressure from European Community partners.[20] However, at the UN World Conference for Action against Apartheid in Lagos in August 1977, Ireland – along with Denmark and the Netherlands

– was critical of western arms supplies to South Africa.[21]

Irish attitudes of anti-imperialism have emphasised the injustice of political domination by settler regimes, and because of Ireland's historical experience are regarded as 'natural', right across the political spectrum. They pervade several areas of foreign policy with relevance to the Third World[22], but their expression with regard to politically contentious issues stops well short of being revolutionary. This may be partly explained by the existence of a second type of value which bears on the Irish view of international justice, the Christian ethic, which exists in a particularly marked catholic form. This is hardly surprising in a country where the Catholic Church is the predominant traditional source of social values, and although the Irish Hierarchy has not always reflected the broader horizons of the central authority of the Vatican, it does have a tradition of articulating its position on the morality (or more usually the immorality) of international affairs.[23] While Irish catholic leaders opposed British imperialism on the grounds of its materialism, by the same token they were not prepared to see the existing evil replaced by international socialism, which offered a more fundamental challenge to their moral authority. Indeed it has been argued that, during the final phase of the independence struggle, the Irish Church was developing a form of religious imperialism of its own through its activism in the missionary field, although the possibility of Ireland becoming a theocratic state disappeared during the civil war.[24]

Catholic values were thus to find explicit expression in the foreign policy of the new state, as in its domestic politics: 'recognition of the sovereignty of God and the moral law is the fundamental basis of any just and stable world order.'[25] But the expression of a value is one thing in the form of a statement of principle; in the form of policy leading to government action it is something yet again. This became clear in 1934, when de Valera was faced with the first significant issue upon which the government had to declare its attitude towards the only communist state then in existence, the Soviet Union. Although tentative moves had been made to establish relations with the Russian regime during the Irish war of independence[26], by the nineteen-thirties this fact had, with suitable embroidery, become a flag waved by de Valera's political opponents, who accused him, among a multitude of other sins, of dealing with Moscow.[27] In spite of this, on the question of Russian membership of the League of Nations Ireland's vote was in favour, even though some other governments opposed the move on ideological grounds. The only concession to catholic indignation at home was a well-publicised speech appealing to the Soviet government to establish religious freedom within its boundaries.[28]

The moral goal had taken second place to the requirements of international security; a pattern was set, to be followed shortly on two issues where catholic feeling ran high. The Irish government's support for League sanctions against Italy after Mussolini's invasion of Ethiopia in 1935 aroused concern, for Italy was a catholic country and Mussolini had the appearance of a champion of anti-communism.[29] The equivocal attitude of the main opposition party, Fine Gael, still associated with the quasi-fascist 'Blueshirt' movement, led to the resignation of its deputy leader, Frank MacDermot, though the party did in the end fall in behind the government. This was not the case with three backbenchers, one of whom declared:

> As an Irishman and as a Catholic – a humble one, I must say – I will . . . not agree to the application of sanctions against Italy, who is going out to civilise and to Christianise a pagan race. I sincerely hope that the Italian race, and Mussolini, the great leader of the Italian people, and defender of our faith in Italy, will be successful in this war.[30]

If pagans (and, it was suggested, Jews) were to be an abomination in the international environment in 1935, the following year, with the outbreak of the Spanish civil war, saw the emergence of a more formidable enemy, international communism, and 'considerable real emotion in Ireland.'[31] The government's policy was non-intervention, and it met with vocal opposition both inside and outside the Dáil. Fine Gael pressed for the recognition of the Franco government and took the line that 'the issue in Spain . . . is God or no God.'[32] A pressure group, the Irish Christian Front, was formed to mobilise opinion throughout the country, and an expeditionary force under the former Blueshirt leader, General Eoin O'Duffy, was smuggled out to fight for Franco. Yet at the general election of 1937 this crusade was made to appear a nine days wonder, and the leader of the Irish Christian Front, Patrick Belton, lost his seat in the Dáil. Not only had the government been unwavering in its concern to dampen a conflict with serious international implications; the point had been made that, however vocal militant catholicism might be, in the long term it was not a critical force in electoral terms.[33]

World War II served only to confuse the ideological issue. The attitudes to Nazi Germany among some militant catholics had been equivocal before the war[34], and reaction after 1939 varied. The general acquiescence in neutrality allowed politicians to approach, or rather avoid, the moral issues in the most general of terms. Only James Dillon argued that opposition to Hitler was justified 'on moral and spiritual grounds.'[35] There was no overt support for Hitler's New Order, but the leading catholic journal, *The Standard,* tended to be isolationist and anti-British. The British press attaché in Dublin, John Betjeman, found an unwillingness to believe in Nazi atrocities, and cases of anti-semitism were not unknown.[36] It is doubtful, however, whether such attitudes had any significant effect on government policy one way or another, for policy was based on other motives. De Valera's only interest in a specifically catholic issue can be seen in his appeal to the belligerents to save Rome from damage in March 1944.[37]

The war was barely over in Europe when Dillon, now an independent TD, urged that Irish foreign policy should be based on an explicit moral position:

> I want to hear in the councils of the world one Catholic voice at least which is allowed and which has the courage to speak, which has the knowledge to speak, which has the solid ground beneath it of a Christian philosophy on which to stand.[38]

The following year, as the Dáil debated membership of the United Nations, one of his colleagues expressed alarm that the UN Charter contained 'no reference to the Supreme Being, to the Creator of the human race'[39]; but the sins of omission of the UN Charter soon paled before the crimes of communist revolution in eastern Europe. The imprisonment of Archbishop Stepinac in Yugoslavia was the occasion of a full-scale debate in the Dáil on 21 November 1946, during which there was general condemnation of religious persecution under communist regimes. The effect was marred, however, by a partisan squabble over procedure, which was not at all Christian in tone, and characteristically the government's form of condemnation was a shade less indignant than that proposed by James Dillon.[40] This was a taste of things to come.

Although over the next few years the increasing polarisation of the cold war met with expressions of catholic militancy, when it came to the point of participating in an anti-communist alliance the Irish government – which included Dillon and other conservative catholics – declined to join NATO. The pursuit of international justice was less important than the pursuit of national unity.[41]

Absence from NATO left the war of words between Irish catholicism and international communism in something of a vacuum, and it was not until Ireland was admitted to the UN in 1955 – as a consequence of a cold war compromise – that religious values were again made explicit in policy. This took the form of the third of Liam Cosgrave's 'three principles', which was enunciated as 'a principle not simply of our policy at the United Nations but of our foreign policy as a whole'. It was: 'to preserve the Christian civilisation of which we are a part and with that end in view to support wherever possible those powers principally responsible for the defence of the free world in their resistance to the spread of Communist power and influence.'[42] When Cosgrave's successor, Frank Aiken, appeared to be neglecting this principle, to say the least, by opposing American policy on admitting communist China to the UN, the Fine Gael opposition joined with clerical authorities in denouncing this betrayal of religious values.[43]

But the nineteen-sixties marked the beginning of a much less explicit statement of catholic attitudes in the discussion of foreign policy. If the government did indeed revert to the third principle in 1961, it justified its position in terms of a general commitment to the 'free world' and American leadership of the struggle to contain communism. This attitude was expressed by the Taoiseach, Seán Lemass, rather than by Aiken, possibly in anticipation of pressure to join NATO if Ireland joined the EEC. It was not in the Fianna Fáil tradition to lean on clerical authority in international affairs (whatever they did at home), and in any case the Catholic Church, after the Second Vatican Council, became less inclined to encourage anti-communist crusades.

The initial bid to join the EEC collapsed in 1963, but government views on international justice remained much the same. Aiken concentrated on his attempt to develop international order but refused to be drawn into public criticism of American leadership of the free world, as manifested in the great moral issue of international politics of the late nineteen-sixties, the war in Vietnam. This met with some opposition from the Labour Party, but Aiken's retirement in 1969, coinciding with the crisis in Northern Ireland and the possibility of negotiations to join the European Community, prevented it from taking the centre of the stage. Even when Ireland participated in the successful revolt against American policy on Chinese representation at the UN, at the 1971 session of the General Assembly, there was little public comment one way or the other.

At the same time the traditional enemy of conservative Irish catholics threatened to appear in the flesh – the possibility was raised by the Fianna Fáil government of establishing diplomatic relations with the Soviet Union. To some extent this produced the traditional Fine Gael response; the foreign affairs spokesman, Richie Ryan, opposed the idea, rejecting 'the suggestion . . . that mother Ireland should suckle the Russian bear as a contribution to world détente.'[44] Nonetheless, he went on to propose that Ireland should have diplomatic contacts with other communist states, such as Poland; the essential immorality of the Soviet Union, it seemed, was not in its communism but in its imperialism. Again, once in office this attitude was no longer evident. Although Richie Ryan moved to another part of government, it was a party colleague, Garret FitzGerald, who was the minister responsible for concluding negotiations with the Russians and exchanging ambassadors in 1974. As is the case with Soviet embassies in western capitals, it is the focus of demonstrations of various groups protesting against Soviet policies, but anti-communism in Ireland has lost its traditional image of being a mass crusade led by the Church militant.

The two traditional Irish views of what a 'just world' consists of – a world free from imperialism, and a world in which Christianity prevails over communism – have in a sense cancelled each other out. Religious conservatism has been an important force inhibiting a radical economics-oriented view of imperialism, while the anti-imperialist instinct has served to deflate some of the crusading tendencies of conservative catholics. Government policy has on the whole been driven, sometimes cautiously, sometimes firmly, down the centre, responding to the requisites of order in the international environment rather than to the aspirations of ideology. As a result there has been an emphasis on declaratory policy and

diplomatic support for the declaratory policies of other governments, but the commitment of other than verbal resources to the
international milieu has been a feature in the issue-area of order
rather than that of justice.

An exception to this generalisation is the increasing concern in
Ireland in recent years over the issue of economic justice in the
world at large, an issue which primarily involves the economic
relations between the industrialised countries of the west and the
less developed countries of the Third World. These relations, it is
argued, should not be based on the potential gains accruing to the
state, but on a notion of distributive justice in which it is assumed
that the state has an obligation to help those living outside its
boundaries to achieve a certain standard of living; the policy goal
is one of national self-denial. In practice, however, the element of
altruism may be difficult to discern, and the world's experience of
development aid policies over the past twenty years leads to
pessimistic conclusions:

> It is not clear . . . that the idea of the community of mankind does
> actually underlie the enterprise of the transfer of resources to any im-
> portant degree; or indeed that the transfer of resources yet has a secure
> and established position as part of the permanent business of inter-
> national society, assailed as it is on the one side by the idea that the
> rich countries should reduce their involvement in the Third World to
> the minimum, and on the other side by the doctrine that aid is essen-
> tially a means of perpetuating domination and exploitation and hence
> prejudicial to the true interests of the "have-nots".[45]

Even where a disinterested concern for international economic
justice is presented as the primary motive for a state's policy
towards less developed countries, other motives may be present, if
not predominant. A critical study of Canadian aid policy, in which
goals are usually articulated in humanitarian terms, points to the
crucial place of specific economic and political objectives. The
author concludes:

> Philanthropy is plainly no more than a fickle and confused policy
> stimulant . . . it is not an objective of government . . . Governments exist
> only to promote the public good; and, as a result, they must act purely
> in the interest of the state they serve. Altruism as foreign policy is a
> misnomer, even if sometimes the fruits of policy are incidentally bene-
> ficial to foreigners.[46]

This is not the place to argue whether these strictures do indeed apply generally, but it is as well to keep them in mind when assessing Irish aid policy. However, two points are worth noting. Irish economic interests in Third World countries are not extensive, and there are few economically significant interests in the limited range of states towards which Irish aid policy could be said to have a particular bias.[47] Nor is there any very obvious direct political interest for Irish governments to support aid programmes. They may share with other western governments a reluctance to accept the establishment of communist influence in less developed countries, but unlike many of these aid donors there is little strategic incentive to make aid, in effect, just another instrument in the state's security policy. This is not to say that individuals or groups, both inside and outside government, do not see development aid as leading in a very general way to a desired political outcome, but such motives are so general as to offer little help in explaining the development of Irish policy towards the Third World. A general instinct to oppose communism may at this level of motivation co-exist with a general instinct to oppose imperialism.

Moreover, if the motivation for Irish aid policies is usually expressed in humanitarian terms, there is some considerable justification for this. A major source, both of attitudes and action, is a particularly strong missionary tradition, representing some of the most fundamental religious and social values associated with popular images of Irish national identity.[48] Indeed, up to the nineteen-seventies it was difficult to find a governmental aid policy that went much beyond regular statements of admiration for the dedication of missionaries, supplemented by nominal subscriptions to UN specialised agencies and intermittent contributions to disaster relief. The targets set under the UN Development Decade — official aid to be 0.7 per cent of GNP by the mid-seventies, overall aid to be one per cent of GNP — proved in general to be beyond either the altruism or enlightened self-interest of the twenty-one developed countries among which Ireland is included. At the beginning of the nineteen-seventies the average contributions from a representative group of western states, the so-called 'DAC group', were 0.34 per cent of GNP for official aid and 0.78 per cent of GNP for overall aid.[49] Ireland, not then a member of the group, according to one contemporary estimate fell even further behind with an official aid contribution of 0.1 per cent of GNP and an overall contribution of about 0.2 per cent.[50] Calculated over the period since Ireland started to make subscriptions to the World Bank in 1957-58, the average figure of official aid would probably be even worse, for contributions tended to be arbitrary and without reference to fixed percentage targets.

Against this background the efforts of the private sector were more impressive. In 1971 it was estimated that there were 'about 6,000 people from Ireland (of whom over 400 are lay people) working in more than sixty developing countries.'[51] Yet these efforts were often uncoordinated, resulting in duplication of effort and expense and an incomplete appreciation of either the opportunities for action or the most appropriate strategies to be adopted. In 1969 the new Minister for External Affairs, Patrick Hillery, had admitted both the importance of non-governmental aid and the deficiencies of government policy, and promised 'a review of the whole aid position.'[52] However, recognition of the problem did not make aid policy one of the government's more obvious priorities for several years; expenditure varied from one year to the next and a comprehensive strategy was slow to emerge.

In 1973 this situation changed, and from this date aid policies started to become a more tangible feature of Irish foreign policy. In part this may have been a consequence of membership of the European Community. The promotion of aid policies at the European Community level had been seen as offering Ireland participation in programmes to reform First-Third World relations which would have overall significance.[53] But although Irish attitudes to the Third World might for historical reasons be more disinterested than those of her European partners, most of which were former imperial powers and still enjoyed rewarding economic relationships with less developed countries, it was not likely that Ireland's views would be respected so long as her aid performance was one of the most dismal in western Europe.

The increase in government aid expenditure since 1973 may thus be seen as an effort to redress this situation. For the first time the government entered into a commitment of a planned increase equivalent to 0.05 per cent of GNP per annum, and accepted a European Community decision to achieve the UN target. In 1974 aid was more than doubled to £2.5 million (0.083 per cent of GNP) and in 1975 was £3.0 million (0.082 per cent of GNP). In 1976 the total official development aid was £4.6 million

(0.104 per cent of GNP) and the target for 1979 – the end of the five year programme – is to reach 0.25 per cent of GNP, still well short of the original UN target but representing some effort by a state with its own problems of structural development.[54]

A feature of aid policy from 1973 to 1977 was the personal commitment of the Minister for Foreign Affairs, Garret FitzGerald.[55] This was made clear at the UN General Assembly and in the European context; acting as president of the Council of Ministers, he described the Lomé agreement of 1975 as 'a test of the understanding between Europe and the developing countries.'[56] The real test of commitment may be seen at the practical level, where strategies for both multilateral and bilateral programmes are handled by a new division in the Department of Foreign Affairs. About half the government's aid expenditure is channelled through the United Nations system and some thirty-five per cent through the European Community; in both bodies FitzGerald supported increased efforts and played a constructive role in de- bate on ways to improve the organisation and implementation of aid programmes.[57] A new programme of bilateral aid, absorbing nearly fifteen per cent of aid expenditure, was started in order to establish specific links with some of the poorest countries and in particular Lesotho, and to develop existing bilateral links, especial- ly those with Zambia.[58]

At the same time as government aid policy began to take shape, the contribution of the private sector was being rationalised to some extent, partly in response to a fall in traditional missionary vocations. The nineteen-sixties has seen the growth of private aid organisations in addition to the established missionary orders; bodies such as Gorta and Concern had a national appeal and placed emphasis on the broadly humanitarian, rather than the purely spiritual, aspects of development aid.[59] An element of policy co- ordination was introduced when the Irish Catholic Bishops estab- lished the Irish Commission for Justice and Peace in 1970 and a fund-raising agency, Trócaire ('Mercy'), in 1973. [60] These organi- sations represented considerable experience of social work overseas and of fund-raising at home – in 1977 the annual collection of Trócaire raised £842,000.

The parallel development of governmental and private aid pro- grammes was facilitated by the creation of new co-ordinating agencies, in themselves further evidence of the increasing government priority given to aid policies. On 28 June 1973 the government approved the establishment of the Agency for Personal Service Overseas (APSO), to sponsor and train volunteers for overseas work and to act as a clearing house for some of the activities of other organisations, through a Voluntary Agencies Liaison Committee.[61] Although not a fund-raising body itself, APSO, which was officially inaugurated in 1974, does have a promotional role, as the pioneering state agency in the aid field.[62] In September 1975 another co-ordinating body, the Development Co-operation Organisation (DEVCO), was established to act as a clearing house for the technical development aid activities of twenty-four semi-state agencies, which between them handled about two-thirds of the state's bilateral aid. Further institutional developments have been advocated. Those concerned outside the government argued that the work of both APSO and DEVCO should be subsumed under a single aid agency, while a national council, representing the major aid organisations both private and governmental, should be formed to advise the government and mobilise public support. Although these proposals appeared to have the support of Garret FitzGerald, they were not accepted as policy before he left office in July 1977.[63]

Development aid, in its broadest sense, is concerned with trade relationships as well as aid programmes. It is often the case that the beneficial effect of the latter is more than cancelled by that of the former, and even where this is not so, economic interests may oppose the objectives of aid policies. To date Ireland has been comparatively free of such constraints.[64] Irish imports from less developed countries are only about ten per cent of total imports, and exports to these markets are relatively lower, well below the European Community average level of trade with the Third World. The major element of dependence is in fuel imports (forty per cent of total fuel imports), and in raw materials (twenty per cent of total). Although structural deficiencies in the Irish economy mean that trade liberalisation is a threat, in the short term even the most vulnerable Irish industries — textiles, clothing and footwear — are protected from Third World competition by the European Community system of generalised preferences. In the long term, Ireland should be in a position to negotiate compensatory European Community aids for these industries, and for the special case of sugar beet production, if, as is likely, the pressures for trade liberalisation increase. Thus the Irish government has so far been able to support a gradualist strategy aimed at redressing the imbalance of world trade in favour of the poorer countries. At the United Nations Conference on Trade and Development at Nairobi in 1976, for example, the Irish delegation was one of a group of sixteen industrialised states which worked for a compromise position on the commodities fund proposed by the Third World governments.[65]

It is probably in this aspect of aid policy, the negotiation of the so-called 'new international economic order' or 'north-south' dialogue, that the limitations of state altruism are most clearly perceived. While a Labour Party Senator, with some political courage, claimed he would 'offer to the Irish people at all times a cut in Irish living standards if it will make world life more possible', elected government spokesmen are more likely to act on the basis that:

> people . . . are willing to make small sacrifices by degrees. They are not willing to face massive unemployment or reductions in living standards as would be required if we were to be utterly consistent with the ideals of the Christian religion or of humanism in our relations with the Third World.[66]

The problem of mobilising popular support is indeed a critical aspect of aid policy, both in encouraging general acceptance of some sacrifice and in devising means of raising funds. A strong traditional sense of moral obligation exists, derived both from religious values and historical anti-imperialist attitudes, but in a country which itself is under-developed by European standards, public support cannot be taken for granted. The bilateral aid programme has been initiated partly because it is a 'visible' manifestation of aid, and can form the basis of public education campaigns with a specific Irish interest. The promotion of an aid ethos is a continuous task, even where aid policies are removed from the area of partisan conflict.[67]

The three facets of the notion of international justice which have been referred to so far – anti-imperialism, catholic-based opposition to communism, and development aid – do of course overlap in confusing and sometimes contradictory ways. A commitment to 'human rights' in a general sense underlies them all, in so far as they all represent particular responses to the evils of political domination and the uneven distribution of wealth. But in a rather narrower sense 'human rights' are a distinct area of concern, in so far as there has developed the idea that the rights of individuals should be incorporated in international law, as well as in the law of the sovereign state to which particular individuals belong. It may be true that in practice there is no 'general protection of human rights, only a selective protection that is determined not by the merits of the case but by the vagaries of international politics'[68]; nevertheless, an important indicator of any state's attitude to the whole corpus of issues referred to here as 'international justice' is the extent to which human rights legislation is incorporated in its foreign policy.

The reasons for its incorporation may of course owe less to a concern for the international environment than to some specific grievance of the government concerned; after all, it is in generalising from the particular that moral norms are formed. Thus in the case of Ireland an important source of a general interest in human rights questions has been the predicament of the 'lost' nationalist minority in Northern Ireland. In 1934, for example, de Valera maintained in the League of Nations that the protection of minorities was 'a sacred duty' and advocated an international convention on individual rights.[69] Another subject of concern was the development of, and adherence to, international legislation on labour conditions, in the form of conventions formulated within the framework of the International Labour Organisation.[70]

Moral revulsion after World War II and the ideological cleavage of the cold war led to an increased awareness of human rights in western Europe, which found expression in the Council of Europe, established in 1949. Ireland was the first state to recognise the jurisdiction of both the European Court of Human Rights and the Human Rights Commission, after signing the European Convention on Human Rights and Fundamental Freedoms. Under the 'jurisdiction' of this process Ireland has been both defendant, in the Lawless case, and plaintiff, in the cases of alleged torture by the British army following internment in Northern Ireland in 1971.[71] The government's persistence with the latter case, in spite of British protests that amends had been made, was justified on the grounds of the broad implications for the protection of human rights.[72] On a pan-European level the Conference on Security and

Co-operation in Europe (1973-75) was the occasion of Irish concern with the question of religious freedom, as well as approval of the principle that rights in general should be actively promoted.

Nevertheless, lacunae persist in Irish policy towards human rights. Several United Nations conventions have not been ratified, and in 1971 a former Minister for External Affairs, Seán MacBride, argued that this 'put into question our sincerity when we profess loudly our attachment to the ideals of human liberty.'[73] MacBride referred in particular to the International Convention on the Elimination of Forms of Racial Discrimination (1965) and the International Covenant on Economic, Social and Cultural Rights (1966), and also claimed that the quality of Irish representation at international conferences on human rights issues was often poor. Delays in ratification may be explained partly by simple legislative inertia, but in some cases they may reflect specific reservations. The controversy about domestic legislation on the question of birth control is an example of an issue where Ireland is reluctant to mount the international human rights bandwagon, while doubts also remain about the compatibility of anti-terrorist legislation and treatment of prisoners with international norms. It is no surprise that the Irish Council for Civil Liberties, formed in July 1976, should pay attention to the international dimension of civil liberties by seeking consultative status with both the United Nations and the Council of Europe, and by drawing public attention to existing obligations.[74]

The existence of reservations in Irish policy on human rights is yet another manifestation of the fact that, although there may be general agreement that the pursuit of international justice is desirable, the notion of justice is essentially subjective. It is not enough to say, as Eoin MacNeill did in 1918, that Ireland's cause 'is the cause of international civilisation, peace, justice and liberty. It is pure.'[75] The position is a good deal more complicated than this. The values described in this chapter as anti-imperialist may incline towards radical change in the international system, but religious values have encouraged a more conservative stance. While there may be an element of synthesis between the two traditions, the inherent tension between them cannot be ignored.

Moreover, the ethical element in Irish foreign policy is shaped not only by an internal debate on moral issues, but it is also affected by a consideration of the costs of moral behaviour, in the form of repercussions on the state's self-regarding, often material, interests. Here, too, the initial expectation that Ireland would 'say plainly the things that everyone is thinking and that other powers are too cowardly to be the first to say' was to be modified in the harsh light of a world where, to a large extent, 'diplomacy consists in kidding the other fellow and obtaining your ends.'[76] If Irish foreign policy has not been altogether self-regarding this is to some extent a reflection of the country's security, the fact that 'owing to our peculiar geographical position and other circumstances, we can afford to take up a high moral tone without having to pay a price for it.'[77] It is also a reflection of the limited geographical spread of Irish interests and of the state's relative insignificance in the hierarchy of powers. On the other hand, if vital interests are seen to be threatened, the flag of international justice may be waved, but only if it adds an aura of legitimacy to the essentially selfish policy of the state.

Even where there is no immediate conflict between moral values and material interests, Irish governments have often been wary of making moral gestures which either achieve nothing in themselves or which threaten unpredictable consequences. On the whole, policy has been based on a widespread and orthodox

> liberal or progressivist view . . . which is inclined to . . . argue that attempts to achieve justice by disrupting order are counter-productive, to cajole the advocates of "order" and of "justice" into remaining within the bounds of a moral system that provides for both and permits an adjustment that can be mutually agreed.[78]

Thus Seán Lemass wrote of Ireland's role in the United Nations as being one of 'softening extreme positions . . . and of promoting compromise formulae.'[79] This desire to build bridges could be seen too when, during the last weeks of the Franco regime in Spain in 1975, there was widespread condemnation of the execution of Basque guerillas, and the Irish government, unlike its European Community partners, did not withdraw its ambassador from Madrid. The decision was justified on the grounds that such a measure was counter-productive, in so far as it would strengthen right-wing support and make a democratisation of the new regime all the more difficult.[80] The case of the Spanish executions also demonstrated the fact that although Irish foreign policy reflects a broadly similar ethical background to that of its Community partners, differences could exist on specific issues both with regard to ends and means. As with issues of international order, the process of political co-operation in the European Community contains a spectrum of governmental opinon. Thus on issues relating to the Third World, Ireland has often been in a minority (as was, up to 1977, the case concerning a Palestinian homeland.)[81] Here the government may well think 'it right to remain for the moment, pending an evolution of opinion within the Community which we hope to see in the direction of our view-point.'[82] The quest for international justice in foreign policy may be hedged around by internal qualifications and external constraints, but it does, nevertheless, persist.

PART III

Problems of Purpose in Foreign Policy

The Irish people has no clear idea of its place in the world nor of what contribution it can make to the world. It is near enough still to foreign rule to know that independence is the essential condition of self-realization. It has not yet possessed independence long enough to appreciate that self-government is not an end in itself but must be justified by the manner in which it is used, not only for our own benefit but for the benefit of those with whom we live. There is, therefore, some lack of a sense of purpose which diminishes . . . every . . . side of life.

James Meenan, *The Irish Economy since 1922* (Liverpool: Liverpool University Press, 1970), Page 393

Chapter 10

The Problem of Design

*We do give some overall policy direction to our foreign relations.
But for a small country like ours, the role of Government is not
to try to impose a grand "foreign policy design".*

Dr Patrick J. Hillery,
Minister for Foreign Affairs,
in the Dáil, 18 April 1972

In the preceding chapters foreign policy has been seen as being
composed of a range of issue-areas, reflecting a variety of motiva-
tions, objectives and actions, and which almost amounts to a
microcosm of the whole range of public policy. It is a matter of
convenience to refer to all of this collectively as 'foreign policy',
but the diversity of interests encountered defy any neat or simple
definition. In the words of a recent Irish practitioner of the art of
diplomacy:

> The foreign policy properly so-called of an Irish Government at any
> particular time is not a single attitude or a simply stated principle or
> slogan. It is the sum of a whole series of actions and decisions at Govern-
> ment level in a wide variety of exchanges – political, trade and econo-
> mic, social and cultural. These exchanges take place with a variety of
> other nations and they vary widely in their importance to us.[1]

By its nature, then, foreign policy tends to lack a clear overall
shape, and it is often difficult to distinguish themes and actions
which can give it coherence. Certainly it relates 'to some aspect or
objective external to a political system, i.e. to some sphere outside
the jurisdiction or control of the polity'[2], but, having said that,
the question arises – to what extent does foreign policy reflect

design? In other words, can it be represented as a plan or scheme of related aims, either conceptually or in terms of actual government behaviour?

To answer this question it is first necessary to establish that there is indeed some degree of interaction between the issue-areas which have already been identified. Instances of such interaction, either in the form of substantive connections or bargaining exchanges, have been referred to in passing, but it is worth briefly summarising the more important cases in chronological order. The Treaty negotiations in 1921 can be seen as the first of six junctures when most, though not necessarily all, the issue-areas were activated; that is to say they were characterised by political controversy, both inside the state and in its diplomatic relations. The 1921 negotiations in fact saw the crystallisation of four of the six issue-areas (the international milieu was not then a major concern) and the outcome of the negotiations – the Irish Free State – reflected very dramatically the efforts of both participants to bargain one issue-area against others. The Anglo-Irish negotiations of 1938 were, in effect, a second round of this contest. Developments within the four original issue-areas and within the broad international environment had reached the point where further comprehensive bargains were expected by both governments. In some cases they were reached, the notable exceptions being the failure of the Irish to achieve any movement with regard to partition and of the British to clarify the position on security.

The third occasion when the major issue-areas became significantly interlinked was during World War II. The themes of independence, security, unity and prosperity were intertwined in one fundamental objective – the survival of the state. There was little chance to influence the hostile international environment, though that environment was a constant preoccupation in every important decision. This critical period was followed by a fourth convergence of foreign policy issues, which reverted to the familiar context of Anglo-Irish relations, from the middle of 1948 to the middle of 1949. Unlike the first two rounds of that uneven duel this was not marked by formal intergovernmental negotiations, though like them decisions taken on the question of the constitutional relationship had important consequences for other issue-areas. Although the international state system in general was undergoing significant changes, particularly in the formation of regional alliance systems,

Ireland's ability to sidestep this process was a measure of the extent to which her foreign policy was not merely a reaction to the main trends in world politics.

In 1961 Ireland's application to join the EEC marked a fifth occasion when foreign policy was more than a random series of decisions in separate issue-areas. The predominant question was now that of economic foreign policy, and the adoption of a free trade strategy in this area began to be felt throughout the foreign policy field, including the issue-areas of international order and justice, which had been developed considerably following the state's accession to the United Nations in 1955. The Gaullist veto of 1963 may have dampened the reverberations this caused, but by the same token, the withdrawal of the veto in 1969 led to a sixth turning-point when the whole foreign policy field became increasingly integrated. This became especially evident during the actual negotiations with the European Community from 1970 to 1972, which were accompanied by a sustained public debate. The economic issue-area predominated both in the substance of the negotiations and in the public response to them, as it has since; nevertheless, reappraisal of the other issue-areas has also been provoked by membership of the European Community. Independence has become important both in the manner of participation in, and with regard to the future development of, the Community's central institutions. Political co-operation and regular head of government contacts in the European Council have set in train a procedure which, if it does not directly modify Irish policies towards the international milieu, does mean that the relevant issue-areas are brought into a setting where bargaining exchanges will at least be facilitated. The Irish tradition in the security issue-area may be perceived as increasingly anomalous.

An exception, to some extent, to this current integration of Irish foreign policy — for the turning-point of 1969 has been prolonged in the continuous negotiation of the Brussels system — is the unity issue-area. The breakdown of order in Northern Ireland coincided with the 'Europeanisation' of Irish foreign policy, and while there have been attempts to link the two questions, the remarkable feature is the way in which they have been kept apart at the governmental level. At the nadir of Anglo-Irish relations on the issue of Northern Ireland, after the imposition of internment in 1971, Ireland and the United Kingdom finalised their negotiations in Brussels and joined the Community together. The Bloody Sunday killings and their aftermath of diplomatic and public protest did not alter this pattern, and little over three months later the Irish electorate, for its part, did not respond to the anti-marketeers' attempts to tar the European Community with the brush of partition.

Nevertheless the relative separation of the Northern Ireland issue-area does not detract significantly from the hypothesis that the Irish foreign policy field has become increasingly integrated in the nineteen-seventies. Even on the northern question the governments in Dublin and London are both reluctant to act with regard either to Northern Ireland or each other in such a way as to upset the susceptibilities of their continental partners, to whom they may at some stage have to turn for assistance. As far as governments outside the British Isles are concerned, Northern Ireland is as legitimate an interest of Irish foreign policy as are any of the questions which form their own relationships with the Irish government.

Indeed, it is partly through the perceptions of other actors that the foreign policy field does acquire a certain unity, in so far as 'Ireland' is herself seen to be an 'actor' in international politics, rather than a conglomeration of disparate groups and interests. Given the substantive connections and potential bargaining exchanges between issue-areas which arguably do exist, does this mean that foreign policy can then be conceived of as a summation of issue-areas, and, if so, what form will this take? The notion of 'the national interest' having been generally discredited as a means of aggregating a state's foreign policy action[3], the most general descriptive category available is that of the state's 'orientation'. This has been defined by K. J. Holsti as the state's 'general attitudes and commitments toward the external environment, its fundamental strategy for accomplishing its domestic and external objectives and aspirations and for coping with persisting threats.'[4] Orientation can be seen in a series of cumulative decisions, and will depend on the structure of the international system, the state's domestic attitudes and needs, policy-makers' perceptions of external threat and, finally, the physical attributes of the state, its geographical location and natural resources.

Holsti identifies three fundamental orientations which he maintains have persistently recurred, no matter what the historical context may have been. These are, first, isolation, second, non-alignment, and third, diplomatic coalitions and military alliances. In the twentieth century an isolationist orientation has become increasingly difficult to adopt, and the case of Ireland is no exception. Thus, although aspirations towards an isolationist position have been expressed by Irish politicians, and although these may be reflected in some policies[5], at no stage has a truly isolationist orientation been implemented. The nearest approach was during de Valera's 'self-sufficiency' phase in the early to mid-nineteen-thirties, but this experience showed clearly the very high costs of even attempting such a strategy.

In practice, therefore, Ireland has adopted one or other of the remaining two fundamental orientations. From 1922 to 1932 foreign policy was framed in the context of a diplomatic coalition – the British Commonwealth. From 1932, however, policy can be seen as directing the state away from this orientation to that of non-alignment, a process in effect achieved in the settlements of 1938, for Ireland was really only a nominal member of the Commonwealth after that date. For Holsti, 'unwillingness to commit military capabilities to others' purposes is the hallmark of non-alignment as a foreign policy strategy.'[6] This unwillingness became one of the key values for all shades of Irish nationalist opinion in 1918[7], though it was not until the return of the ports twenty years later that it could be translated into an orientation of non-alignment, or what in Ireland is generally referred to as 'neutrality'.[8] This orientation has its roots in several issue-areas: in the desire to keep British influence at arm's length, to stay out of continental wars, and to underline the anti-partition case. It has been a means of mobilising domestic political support, and is often assumed to be a means of increasing diplomatic influence and manoeuvrability. Thus Garret FitzGerald's first major policy statement in 1973 referred to the possibility of Ireland's role being 'imaginative and constructive – all the more so as we are not involved in any military alliance.'[9] Similarly in 1975 his successor, the Fianna Fáil opposition foreign affairs spokesman, Michael O'Kennedy, was reported to have claimed that 'our traditional neutrality in international affairs is a strong foundation on which to build our foreign policy programme.'[10]

Whether in fact the non-alignment orientation is an essential prerequisite to the sort of foreign policy roles Ireland has developed in the international environment is open to question. Countries such as Canada, Denmark and the Netherlands have been able to adopt policies on peace-keeping, disarmament, and relations with less developed countries which are in many ways similar to those of Ireland, while at the same time belonging to the military alliance system which Ireland has so scrupulously avoided. A more basic ambiguity in Ireland's adoption of a non-alignment orientation is that it has always been at odds with one important issue-area, that of economic foreign policy. The latter can even be represented as the Achilles heel of non-alignment; the decision to join the EEC in 1961, and its eventual implementation in 1973, amount to a reversion to the original orientation of participation in a diplomatic coalition. In terms of Holsti's classification, therefore, so long as ambiguity persists concerning both the European Community's involvement in military matters and Ireland's possible adaptation to such an involvement, Ireland is, in effect, straddling the only two fundamental orientations which are generally found in the present international state system.

This reduces the usefulness of Holsti's analysis as a means of summarising Irish foreign policy, though it is only fair to point out that the concept of orientation can be used in a rather different way, to refer to the sphere of diplomatic activity in broadly geographical terms.[11] Thus it could be said that Irish foreign policy was first marked by a 'British' orientation — ostensibly a British Commonwealth orientation, but perhaps more accurately seen in terms of the British Isles as a sub-system of the international system. This asymmetrical bilateral relationship was balanced, where possible, by a preoccupation with a 'universalist' orientation, encompassing the issues relating to the international milieu, and to some extent by an 'Atlantic' orientation, in as much as Ireland had, even before the creation of the state, looked to the United States as a means of counteracting the weight of British influence. The decision to 'go into Europe' in 1961 thus marks a distinctive re-orientation of Irish foreign policy, in which all issue-areas are affected in some way.

However, the identification of connections between issue-areas and the notion of orientations provide the foreign policy field with at best only a very general and *de post facto* coherence; they do not offer policy-makers clear guidelines for the overall direction of policy. Yet policy-makers recognise, as Dr Hillery put it in 1972, that governments exist in order 'to steer and develop our many existing contacts in accordance with some general ideas of what we stand for and what we want to achieve.'[12] In attempting to explain this process, practising politicians and diplomats often speak in terms of the roles their country can play in the international arena. The idea of 'national roles' has been defined by K. J. Holsti as 'the policy-makers' definitions of the general kinds of decisions, commitments, rules and actions suitable to their state, and of the functions their state should perform in a variety of geographic and issue settings.'[13]

Analysing policy statements pertaining to seventy-one states during the period 1965 to 1967, Holsti has identified sixteen types of foreign policy role. With regard to the present epoch, ten years later, it can be argued that at least five of these roles are reflected in Irish foreign policy. The role of 'mediator-integrator', where the state is seen as being able and willing to undertake mediation tasks can be seen in the Irish commitment to UN peace-keeping. A rather similar, but more far-reaching and continuously demanding role is that of 'regional-subsystem collaborator', which Ireland plays in maintaining and developing the European Community. A third role which has recently received much emphasis in Irish policy statements is that of 'developer', in which the obligation to assist less developed countries is followed. A fourth role, which does not necessarily involve much action, is that of 'bridge'. Here policy-makers refer to what are assumed to be unique features of location or culture which allow them to bridge gaps in international communication or understanding. In the Irish context this arises in frequent references to the circumstances of the country's historical development, which are seen as giving Irish governments a special insight into the problems of the newer, non-European states. Finally, there is the role of 'independent' in which policy-makers simply declare their policy to be based on the state's self-interest.

Holsti's list of role-types is not exhaustive, and in the case of Ireland the role of 'minority protector' could perhaps be added with regard to the position of Northern Ireland. It does give some indication, not only of the extent of involvement of Ireland in international politics[14], but of the possibilities of policy development which are open to Irish governments. Yet the policy-maker is concerned not merely to articulate the purposes for which foreign policy is to be formulated and implemented; an equally important task is 'to order them in some scheme of relative importance.'[15] The establishment of priorities is an essential feature of the design of foreign policy.

On rare occasions Irish policy-makers have attempted to present a very general rationale for the establishment of priorities. During the first thirty years of the state's existence an overwhelming preoccupation with Anglo-Irish relations was usually an implicit, self-evident framework for policy, but subsequently the development of a greater variety of interests has encouraged foreign ministers to present their policies in a more systematic fashion. Thus, after Ireland joined the United Nations in 1955 Liam Cosgrave produced his 'three principles' upon which Irish foreign policy was to be based.[16] However, these principles, especially the second and third, were arguably not so much an ordering of priorities as a recognition of the tension between the 'neutralist' and 'western' poles in Irish foreign policy; the real decisions as to which direction was to prevail remained for the future. Patrick Hillery, after nearly three extremely hectic years in office, attemtped to rank foreign policy priorities in terms of 'concentric circles of interest.'[17] The first circle contained the whole spectrum of Irish relations with Britain, in which the unity issue-area was seen as the major outstanding difficulty. The second circle of interest was the European Community, regarded not merely as a setting for the development of economic foreign policy but also for the pursuit of milieu goals. A third circle was described as a network of bilateral relations with other developed countries; a fourth was represented by involvement in other intergovernmental organisations, especially the United Nations, and a fifth by relations with Third World states. Within each circle of interests, but also cutting across all of them, was the need to balance 'interests' against 'ideals', a distinction also made by Hillery's successor, Garret FitzGerald.[18]

Given this framework, Hillery claimed that 'we still have a considerable area of choice in foreign affairs.'[19] It is probably in the area of 'ideals' — that is to say, with regard to the international milieu in general — that freedom of choice emerges most clearly, for the foreign minister at least. Frank Aiken seems to have been given a good deal of scope, both by international and domestic developments, to impose a measure of design on Irish United Nations policies. In particular, he had considerable latitude in pursuing his interest in disarmament. In a similar way Garret FitzGerald was able to choose to expand governmental activities in the area of development aid. Both these policy strategies were not merely reactive; circumstances did not compel the ministers to promote these policies to the extent and in the way which they did. On the contrary, they were able to think in terms of identifying objectives, calculating the means to be applied, taking decisions and implementing them – in short, in these cases they could design their policy.

On the other hand, the area of choice is generally more restricted in other issue-areas, and policy direction tends to become a matter of adapting to external pressures as they arise. In retrospect the campaign to clarify Ireland's constitutional status may have the appearance of a masterminded strategy, but the reality was a succession of short-term adaptations to a complex and fluid situation. If de Valera saw his attempts to develop self-sufficiency in strategic terms, it was not a strategy marked by much success; his maintenance of neutrality during World War II did succeed, but it was a policy developed almost on a day-to-day basis, and which to its author often seemed like a gamble against impossible odds. Re-unification policies contained tentative explorations of alternative strategies, such as diplomatic and propaganda pressures or functional co-operation, but have often contained internal inconsistencies and misconceptions and, meeting with little success, have been punctuated by long periods when the best policy seemed to be to do nothing. This is not to argue that there is no choice at all, but rather that the range of choice is extremely limited and it is based on a tactical rather than a strategic appreciation of the situation. Nevertheless, the quality of such tactical decisions is extremely important, for it is all too easy to turn an inevitable retreat into a rout.

In one particular issue-area the constraints on governmental choice are noticeably marked. Where economic foreign policy is concerned, difficulties posed by the international environment are often no less intractable than those relating to security or unity, but the policy-maker does not have the relative freedom of action from domestic pressures, which for long periods he may enjoy with regard to the latter. Indeed, it has been argued that in modernised, industrialised states 'the principal set of determinants of foreign policy can be thought of as relating to domestic social structure.'[20] Certainly, within the European Community system those responsible for framing Irish foreign policy cannot hope to escape the continuous and often competing demands arising from within the state. They may still have some latitude in the more traditional foreign policy issues which arise within the political co-operation process, but in welfare matters they are caught in the middle of the paradox of 'modernised' foreign policy. At the same time as governments face increasing domestic demands that they should pursue welfare goals in foreign policy, they find themselves increasingly sensitive to external events which affect their capacity to pursue such goals.[21] Interdependence, particularly with regard to economic interactions, makes the design of foreign policy more problematic than ever before; while in blurring the boundaries between 'foreign' and 'domestic' policy it raises the associated problem of the policy-making process in an acute form.

Chapter 11

The Problem of the Policy-Making Process

Which is the driving Department? Is there any one person or any one Department charged with looking after the thing as a whole, to push it definitely?

Eamon de Valera, TD,
in the Dáil, 7 March 1951

The range of interests and values which arise in the field of foreign policy, combined with the complexity and unpredictability of the world outside the state, make it difficult to conceive of foreign policy in terms of its overall design. But in so far as an element of design does exist, in attempts to articulate goals and establish priorities, the process of policy-making lies between it and the actual behaviour of the government. In this process purpose and design often become further diluted, if not distorted, and the actions of the state may be characterised by hesitation, misconceptions and confusion.

Ideally, the policy-making process is an enduring marriage of ends and means, presided over by an omniscient policy-maker, but the facts of international history give the lie to this image. Although the structure of policy-making systems and the intentions of the policy-makers themselves may reflect the assumptions of this ideal type − the 'rational policy model' − policy outcomes can often be explained with equal, if not greater, plausibility by reference to alternative models.[1] The nature of the administrative structures created for policy-making and policy-implementation narrows the range of choice and reduces the flexibility of governmental response to events. Furthermore, there is not, even in dictatorships, a unitary policy-maker, but rather a group of individuals whose interests and involvement in particular issues may vary widely:

what 'the government' eventually does is often strongly influenced by the internal struggles of this group.[2]

The policy-making process is, then, in itself an important factor to be considered when trying to understand the foreign policy behaviour of the state. Three particular problems arise with relation to foreign policy. First, the possession and understanding of information is especially critical, for the source of relevant information can be anywhere on the globe. Then there is the problem of co-ordinating governmental activities across the varied issue-areas in the foreign policy field when in practice the policy-making process may differ significantly between one issue-area and another. Finally, the question may be posed as to what extent public control can or ought to be exerted over the making of foreign policy. Speed of response and flexibility in negotiations with other governments often seem to call for a degree of secrecy which is repugnant to the ethos of representative democracies, yet in the long term a government ignores public opinion at its peril.

*   *   *

These problems will be examined below in the context of Irish foreign policy-making in the nineteen-seventies. Prior to this, patterns of policy-making had assumed different forms within similar constitutional structures; these are worth describing briefly, since they throw some light on the political and administrative traditions on which the current policy process is based.[3]

During the first ten years of the Irish Free State, from 1922 to 1932, the policy process seems to have focused on the cabinet (Executive Council) as such; the period can be labelled as one of 'cabinet policy-making' as far as external relations were concerned. The civil war and its aftermath and the need to establish a national political system were the principal preoccupations of public debate. Foreign policy questions were restricted and often treated dismissively by parliamentary representatives.[4] The issue-areas that were important only intermittently impinged on the parliamentary arena. Unity was a matter for confidential intergovernmental negotiations, both before and after the remote deliberations of the Boundary Commission, and constitutional independence was the subject of a legal debate pursued during and between infrequent Imperial Conferences or in Geneva. The policy-makers were of course answerable to the Dáil, and by later standards were quite forthcoming in this respect, but the cliché that foreign policy was the prerogative of the executive rather than the legislature certainly held true.

Within the cabinet the most striking feature was the extent of collective participation in decision-making, possibly arising from the youth and inexperience of most of its members. This characteristic was also facilitated by W. T. Cosgrave's own reluctance to become deeply involved in foreign policy; apart from his contributions 'at the summit' on questions of independence and unity, he was content to preside over collegiate discussion in the cabinet room.[5] This was by no means a question of giving assent to ministers with clearly defined departmental responsibilities, nor were tasks necessarily undertaken by the obvious minister.[6] Up to 1927 the Vice-President and Minister for Justice, Kevin O'Higgins, played an increasingly important role, being given the External Affairs portfolio a matter of weeks before his assassination. The Minister for Education, Eoin MacNeill, was not only the government's nominee for the Boundary Commission, but shortly afterwards wrote the speech which Cosgrave delivered in Geneva when the Irish Free State was admitted to the League of Nations.[7] Later in the nineteen-twenties another minister who took a serious interest in League affairs was Ernest Blythe, Minister for Finance, who on occasion led the Irish delegation.

This sharing of activities at cabinet level reflects an uncertain relationship, to begin with at any rate, with the administrative level of the policy-making system. Foreign policy was one of the principal gaps in the developed administrative system which had been inherited from British rule. Early experience with envoys overseas had not been of the happiest, and it had proved difficult to build up a reliable diplomatic service overnight.[8] Thus the government's handling of the Boundary Commission crisis late in 1925 was marked by a reluctance to use official departmental channels and relied instead — and possibly to the detriment of policy — on direct ministerial contacts.[9] However, in the vital issue-area of constitutional independence, a close working relationship began to develop between policy-makers at the political and administrative levels. In the Department of External Affairs officials such as Joe Walshe, J. J. Hearne, Seán Murphy, and towards the end of the nineteen-twenties, F. H. Boland, began to develop the technical expertise, particularly on legal matters, on which ministers were increasingly compelled to rely.[10] By the late twenties this small group of professional civil servants was on equal terms with political leaders, being of the same age and background, and its subsequent influence on the development of the Irish diplomatic service and on foreign policy was to stretch as far as the early nineteen-sixties. A similar pattern began to emerge with regard to the more passive issue-area of economic foreign policy, as officials in the Department of Finance became the source of conventional wisdom.

With the change of government a new pattern of policy-making was introduced. From 1932 to 1948 the head of the government, Eamon de Valera, assumed direct responsibility for the External Affairs portfolio; the result was a concentration of the foreign policy-making system at the highest level. Although he was faced with a parliamentary opposition that was well-informed following its experience of government, de Valera was backed by a disciplined party which controlled a parliamentary process which might have been designed to reduce his domestic anxieties to a minimum.[11] Moreover, within his cabinet de Valera seems to have received a good deal of latitude, derived not merely from his personal authority, but also from his direct control of the Department of External Affairs.

This pattern of concentrated high-level policy-making could be seen even in the most politically sensitive issue-area – that of constitutional independence – where there was a relatively high degree of electoral and party interest and, because of the legislation involved, a necessarily high degree of involvement of parliamentary institutions. This implied that the goals of policy had to be articulated and justified a good deal in public, but when goals had to be translated into action the extent of de Valera's personal control was remarkable, particularly when it came to communicating and negotiating with the British government. The secret talks which started in 1936 with Malcolm MacDonald, the British Secretary of State for the Dominions, were kept out of the cabinet, de Valera's direct contribution being supplemented by that of the Irish high commissioner in London, J. W. Dulanty.[12] When it came to the full-scale negotiations in 1938, which covered the greater part of the foreign policy field, de Valera established firm leadership over the Irish delegation, which included the

Ministers for Finance, Industry and Commerce, and Agriculture as well as their civil service advisers. Although he claimed to be acting under strict instructions from his cabinet (and mindful of the cabinet-delegation misunderstandings of 1921 the delegation did indeed refer back to the full cabinet quite frequently during these long negotiations), de Valera's grasp of the background to the negotiations placed him at a clear advantage over his cabinet colleagues, his civil servants and outside forces. If he was intransigent on partition it was not because of the pressure of northern nationalists who followed him to London, but rather on account of a strong personal commitment on this point. Certainly, to his British opponents he appeared to be master in his own house.[13]

In other foreign policy issue-areas de Valera's personal authority became equally marked. Given the goal of self-sufficiency, economic foreign policy came to the fore and gave much scope to a dynamic young Minister for Industry and Commerce, Seán Lemass. However, Lemass had to act within the constraints of his leader's campaign for constitutional revision, as did his principle colleague in economic matters, the Minister for Finance, Seán MacEntee. Policy on the 'economic war' was drawn into the ambit of External Affairs rather than Finance, and the coal-cattle pact of 1934 was the result of an initiative by Dulanty.[14] The final financial settlement with Britain in 1938 also appears to have been the result of de Valera's and Dulanty's activities, and there is no clear evidence as yet that MacEntee was consulted about the Irish concessions.[15] Finally, with regard to issues which clearly came within the competence of the External Affairs portfolio the cabinet does not appear to have shown much desire to intervene. Two examples of such a readiness to act as 'a rubber stamp' can be found in the course of one cabinet meeting on 22 December 1936. Faced with two issues which at that time could arouse political controversy in the Dáil – the opening of diplomatic relations with the conquerors of Ethiopia, and the non-intervention policy towards the Spanish civil war – the response of the cabinet was simply that 'decision . . . was left to the President.'[16] As far as the public was concerned, by the late nineteen-thirties even de Valera's political opponents had reluctantly to concede that he was not only the principal source of foreign policy, but a competent manager of the state's diplomacy.

This pattern of policy-making was, not surprisingly, reinforced during World War II. Strict censorship reduced public debate to a minimum, the Dáil – apart from James Dillon – was quiescent, and the all-party Defence Conference was restricted to consultation on the implementation of policy measures.[17] De Valera kept a tight control over the day-to-day evolution of neutrality policy. Other members of the cabinet were of course involved in the course of their departmental duties and in full cabinet, but it is doubtful if they had access to much of the pertinent information from either diplomatic or military intelligence sources.[18] De Valera's closest collaborators came from the professional administration, and above all from his 'additional' department, External Affairs. The names of Joe Walshe, F. H. Boland and, abroad, of Dulanty in London and Robert Brennan in Washington, recur frequently in accounts of this period.[19] An impression of the working methods employed may be seen in the formulation of a reply to the 'American note' of February 1944, demanding the expulsion of Axis diplomats from Dublin. De Valera was provided with drafts by Walshe, Secretary of the Department of External Affairs, Maurice Moynihan, Secretary to the Government, and Frank Gallagher, Director of the Government Information Bureau, but 'as usual, the document he produced was completely his own.'[20] The issue was certainly discussed in the cabinet, but de Valera's colleagues took only fifteen minutes to approve the final draft on 6 March 1944, subject to 'any verbal alterations that might subsequently be decided upon by the Taoiseach.'[21]

In retrospect it can be seen that this pattern of policy-making was a product of particular circumstances as well as of the personal authority of de Valera. Even before the development of the post-1945 international economic system some of the Department of External Affairs's trade responsibilities had been reassigned to the temporary Department of Supplies, under Seán Lemass, a small portent of the pattern of 'fragmented policy-making' that was to emerge gradually after World War II. 'Fragmentation' or 'compartmentalisation' resulted from the increasing scope of government intervention in all types of public policy, and the consequent degree of specialisation introduced into what had hitherto been quite small and simple administrative structures. It reflects a situation where

> problems are segmented into constituent elements, each of which is dealt with by experts in the special difficulty it involves. There is little

emphasis or concern for their inter-relationship . . . Things are done because one knows how to do them and not because one ought to do them. The criteria for dealing with trends which are conjectural are less well developed than those for immediate crises.[22]

When de Valera left office in 1948 changes in the international state system favoured the fragmentation of foreign policy although it was not until the mid-nineteen-fifties that the phenomenon emerged clearly in Ireland. Partly this was a consequence of a reluctance by conservative policy-makers in the economic sector to seize directly the opportunities that were open to them, with regard to Marshall Aid, the development of trade and the management of the balance of payments. Indeed, under Seán MacBride, from 1948 to 1951, the Department of External Affairs often appeared to be as much involved in such matters as were the Departments of Finance or Industry and Commerce.[23] But once the notion had taken root in the Irish civil service that the economy was there to be directed, the era of 'big government' and of the 'economic departments' had arrived. By the time Seán Lemass became Taoiseach in 1959 the separation of economic foreign policy from other foreign policy issue-areas was marked. Lemass, as Minister for Industry and Commerce, had chaired the cabinet committee concerned with economic development and which finally accepted the change from protection to free trade. This committee was advised by the Secretaries of the Departments of Finance, Industry and Commerce, Agriculture and External Affairs; the dialogue between Finance and Industry and Commerce was, it seems, the focus of the debate.[24] On the other hand, the main preoccupation of the Minister for External Affairs, Frank Aiken, was the development of policies concerning the international milieu at the United Nations.

This pattern of fragmentation between economic foreign policy and other issues continued until 1969. As a consequence Irish membership of the European Economic Community was often presented to the public as a complex technical adjustment rather than a diplomatic alignment, while the term 'foreign policy' became almost exclusively attached to the pursuit of milieu goals in New York. This arrangement seemed to suit the ministers concerned, for Frank Aiken showed very little interest in 'Europe'; it may also have suited the Department of Industry and Commerce

which would have been responsible for the original EEC negotiations, and the Department of Finance which, under Whitaker's
leadership, was energetic in considering the implications of EEC
membership. Although at the official level the Department of
External Affairs maintained contact with Brussels, there seemed to
be a question mark over the future of a diplomatic service which
was given less to do of any substance. Even in the unity issue-area
Lemass had recourse to the ubiquitous Whitaker in arranging his
initial meeting with Captain O'Neill in 1965, rather than to the
Department of External Affairs, which in spite of the continuing
tradition that 'the north was the Taoiseach's preserve', had nevertheless maintained what day-to-day contacts did exist across the
border. Lemass's pragmatic and deliberate fragmentation of the
foreign policy field had the virtue of flexibility so long as he maintained overall supervision, but there were always doubts about the
co-ordination of foreign policy under this lop-sided allocation of
departmental tasks, and the government does not seem to have
been noticeably well-prepared to meet the two-faced crisis of
1969, when EEC membership and Northern Ireland both became
critical issues.

The crises of the late nineteen-sixties did, however, see the
gradual rehabilitation of the Department of Foreign Affairs (as it
was known from 1971 onwards). Under Patrick Hillery it, rather
than Finance or Industry and Commerce, co-ordinated the
European Community negotiations from 1970 to 1972. And while
ministerial responsibility for Northern Ireland matters was still
primarily a matter for the Taoiseach, the vastly increased day-to-
day exchanges with northern groups and with the British government were channelled through Foreign Affairs. By 1972, the
foreign policy field was still fragmented, as is perhaps inevitable
in a modernised administrative system, though the fragmentation
as between government departments looked a good deal less lop-
sided than it had ten years earlier. But the policy-making process
was from now on to be of sufficient complexity to place new
strains on the attempts of governments to reconcile ends and
means in a coherent and satisfactory manner.

The current policy-making process must first be seen in the light
of developing administrative structures. The most remarkable
change in this respect has been the growth of the Department of
Foreign Affairs itself.[25] In 1967, before the Northern Ireland and

European Community issues were activated, the total number of officials of foreign service or equivalent grades was 115, forty-one of whom served at headquarters and seventy-four overseas. By 1972, following the negotiations at Brussels and more intensive contacts with the British government over the northern question, the total had risen to 153, sixty-eight in Dublin and eighty-five overseas. The first three years of European Community membership saw a continuation of this growth; by the Summer of 1977 the total number of officials was 214, ninety-four in the headquarters organisation and one hundred and twenty overseas. At the political level, in February 1975 the department for the first time had a Parliamentary Secretary attached to it, John Kelly (who was also Parliamentary Secretary to the Department of the Taoiseach). On the change of government in 1977 this practice was continued, with the appointment of David Andrews; in November the office was elevated to that of Minister of State, to a large extent a reflection of the increased demands made by international affairs.

An expansion on such a scale and at such a pace was unprecedented in the department's history. Its significance with regard to policy-making may be seen particularly in the development of the headquarters in Dublin, which were almost doubled in size in less than ten years.[26] The 1967 department was organised on the basis of three divisions, corresponding rather loosely to the administrative, economic and political information work of the department, and co-ordinated by four Assistant Secretaries. In 1977 co-ordination was the responsibility of a Deputy Secretary and five Assistant Secretaries, supervising six divisions based on a greater degree of functional specialisation. Of the old structure the most recognisable elements are the Administration Division (which has however lost its legal section, which has become a division in its own right), and the Economic Division. The latter has been one of the department's major growth points, employing twenty-nine officials (ten in 1967), and is divided into four sections, which are further broken down into precisely defined policy areas. For the most part these match the functional divisions of the European Community system, and form a direct link to the largest overseas mission, the Permanent Representation in Brussels. The economic element in the department can also be seen in a separate Overseas Development Division which includes six foreign service officials. There was no corresponding unit in 1967, or even in 1972.

A further innovation since the late nineteen-sixties has been the explicit concentration on Anglo-Irish relations, particularly on the Northern Ireland issue, in the eight-strong Anglo-Irish affairs section in the rather heterogenous Anglo-Irish and Information Division.[27] But even more striking has been the development of a fully-fledged Political Division. Starting from the same root as the Anglo-Irish affairs section — the General Political and UN section, which in 1967 consisted of only four officials — this division currently has a strength of seventeen officials. This growth can be explained almost wholly by the increased range of Irish interests since joining the European Community in 1973, for in the previous year only twelve officials were working in what was then a mixed Political and Cultural Division. Within the Political Division there has been a new departure in the Irish foreign service — the allocation of responsibility on broad geographical lines, or what is usually called the 'desk' system, with the world divided into six 'desks', each of which is covered by two officials.[28] One of the four Counsellors in this Division is the 'Correspondent' in the European Community member-states' political co-operation process.

The policy-making role of the Department of Foreign Affairs is highlighted both by the increasing number of officials involved and the greater degree of specialisation which is now possible in the headquarters organisation. Growth at home has also been paralleled in the expansion of overseas representation. Since becoming a member of the European Community Ireland has established diplomatic relations with no less than twenty-four states.[29] However, the greater part of this new diplomatic network consists of non-residential accreditation which does not involve setting up a new permanent mission, but rather a pattern of regular visitations by a diplomat based outside the country to which he is accredited. In 1974 representation of this type was established with Singapore and with six states in the Middle East (Bahrain, Israel, Kuwait, Qatar, Saudi Arabia and the United Arab Emirates). The following year the three Maghreb states, Algeria, Morocco and Tunisia were added, as well as Brazil, Greece, Thailand and in Eastern Europe, Czechoslovakia. The latter was joined by Hungary and Poland in 1976, in addition to Mexico; in 1977 Yugoslavia and Libya were added to the list.

More significant, from the point of view of the policy-making process, has been the establishment of new residential overseas missions. Eight of these have been set up since the Summer of 1973, representing the first new overseas missions to be established since the mid-nineteen-sixties. In 1973 Luxembourg, which had formerly been a non-residential posting, received its own mission, while a completely new element in the overseas network was Japan. Another former non-residential accreditation, Austria, was added to the list of residential missions in 1974, though the major departure of that year was the exchange of ambassadors between Dublin and Moscow. The Middle East also became an area of immediate concern. An Irish mission was established in the Lebanon, providing a diplomatic 'service centre' for non-residential representation in the Arab states until the Lebanese civil war compelled a move to Saudi Arabia; a chargé d'affaires was also sent to Egypt. A further residential mission was set up in the Middle East in 1976, in Iran, while the following year saw a residential mission being established in Athens. Although none of these new missions is served by more than three officials, and most of them by less, they do reflect the broadening of the Irish diplomatic network beyond its traditional 'Atlantic' focus.

The expansion of the Department of Foreign Affairs has undoubtedly raised the morale of the Irish Diplomatic Service. There is much greater mobility within the service, allowing for more attractive promotion opportunities, and an alternative career outlet in so far as the diplomat may be well-equipped to work in the central institutions of the European Community. The work itself is more varied, offering a wider range of opportunities for at least a partial involvement in policy formulation rather than an unrelenting administrative routine. The department and its personnel can no longer be viewed as an eccentric and peripheral element in the Irish administrative system.

But the rehabilitation of the Department of Foreign Affairs is not the only recent structural development in the foreign policy-making process. Closely associated with it there has occurred a less visible, but nonetheless important, institutionalisation of inter-departmental co-ordination, which makes explicit the involvement in foreign policy of the major economic departments.[30] The need to formulate national policy positions on issues affected by membership of the European Community led to the creation of the 'Committee of Secretaries', which co-ordinated Irish policy during the negotiations in the early nineteen-seventies. This body included the Secretaries (and sometimes Assistant Secretaries) of the Departments of Foreign Affairs, Agriculture and Fisheries, Industry and Commerce and Finance, and was sponsored by the latter department, thus reflecting Finance's claim, established under Whitaker and Lemass, to co-ordinate economic foreign policy. With European Community membership it has become the 'European Communities Committee', and is now sponsored and serviced by the Department of Foreign Affairs, in itself a reflection of the new standing of that department. The committee also includes the Department of the Taoiseach, and other departments when they are directly concerned, and meets at both Secretary and Assistant Secretary level. At a lower level, inter-departmental working parties were also set up in ten policy areas with the intention of providing long-term planning. In practice some quickly became moribund and others ensnared in short-term operational details, although two or three have worked as originally envisaged. In so far as a 'community policy-making system' exists in Dublin, it operates through the European Community units in the major departments which then attempt to co-ordinate departmental positions at the European Communities Committee.

Formal interdepartmental co-operation with regard to the European Community is not restricted to Dublin. The Irish Permanent Representation to the European Community in Brussels is ostensibly the largest diplomatic mission overseas, but in composition it is an interdepartmental unit in which less than half of the officials are career diplomats.[31] The latter do, however, form the largest single element in the Permanent Representation; in 1977 this represented eight of the twenty administrative grade officials, including the Permanent Representative himself and his Deputy, three of the seven Counsellors and three of the twelve First Secretaries. The Department of Foreign Affairs has therefore an important role in managing the affairs of the mission. At this time the Department of Finance had three officials (one Counsellor and two First Secretaries), Agriculture and Fisheries had two (one Counsellor and one First Secretary), Industry and Commerce had three (one Counsellor and two First Secretaries), Transport and Power had two (one Counsellor and one First Secretary), while Labour, Local Government and Health had one

First Secretary each. In conjunction with the European Communities Committee in Dublin the Permanent Representation
embodies a degree of formal, institutionalised interdepartmental
co-ordination which is unusual in the context of Irish administrative practice. Nevertheless, the number of officials who participate
is still relatively small, and they enjoy a high degree of personal
knowledge and flexibility in their relationships with each other.
Consequently co-ordination mechanisms are not so centralised or
rigid as those employed in some of the other European Community
member-states.[32]

The institutional framework of the foreign policy-making
system in the nineteen-seventies is, therefore, characterised by
increasing specialisation and the simultaneous fragmentation and
growth of bureaucratic structures. These characteristics affect
both the design and outcomes of policy throughout the foreign
policy field, as do the increasing complexity, uncertainty and pace
of change which can be seen in nearly all the issue-areas of which
it is composed. In these circumstances the collection and processing
of information can pose serious problems; it has even been
suggested that the governments of small states in general, because
of their limited information base and their narrow perception of
their external environment, tend to behave unpredictably, and
ineffectually.[33] Prior to joining the European Community Ireland's
information base was indeed limited, being restricted by a small
diplomatic network in which the delegation at the United Nations
was the principal window on the diplomatic world. But in the
nineteen-seventies this base has broadened significantly. With
regard to economic foreign policy, formerly dependent on the
OECD and some of the UN specialised agencies, the Irish policy-
maker is now at the receiving end of a constant bombardment of
information through the process of interaction with the central
institutions of the European Community. Less generally appreciated, perhaps, is the amount of information received by way of
the political co-operation process; even if they do not arrive at
common positions on the more sensitive issues, the governments
of the Nine do 'know each other's minds' to an extent that is
unusual in international politics.[34]

For a state with Ireland's traditionally restricted involvement in
international affairs, the significance of plugging in, as it were, to
this endless diplomatic conversation with some of the world's

most significant states is considerable. One consequence, as we have seen, has been the establishment of a Political Division within the Department of Foreign Affairs, which is sizeable by Irish standards and which allows an unprecedented measure of specialisation. The expansion of the department's own external information system, at least so far as the new residential missions are concerned, also represents an improvement in the policy-maker's information base; first-hand assessments are still a valuable means of reducing the distortion which inevitably creeps into the information supplied by other governments and the international, but nationally biased, press agencies.

Improved access to information is one thing, the ability to comprehend it and use it is quite another. The recent structural changes, in particular the desk system, may permit Irish policy-makers to cope with external information so far as it concerns Ireland directly, but it would be a mistake to assume that the government has the intelligence resources to make a serious contribution on the whole range of issues which confront it, either inside or outside the European Community context. Thus with regard to the international milieu in general only a few topics, such as disarmament or development aid, can be selected and even these cannot always be pursued in great depth. Moreover, the Irish policy-maker still does not enjoy the benefits of a serious public debate outside his immediate circle; thus information is not only 'wasted' because he does not have the resources to cover it all, but some relevant information may evade him because his preconceived categories are rarely exposed to probing questions by outsiders.[35] For a small state Ireland may be relatively well-informed, but the policy-maker's view of the world is nonetheless necessarily very selective.

A second major source of possible distortion in policy-making is the need to co-ordinate the activities of the various elements in the policy-making system. As interdependence between states, particularly in economic foreign policy, has increased throughout the western world since World War II, the associated fragmentation of policy-making has become a widespread phenomenon. In Ireland, in the nineteen-sixties, it was manifested in the tacit division of the foreign policy field between Lemass and Aiken; in the nineteen-seventies it takes a more complex form, deriving from the expanded foreign policy field resulting from membership of the European Community system.

The Brussels policy-making system virtually imposes fragmentation on national governments. It pulls a wide range of government departments into a process of continuous interaction with their counterparts in other member states, and interest groups follow where they can. The line between foreign and domestic policy, never clearly defined in the contemporary era, becomes increasingly blurred, so that it has been argued that there is in effect a third type of policy – 'community policy' – which shares some of the characteristics of both.[36] One of the most striking features of 'community policy' is the difficulty which governments find in controlling the activities of their component parts; this may lead to the phenomenon of 'transgovernmental relations', in which direct contacts are made and positions agreed between states at the departmental level without the higher co-ordinating organs of government in either state really controlling the outcome.[37] Of course the advocates of political integration want this to occur, but equally obviously the leaders of national governments do not see their position being eroded with equanimity.

Up to the early nineteen-seventies the national governments in the European Community did on the whole maintain control through various systems of co-ordination, in which there was a general tendency for the foreign ministry to assume a key role, though not without a struggle with the leading economic departments.[38] Ireland conformed to this pattern, with the Departments of Foreign Affairs and Finance matching each other's claims by reference to continental practice, and Foreign Affairs emerging as the sponsoring department in the European Communities Committee in Dublin, and as the core of the Permanent Representation in Brussels. Yet experience in the expanded European Community has raised doubts as to whether effective national co-ordination is being maintained; especially with recurring crises in exchange rate and agricultural policies the relevant departments often appear to go their own way. The latter phenomenon can be seen in the Irish Department of Agriculture's direct involvement in the management of the Common Agricultural Policy through the CAP's Management Committees, without being channelled through the normal interdepartmental structure; the Department of Finance, too, is necessarily secretive about exchange rates.

Nevertheless, agriculture is still viewed as a special case, and most other issues involve more than one department. In these circumstances attempts by any one department to by-pass either the interdepartmental committee in Dublin or the Permanent Representation have been rare, and when discovered have caused serious rows. After some early difficulties, co-operation in that part of the co-ordinating system which operates continuously — the Permanent Representation — has proved to be the norm, partly because the ultimate decisions emanate from Dublin and the Permanent Representation only has discretion when policy lines are already clearly established.[39] Communication between Dublin and Brussels seems to be straightforward. The Irish do not bring their national decision-making into meetings of the Committee of Permanent Representatives (COREPER) or the Council of Ministers, as the Italians have sometimes done; nor, like the French, have they felt it necessary to formalise and centralise their co-ordinating system to a high degree. At present, at any rate, with regard to European Community policy the Department of Foreign Affairs seems to be accepted in the role of gatekeeper.

The ability of the Irish foreign ministry to maintain this position may have owed more than a little to its ability to present a single departmental position to outsiders — that is to say it manages to co-ordinate its own activities, which of course spread right across the foreign policy field. Although the department has itself expanded and has two strong, 'political' and 'economic' divisions, it has so far been possible to keep them apart.[40] Moreover, the department, like the administration as a whole, is still relatively small and more clearly committed to its overall policy goals, especially in the European Community context, than are some of its counterparts in other states in the Nine. The success with which it managed the Irish presidency of the European Community during the first six months of 1975[41] is evidence that the fragmentation of responsibilities and the diffusion of government control has not yet advanced as far in Ireland as in some other west European states. Whether the 'leadership' of the Department of Foreign Affairs will last is another matter. It has been suggested that as Ireland settles into the routine of membership the large economic departments, particularly the Department of Finance, will tend to go their own way.[42] Also there is the possibility that, with the developing role of the European Council, the Department of the Taoiseach will become a more important instrument of policy co-ordination.[43]

Whatever form it assumes, the development of formal inter-departmental co-ordination does suggest that in one important respect the pattern of policy-making is being transformed, though it is difficult to say to what extent. Traditionally the cabinet has been the primary co-ordinating agency, and it still is 'above' the interdepartmental system in so far as its members are responsible for the ultimate decisions taken. There is also a cabinet committee for European Community matters, consisting of the Ministers for Foreign Affairs, Finance, Industry and Commerce, and Agriculture and chaired by the Taoiseach; this is one of a number of cabinet committees which proliferated when the Fine Gael-Labour coalition came into power in 1973.[44] It is the ministerial counterpart of the civil servants' interdepartmental committee, and it is an obvious forum in which serious inconsistencies between departmental policies can be reconciled, and a homogenous national policy maintained. The cabinet committee has been used to discuss very broad policy options, such as the Tindemans proposals for European Union in 1976, but it is significant that, as a manifestation of ministerial co-ordination, it generally intervenes at a late stage in the policy-making process. Neither the cabinet committee nor the full cabinet is an important source of policy initiatives, for in so far as initiatives stem from ministers this is usually through departmental channels. Rather, the cabinet committee, which meets on an *ad hoc* basis, appears to act as a court of appeal, in order to reconcile departmental differences in which the policy options have already been drastically reduced.

Thus the extent to which either the cabinet or its committee can be said to control policy-making is limited. Indeed, on occasion it has been shown in a poor light. For example, in 1975 one of its members, the Minister for Labour, Michael O'Leary, put his support behind European policy for equal pay for women; barely six months later the government decided it could not afford to accept the Community's directive and entered a well-publicised confrontation with the Commission. The subsequent recriminations, including an attack on the Irish Commissioner on party political lines, gave the impression that the cabinet had been incapable of co-ordinating its activities, either in the formulation of the original policy or in its clumsy attempts to obtain a derogation from the consequences. Another instance of confusion at the highest level was the decision to appoint a separate Minister for Fisheries on 4 February 1977 in the middle of an attempt to change the Community's fishery policy. The new minister, Paddy Donegan, often appeared to be at cross-purposes with his colleague in Foreign Affairs, Garret FitzGerald, and the ensuing public comment can hardly have helped Ireland's negotiating stance at Brussels.

However, public manifestations of executive confusion are relatively rare. Many issue-areas in the foreign policy sector have not traditionally been a matter of immediate public concern, and the instruments of public control over foreign policy, particularly so far as parliament is concerned, have been notoriously weak in Ireland.[45] But welfare issues, such as the equal pay controversy, are typical of the blurring of the domestic-foreign categorisation which can only increase with participation in the European Community political system. Indeed, it is in response to membership of that system that there has occurred the principal innovation in trying to improve public control over at least a part of the foreign policy field.

In the Summer of 1973 a Joint Committee of the Dáil and Seanad was established to scrutinise the secondary legislation of the European Community, and was given powers to examine proposals made by the central institutions of the Community as well as the implications for Ireland of Community acts.[46] The Joint Committee made a hesitant start; for nearly two years it encountered difficulties in obtaining civil service staff for its secretariat. This reflected widespread suspicion on the part of professional administrators, for it was the first Irish parliamentary committee established to cover a particular area of public policy and seemed to threaten the principle of ministerial responsibility.[47] Ironically, when the Joint Committee did get off the ground, in the Spring of 1975, it found it easier to establish a satisfactory working relationship with government departments than with its own parliamentary parent bodies. Each department has a liaison officer, supplies written memoranda at the Joint Committee's request, and permits senior officials to give oral information in the private sessions of the Joint Committee's four sub-committees. This latter innovation has generally been well received on both sides, and the informal and useful pattern of communication which has resulted has allowed the Joint Committee to produce reports which have some influence in the policy-making process within the administration.[48]

But the weak link in this new system of public control is found in the Joint Committee's relationship with the Dáil and Seanad. Neither house has arranged a regular procedure to discuss its reports. The same fate has faced the government's own six-monthly reports on developments in the European Community; the first two were debated in both houses, the Dáil adjourned its debate on the third and fourth, the sixth was discussed in the Seanad, while the fifth to the ninth were disposed of in one day after a delay of over two years! Although the knowledge and interest of individual parliamentarians in the European Community has probably increased since 1973, parliamentary procedures still stand in the way of effective public control of community policy. The position is a far cry from that found in Denmark, where the Market Relations Committee can in some instances virtually impose a veto on their ministers' actions at Brussels.[49]

Moreover, the Joint Committee's terms of reference limit it to only one part of the foreign policy field, even though it is an important part. It does not consider policy arising under the heading of the political co-operation process of the Nine, nor does it reach beyond strictly European Community issues.[50] For such matters the only measures of public control are the traditional ones of parliamentary questions and more or less annual estimates debates, together with such special opportunities the government sees fit to provide to discuss specific issues. However co-operative the foreign minister may be, this is a weak and intermittent influence on policy.[51] In recent years parliamentary debate on Northern Ireland may be more frequent, but the limits of bi-partisanship on this subject have precluded the Dáil's *ad hoc* all-party committee, established in 1972, from becoming an effective instrument of influence on policy.

Outside the central parliamentary organs of public control, the activities of policy-makers in most western, 'modernised' political systems come under the informal scrutiny of the 'foreign policy community', composed of specialised journalists, the personnel of academic and research institutes and spokesmen for the major interest groups. Although there has been an increasing awareness of the importance of foreign policy throughout the nineteen-seventies, the Irish 'foreign policy community' remains a shadowy source of influence. Press and television coverage has become more specialised and both governmental and non-governmental partici-pants in the policy-making process have now amassed considerable experience, but there is still relatively little independent research on foreign policy problems. There has been increased interest in the universities since 1973, but this has mostly been channelled into teaching rather than research.[52] In 1976 the Royal Irish Academy decided to establish a National Committee for the Study of International Affairs, which commenced its activities during the Winter of 1977-78. This could prove to be the focus of the foreign policy community, and the basis for a more informed public opinion, but if research is to be produced and disseminated (rather than merely talked about) a more significant commitment of financial resources will have to be made in future years.

Where the means of public control of the foreign policy field are not effective, policy-makers may have a certain short-term freedom of action, but in the long term their position may be adversely affected. An ignorant, indifferent or frustrated domestic opinion will not be aware of the extent to which interdependence between modern states constrains national governments. On the facile assumption that the state is indeed a truly autonomous entity, expectations are aroused, only to be disappointed by unforeseen and often drastic changes in the external environment. If policy is to be purposeful, even to a limited extent, the policy-maker must ensure his own support by preparing the public for future change; one of the first steps in this is to educate the public in the complexities of the present. Only then can he attempt the impossible himself, by trying to make policy for an uncertain future.

Chapter 12

The Problem of the Future

*The fact is that while there is a great desire to know what the
future of world politics will bring, and also to know how we
should behave in it, we have to grope about in the dark with
respect to the one as much as with respect to the other. It is
better to recognise that we are in darkness than to pretend that
we can see the light.*

Hedley Bull, *The Anarchical Society:
A Study of Order in World Politics*

In the preceding two chapters it has been argued that it is often
difficult to find a clear sense of purpose in foreign policy. Partly
this derives from the problem of design, the difficulties inherent in
the task of integrating the wide range of issue-areas which come
within the foreign policy field; partly it derives from the nature of
the policy-making processes through which this integration is
necessarily attempted. But confusion about purpose also stems
from the degree of change in the international system as a whole,
and the consequent uncertainties this poses.

When the Irish state was established in the early nineteen-
twenties, the international system had the appearance of a new
type of international order, based on the precepts of national self-
determination within a framework of collective security in the
League of Nations. In retrospect this period can be seen as no more
than the illusory calm in the eye of the storm, as a truly revolutionary phase in international politics succeeded the relative
stability of the mid-nineteenth century. During the last hundred
years the number of states has almost trebled and international
organisations have proliferated; European states reached the peak
of their power in the 'new imperialism' which laid claim to nearly

all of Africa and much of Asia, only to lose control of these empires and of the international system itself; technological change permitted unprecedented economic growth and international economic interactions expanded accordingly, but technological change also led to increasingly destructive consequences when force was used to settle disputes between states. Interstate conflict was rendered more complex by differences over ideological principles, as well as the competition of material interests.[1]

The course of Irish foreign policy has to a large extent been determined by these often unpredictable, erratic and disruptive changes in the international system. Although geographical location did for some time ensure a degree of insulation from many of the most harmful effects of conflict within the European region, the subsequent development in that region of more controlled forms of competition has seen Ireland become intensively involved in European politics. Similarly, Ireland's principal bilateral relationship with the United Kingdom has been altered, not so much by what the Irish or even the British governments have done in the framework of Anglo-Irish relations, but by the steady decline in the United Kingdom's position, from being a great power with global responsibilities to being a secondary power with primarily regional concerns.

It is easy enough to summarise such large changes with the benefit of hindsight, and to forget that the policy-makers who have to deal with such trends can see neither the final outcomes nor the often tortuous paths by which they are reached. For them, change means bewilderment and a loss of direction at worst, and, at best, persistent anxiety about the uncertainties of the future. Attempts to deal with this problem in a systematic way, whether they take the form of the academic activity of 'futurology' or of the statistical projections of government agencies, have not to date been notably successful. Although techniques for extrapolating observed trends have improved, prediction depends on a clear understanding of the way in which the international system works, and on this question there is little agreement. It may well be that the academic observer must accept that 'we have to grope about in the dark.'[2]

On the other hand, if any value at all is placed on the preservation of national autonomy, governments have at least to try to understand how the external environment is changing and the implications this may have for their foreign policy. Informed speculation may fall a long way behind prediction, but it is nevertheless an advance on either a blind fatalism or the common assumption that the future will be like the past, but more so. Informed speculation in the foreign policy field is in itself a major undertaking. This can be seen even in the following brief survey of current developments and prospects at the three levels of international activity which impinge on Irish foreign policy — the global level, the regional level (western Europe and especially the European Community), and the level of the 'British Isles subsystem'.

Change at the global level of international politics must be seen against certain elements of stability which have persisted since the end of World War II. The emergence of two superpowers, the United States and the Soviet Union, and the rivalry between them ensured up to the early nineteen-sixties that world politics was primarily concerned with security issues, especially that of nuclear deterrence, in a bipolar structure characterised by extensive alliance systems. During the sixties this image of 'east-west' conflict became blurred; strains were evident in the alliances on both sides, and the large number of new, less developed states were reluctant to see their claims for economic justice as secondary to the security preoccupations of the superpowers. Nevertheless, it did prove possible for those governments with some capacity to 'manage' the international system, above all the United States, to keep security politics and international welfare issues apart for most of the time.

In the nineteen-seventies, however, a considerably more complex international system has emerged.[3] Superpower security relations are still a major preoccupation; the search for arms control, the persistence of bureaucratised alliance systems and ideological distrust are fundamental characteristics of the politics of détente. But the management of these issues has been made more complicated in so far as they now arise in a triangular relationship, including China, or even in a pentangular relationship, if Japan and the European Community are added as further 'centres of influence'. The enduring elements in this new structure of power are difficult to discern, but it is at least clear that the future of international politics at the global level can no longer be analysed in terms of a bipolar model. An equal source of complexity is to be found in the substance of international politics, for in addition to security issues an extensive range of welfare issues have become politicised at the global level. In August 1971 the question of the control of the international monetary system became a matter of recurrent controversy when the United States government unilaterally ended the convertibility of the dollar. In October 1973 the oil embargo associated with the Arab-Israeli war not only made energy resources a world issue, but demonstrated the vulnerability of energy-dependent developed states and the possibilities of collective action by less developed primary-producer states. Subsequently the conditions of the 'north-south' dialogue, or the search for a 'new international economic order', became more favourable to the less developed states than they had been at any time during the nineteen-sixties, and there were significant pressures to modify trading conditions and patterns of develop- ment aid. The control of food resources, population, pollution and the exploitation of the sea-bed are further welfare issues raised at the global level.

None of these issues is amenable to easy short-term solutions and are likely to remain on the international agenda for some considerable time, the more so since many states display an acutely nationalistic attitude towards proposals that these problems be tackled by way of international rule-making.[4] Thus there will be no shortage of material for Irish governments in the broad international milieu; the problem will be to select those issues where Ireland can make some worthwhile contribution out of her limited resources. Traditional concerns, such as disarma- ment and development aid, might in themselves be more than enough to handle. But global issues will also impinge on other issue-areas in Irish foreign policy, and particularly on that of economic foreign policy. The regulation of international trade and the international monetary system, the control of demographic development and the freedom of movement of labour are arguably no longer merely desirable background conditions against which Irish welfare can be pursued, but are urgent issues which demand specific responses from Irish governments.

The effect of global issues on foreign policy is increasingly being met at the regional level, in the framework of the patterns of inter- dependence which are developing among particular groups of states. It is largely through the European Community that Ireland now faces the world, and the future of Irish foreign policy must be seen in the light of the evolution of the Community. If experience teaches anything in this respect, it is that expectations of the European Community becoming a single actor on the world stage have time and again been disappointed; interdependence between the member-states is an undoubted reality, but it seems a far cry from the political form of a federal union, as originally conceived by the founding fathers. Indeed, a plausible case may be advanced for the hypothesis that the European Community is perceived by member governments above all as a means (and not always the most important one) of reducing the effects of external threats to their own societies. This national introversion has been accompanied by an increasing disparity in economic performance, which makes it even more difficult to advance the integrationist cause significantly beyond its present position. In facing the outside world this closely linked, but far from monolithic, group of states is more likely to play a broadly conservative role than to indulge in attempts to establish a position as a leading centre of influence.

If the European Community is to remain much as it is now – a heavily bureaucratised intergovernmental arrangement – for the next few decades, if not longer[5], it will nonetheless be of considerable significance in Irish politics. Even incremental changes in the Community's political system, such as direct elections to the European Parliament, will lead to modified attitudes and practices in terms of Irish electoral politics, and the political development, no matter how gradual, of the Brussels system is likely to remain a recurrent issue in Irish political debate. More important, though, will be the effect of specific Community policies, in the policy areas of agriculture, regional policy, social policy and so on, for it is here that domestic groups have an obvious stake in the continual negotiations which are a characteristic of bureaucratised interdependence.

Beyond the direct consequencs of participation in Community policies there is the transformation of the setting of Irish diplomacy which occurred in the early nineteen-seventies. In this Ireland moved from a pattern of intermittent bilateral relations with a limited number of states to participation in what is virtually a standing diplomatic conference, which is the major point of contact with the wide range of global issues referred to above. In spite of the fact that it is premature to speak of European foreign policy, the future presents Ireland, along with the other member governments, with several critical choices. One of the most pressing, and one which could well recur over the next fifteen or twenty years, is that of the enlargement of the membership of the Community. With Greece already negotiating for full membership, and Portugal and Spain in the wings, both the economic and political natures of the Community are called into question, whether by increasing yet further the economic heterogeneity of the members, or by over-burdening an already cumbersome policy-making process. Then there are the persistent 'noises off' concerning the Community's lack of direct involvement in the military aspect of global security issues, a question which is not only of interest to Ireland, where a change in policy might have substantial consequences, but which represents an important element in the overall shape of the Community and the way in which it is perceived by the outside world. While the arguments against a significant European Community defence role seem to reflect many of the constants of the post-1945 international system, defence remains on the agenda of all Ireland's partners in the Community. Irish foreign ministers may prefer to talk about the Community's relations with less developed countries, but preoccupation with enlargement and defence will not always make it easy for these preferences to prevail.

A third level of international politics where change may prove to be problematic is that of the 'British Isles sub-system' of the international system. This inelegant terminology is used deliberately in place of what in the past has more commonly been labelled 'Anglo-Irish relations', in order to indicate that the division of the British Isles into two sovereign states can no longer be taken for granted. The mid-nineteen-seventies have seen two quite different assaults on the structure of this international sub-system, which represents Ireland's immediate external environment. On the one hand, separatism has become a political issue on the larger island, primarily in the form of Scottish nationalism and the British government's attempts to contain this within a controversial framework of parliamentary devolution. On the other hand, in that part of the United Kingdom where devolution was actually practised from 1921 to 1972, the possibility of independence has from time to time been raised as a means of breaking the deadlock. Whatever reservations may be held against independence for

Northern Ireland as a solution to the conflict between Irish nationalists and supporters of the union[6], no Dublin government can afford to ignore it as a possible contingency. As such, it could arise in several forms — as a settlement negotiated between the opposing groups within Northern Ireland, with the support of the British and Irish governments, as a unilateral declaration by former unionists, or, as a result of a full-scale civil war, British withdrawal and probable repartition by force. All of these possibilites have serious implications for Irish diplomacy and security, as would the shape of the ultimate outcome. The notion of a British Isles Confederation, composed of Scotland, Northern Ireland, Ireland and England (plus or minus Wales) as sovereign states has been mooted[7]; should such a development occur, it would in itself bring in its train a host of diplomatic problems. In addition to the question of the distribution of the Confederation's 'internal' resources and the management of its interdependent economies, agreement would have to be reached on its association with existing diplomatic coalitions, such as the European Community, the Commonwealth and with the military alliance system, NATO, in which all except Ireland now participate. If this does indeed prove to be the direction in which the British Isles sub-system travels during the next decade, Irish foreign policy will undergo a fundamental reassessment, which could distract attention (and possibly resources) from some of the more general concerns, such as development aid, which have recently come to the fore.

It will not of course require the political disintegration of the British Isles sub-system to ensure that Northern Ireland remains a major preoccupation of Irish foreign policy for years to come. On the assumption that the outcome will be that reflected in the existing policies of the Irish government and, more ambiguously, its British counterpart — that is to say a devolved government within the United Kingdom, based on some form of power sharing — the sensitive issue of Dublin-Belfast relations will have to be grasped, with the possibility of constitutional change within the Republic. On the assumption of prolonged conflict, or even repartition, whether by force of arms or agreement, it is obvious that the Dublin-London side of the triangle will continue to be subjected to the tensions inherent in attempts to co-operate on security policy. And, whatever the direction of events, Irish governments will seek to mobilise and maintain diplomatic support for their Northern Ireland policy, and may find themselves requesting external aid, possibly of massive proportions, from the European Community or the United States to assist in the reconstruction of Northern Ireland.

It is clear, then, that at all three levels of international activity the future promises a wide range of uncertainties which impinge on all the issue-areas in the foreign policy field. Choices have to be made, not only of long-term policy objectives and the allocation of resources to them, but of urgent responses to an external environment which can be relied on to produce the unforeseen. Irish governments have often been secretive about their contingency planning, partly because they have been reluctant to offer hostages to political fortune, and partly because they have been reluctant to devote the considerable resources necessary to engage in systematic policy planning in the first place. There is no separate policy planning unit in the Department of Foreign Affairs, and, given the relatively small size of the department and indeed of the state as an international actor, this is not altogether surprising.[8] However, the department is in some respects better equipped to anticipate external problems than at any previous period in its history. It has access to a major information network in the European political co-operation process, and the new desk system in its Political Division allows the development of a broader range of expertise. On economic matters participation in European Community policy-making and the national interdepartmental consultations this entails provide further opportunities for the Irish government to inform itself.[9]

Information is a necessary, though not sufficient, condition for any government facing the truly awesome task of adapting to external forces. Adaptation also depends on the skill with which political leaders reconcile the aspirations and expectations which they or their predecessors have encouraged with the inconvenient realities of international politics. There can be no easy prescriptions, especially for the policy-maker in the small state, whose margin for error is often barely perceptible. Although Ireland is fortunate in being located in a part of the world where violent inter-state conflict has been 'unthinkable' for the last thirty years, there can be no guarantee of such good fortune in the future. In the last resort, to 'have a foreign policy' is to live on one's wits.

Introduction

1. Denis J. Gorey in the Dáil, 16 November 1923 (Dáil Debates: 5,940).
2. See Patrick Keatinge, *The Formulation of Irish Foreign Policy* (Dublin: Institute of Public Administration, 1973), Part III.
3. For the concept of issue-areas, see James N. Rosenau, *The Scientific Study of Foreign Policy* (New York: The Free Press, 1971), chapter 5. Rosenau also developed the concept, not on the basis of a *value* typology as used here, but rather as a means of grouping issues according to the kind of *units* in or for which they are contested, thus distinguishing 'domestic' and 'foreign' policies as different issue-areas: ibid, chapter 13. Another way of classifying issue-areas, by 'substantive content', is used in Michael Brecher, *The Foreign Policy System of Israel* (London: Oxford University Press, 1972), pp. 13-14.
4. See A. I. Dawisha, 'Foreign policy models and the problem of dynamism', *British Journal of International Studies,* Vol. 2, No. 2, July 1976.
5. In the Spring of 1976 the cabinet minutes and some of the relevant papers for the period up to June 1944 were opened to public inspection — the first manifestation of a serious policy on Irish government archives. The release of departmental archives is still constrained, but the constraint appears to be because of a lack of administrative resources rather than the principle of eternal secrecy.
6. For an attempt to define the boundaries of the foreign policy field, see Rosenau, op. cit., chapter 13.

Chapter 1

1. In a letter to Eamon de Valera, 13 August 1921, quoted in Dorothy Macardle, *The Irish Republic* (London: Corgi edition, 1968), pp. 450-51.
2. These interventions are summarised in Ruth Dudley Edwards, *An Atlas of Irish History* (London: Methuen, 1973), pp. 41-42.
3. See below, pp. 45-46.
4. Quoted in Oliver MacDonagh, *Ireland* (New Jersey: Prentice Hall, 1968), p. viii.
5. Michael Hurst, *Parnell and Irish Nationalism* (London: Routledge and Kegan Paul, 1968), p. 5.
6. For brief summaries of the major aspects of Irish economic development, see Edwards, op. cit., chapters 7-12.
7. Joseph Lee, *The Modernisation of Irish Society 1848-1918* (Dublin: Gill and Macmillan, 1973), p. 35.

8. Hurst, op. cit., p. 3.
9. Oliver MacDonagh, *Ireland: The Union and its Aftermath* (London: Allen and Unwin, 1977), p. 16.
10. For the significance of the Act of Union, see ibid., chapter 1.
11. ibid., pp. 13-14.
12. ibid., p. 9.
13. See Edwards, op. cit., chapter 6, for a concise survey of Irish emigration.
14. F. S. L. Lyons, *Ireland Since the Famine* (London: Fontana, revised edition, 1973), p. 123.
15. For an analysis of the Irish-American community, see Thomas N. Brown, *Irish-American Nationalism 1870-1890* (Philadelphia and New York: Lippincott, 1966), chapter 3.
16. See below, pp. 48-50.
17. Lyons, op. cit., p. 16.
18. MacDonagh, *Ireland*, p. viii.
19. See below, pp. 32-35, 37.
20. See Donal McCartney, 'MacNeill and Irish Ireland', in F. X. Martin and F. J. Byrne (eds.), *The Scholar Revolutionary, Eoin MacNeill, 1867-1945, and the Making of the New Ireland* (Shannon: Irish University Press, 1973), pp. 75-97.
21. Edwards, op. cit., pp. 142-45.
22. Patrick O'Farrell, *Ireland's English Question: Anglo-Irish Relations 1534-1970* (London: Batsford, 1971), p. 13.
23. See below, pp. 176, 177, 182-83.

Chapter 2

1. Robert O. Keohane and Joseph S. Nye, Jr. (eds.), *Transnational Relations and World Politics* (Cambridge, Mass: Harvard University Press, 1970), p. xi.
2. For a concise account of this period, see E. Rumpf and A. C. Hepburn, *Nationalism and Socialism in Twentieth-century Ireland* (Liverpool: Liverpool University Press, 1977), chapter 1. Other useful short surveys are Oliver MacDonagh, *Ireland: The Union and its Aftermath* (London: Allen and Unwin, 1977) and Patrick O'Farrell, *England and Ireland Since 1800* (London: Oxford University Press, 1975), while Nicholas Mansergh, *The Irish Question 1840-1921* (London: Allen and Unwin, third revised edition, 1975) is an essential analysis. The best detailed histories are F. S. L. Lyons, *Ireland Since the Famine* (London: Fontana, revised edition, 1973) and Robert Kee, *The Green Flag: A History of Irish Nationalism* (London: Weidenfeld and Nicolson, 1972).
3. See above, p. 16.
4. Kevin B. Nowlan, *The Politics of Repeal* (London: Routledge and Kegan Paul, 1965), p. 9.

5. Charles Gavan Duffy, *Young Ireland 1840-50,* Vol. I (London: Fisher Unwin, second edition, 1896), p. 153.
6. ibid., chapter 9.
7. Nowlan, op. cit., pp. 65-68.
8. Gavan Duffy, op. cit., p. 152, note 1.
9. *Nation,* 1 November 1845.
10. ibid., 11 March 1848.
11. For a detailed account, see Nowlan, op. cit., pp. 182-93.
12. Quoted in ibid., pp. 191-92.
13. See, for example, the differences between Irish and Italian nationalists: Mansergh, op. cit., pp. 87-88.
14. So conspiratorial was the IRB that for many years even its members were not sure whether the 'R' stood for 'Revolutionary' or 'Republican'.
15. See below, p. 50.
16. See Michael Hurst, 'Fenianism in the context of world history' in M. Harmon (ed.) *Fenians and Fenianism* (Dublin: Scepter, 1968).
17. MacDonagh, op. cit., p. 59.
18. Lyons, op. cit., p. 136.
19. See Brown, *Irish-American Nationalism,* pp. 38-41.
20. For details, see David Thornley, *Isaac Butt and Home Rule* (London: MacGibbon and Kee, 1964), pp. 98-102.
21. For details of fund-raising in the United States, see Brown, op. cit., *passim.*
22. ibid., p. 68.
23. Lyons, op. cit., p. 302.
24. For details, see Alan J. Ward, *Ireland and Anglo-American Relations 1899-1921* (London: Weidenfeld and Nicolson, 1969), pp. 11-21.
25. ibid., p. 18.
26. ibid., p. 13, note 1.
27. Lyons, op. cit., p. 257.
28. For details of separatist support between 1900 and 1910, see Ward, op. cit., pp. 23-27 and 51-52.
29. Basil Chubb, *The Government and Politics of Ireland* (London: Oxford University Press, 1970), pp. 43-44.
30. The foreign policy image is in many respects analogous to the concept of the 'orientation' of an existing state. See below, p. 196.
31. Nowlan, op. cit., p. 8.
32. ibid., pp. 74-75.
33. Thornley, op. cit., p. 381.
34. Quoted in Denis Gwynn, *The Life of John Redmond* (London: Harrap, 1932), p. 52.
35. Ward, op. cit., pp. 19-20. And for Redmond's stance in 1914, see below, pp. 43-44.
36. F. S. L. Lyons, *John Dillon* (London: Routledge and Kegan Paul, 1968), p. 322.
37. See Alan O'Day, *The English Face of Irish Nationalism: Parnellite Involvement in British Politics 1880–86* (Dublin: Gill and Macmillan, 1977), chapter 10.

38. Quoted in Kee, op. cit., p. 387.
39. From a speech in January 1885, quoted in Lyons, *Ireland Since the Famine*, p. 186.
40. See F. S. L. Lyons, 'The Political Ideas of Parnell', *The Historical Journal*, xvi, 4 (1973), for a concise analysis of Parnell's political thought. See also Professor Lyons' biography, *Charles Stewart Parnell* (London: Collins, 1977).
41. Hurst, *Parnell and Irish Nationalism*, p. 98.
42. MacDonagh, op. cit., p. 62.
43. Kee, op. cit., p. 201.
44. Nowlan, op. cit., p. 13.
45. *Nation*, 1 November 1845.
46. O'Farrell, *Ireland's English Question*, p. 139.
47. Mansergh, op. cit., p. 287.
48. O'Farrell, *Ireland's English Question*, p. 204.
49. Mansergh, op. cit., p. 99.
50. Mansergh, op. cit., p. 68. In chapters 2 and 3, Professor Mansergh analyses the attempts of the Italian nationalists and of Marx and Engels to interpret Irish nationalism.
51. It is only fair to Griffith to note intermittent Irish interest in the Hungarian situation since the eighteen-forties. See Kee, op. cit., p. 449.
52. Lyons, *Ireland Since the Famine*, p. 251.
53. Richard Davis, *Arthur Griffith and Non-Violent Sinn Féin* (Dublin: Anvil, 1974), pp. 106-07 and 130.
54. For Griffith's views on economic nationalism, see ibid., chapter 9.
55. ibid., p. 69.
56. See Rumpf and Hepburn, op. cit., pp. 10-13. For examples of Connolly's views, see Owen Dudley Edwards and Bernard Ransom (eds.), *James Connolly: Selected Political Writings* (London: Jonathan Cape, 1973), esp. pp. 225-40.
57. O'Farrell, *Ireland's English Question*, p. 212.
58. Mansergh, op. cit., p. 293.
59. From a letter to Bulmer Hobson, 10 August 1905, quoted in Kee, op. cit., p. 458.
60. See Brian Inglis, *Roger Casement* (London: Hodder and Stoughton, 1974), Part II, chapter 2.
61. *Irish Review*, Vol III, July 1913, 217-27. See also Inglis, op. cit., pp. 227-29.
62. *Irish Review*, op. cit., pp. 224-25.
63. ibid., p. 225.
64. For the alliance with Germany, see below, pp. 45-46.
65. See above, p. 20.
66. Mansergh, op. cit., p. 88.
67. O'Farrell, *Ireland's English Question*, p. 215 and pp. 234-35.
68. MacDonagh, op. cit., pp. 76-77.
69. Hurst, *Parnell and Irish Nationalism*, p. 35.
70. Mansergh, op. cit., p. 211.
71. MacDonagh, op. cit., p. 26.

72. For a concise survey of the historical background, see T. W. Moody, *The Ulster Question 1603-1973* (Cork: Mercier, 1974), chapters 1-4.
73. Lee, op. cit., pp. 129-31.
74. Lyons, *Ireland Since the Famine*, pp. 289-90.
75. For example, in the work of James Connolly: see Conor Cruise O'Brien, *States of Ireland* (London: Panther, revised edition, 1974), pp. 89-97.
76. O'Farrell, *Ireland's English Question*, pp. 246-47.
77. Mansergh, op. cit., p. 211.
78. Quoted in Mansergh, op. cit., p. 228.
79. Translated from the Irish and quoted in Padraic Colum, *Arthur Griffith* (Dublin: Browne and Nolan, 1959), p. 32.

Chapter 3

1. For an account of this period, see Lyons, *Ireland Since the Famine*, pp. 287-329.
2. Gwynn, *The Life of John Redmond*, pp. 354-55.
3. By 1915 Redmond was giving financial aid to his American fund-raising organisation! See Ward, op. cit., pp. 79-80.
4. Lyons, op. cit., p. 330.
5. There was also some clerical support for the central powers on sectarian grounds – France was seen as a 'Freemason infidel gang of anti-clericals': O'Farrell, *Ireland's English Question*, p. 274.
6. In the Proclamation of the Provisional Government of the Irish Republic, cited in Macardle, *The Irish Republic*, pp. 155-56.
7. See above, p. 39.
8. For details of Irish-American involvement in the German alliance, see Ward, op. cit., pp. 73-78 and 91-94. Casement's adventures are related in Inglis, *Roger Casement*, pp. 275-328.
9. See Mansergh, *The Irish Question*, pp. 293-94.
10. Lyons, op. cit., p. 371.
11. *Memoirs of Desmond FitzGerald 1913-1916* (London: Routledge and Kegan Paul, 1968), pp. 140-41.
12. Ward, op. cit., pp. 117-27.
13. MacDonagh, *Ireland: The Union and its Aftermath*, p. 88.
14. ibid., pp. 88-89. For a detailed analysis of the Convention of 1917, see R. B. McDowell, *The Irish Convention 1917-1918* (London: Routledge and Kegan Paul, 1970).
15. See Brian Farrell, *The Founding of Dáil Eireann* (Dublin: Gill and Macmillan, 1971), chapter 2.
16. Alan J. P. Taylor, *English History 1914-1945* (Oxford: Clarendon Press, 1965), p. 104.
17. The Irish Party was now led by John Dillon, Redmond having died in March 1918.
18. Lyons, op. cit., p. 393.

19. Reproduced in Macardle, op. cit., pp. 850-51.
20. ibid., p. 255.
21. See Farrell, op. cit., p. 61.
22. Patrick McCartan, *With De Valera in America* (Dublin: Fitzpatrick, 1932), p. 2.
23. 'Surprisingly for a man of his realistic intelligence', commented an IRB supporter, Patrick S. O'Hegarty, *A History of Ireland under the Union 1801 to 1922* (London: Methuen, 1952), p. 717.
24. For the manifesto, see Macardle, op. cit., pp. 842-44.
25. O'Hegarty, op. cit., p. 727.
26. For Irish-American involvement in the peace conference policy, see Ward, op. cit., chapter 8, and Mansergh, op. cit., pp. 299-304.
27. Lyons, p. 423. For the importance of the American contribution to the Dáil's finances, see Ronan Fanning, *The Irish Department of Finance 1922-58* (Dublin: Institute of Public Administration, 1978), pp. 21-23.
28. See Keatinge, *The Formulation of Irish Foreign Policy*, pp. 107-08.
29. I am grateful to Richard Davis for pointing out that Irish propaganda made extensive use of parallels with India.
30. Ward, op. cit., pp. 214-15.
31. For McCartan's dealings with the Soviet Union, see McCartan, op. cit., chapter 23. The draft treaty is reproduced in Appendix 7.
32. For an account of Irish-Soviet relations at this time, see Marcus Wheeler, 'Soviet Interest in Ireland', *Survey*, No. 3 (96) Summer, 1975.
33. For de Valera's attempts to gain recognition, see Ward, op. cit., chapter 10.
34. For a survey of the strengths and weaknesses of Irish-American pressure internationally, see ibid., chapter 12.
35. Farrell, op. cit., p. 83.
36. De Valera's career up to this time is examined in The Earl of Longford and Thomas P. O'Neill, *Eamon de Valera* (London: Arrow, revised edition, 1974), chapters 1-7. For a critical assessment of his performance between 1918 and 1923, see MacDonagh, op. cit., pp. 105-06.
37. Childers' career is examined in Andrew Boyle, *The Riddle of Erskine Childers* (London: Hutchinson, 1977).
38. Longford and O'Neill, op. cit., p. 148.
39. Made in an interview of 6 February 1920 in the *Westminster Gazette*: see Macardle, op. cit., pp. 339-40.
40. McCartan's account is in McCartan, op. cit., chapter 18.
41. See Keatinge, op. cit., p. 137.
42. For McCartan's complaints, see his letter to de Valera in McCartan, op. cit., pp. 203-07.
43. MacDonagh, op. cit., p. 97.
44. Lord Longford, *Peace by Ordeal* (London: Sidgwick and Jackson, revised edition, 1972), pp. 256-57.
45. See Ward, op. cit., pp. 251-55.
46. For a detailed account, see Lord Longford, op. cit., *passim.* See also Thomas Jones, *Whitehall Diary, Vol. III: Ireland 1918-1925,* edited by Keith Middlemas (London: Oxford University Press, 1971) and Macardle, op. cit., which contains some of the most important documents.

47. The consequences for Irish economic foreign policy are examined below, chapter 7.
48. Lord Longford, op. cit., p. 93.
49. See below, pp. 103-04.
50. See Macardle, op. cit., pp. 863-55.
51. Even the prospects of the Irish constructing their own submarines filled British strategists with alarm. For the further development of security issues, see below, chapter 5.
52. Longford and O'Neill, op. cit., p. 139.
53. MacDonagh, op. cit., p. 98.
54. For the Treaty debate, see F. S. L. Lyons, 'The Great Debate' in Brian Farrell (ed.), *The Irish Parliamentary Tradition* (Dublin: Gill and Macmillan, 1973). For an analysis of the social and economic factors underlying the Treaty split, see Rumpf and Hepburn, *Nationalism and Socialism in Twentieth-century Ireland*, chapter 2.

Chapter 4

1. See Stanley Hoffmann, *The State of War* (London: Pall Mall, 1965), pp. 119-22.
2. *Dáil Eireann. Official Report: Debate on the Treaty between Great Britain and Ireland signed in London on 6 December 1921* (Dublin: 1922), p. 32.
3. For the economic and security issues, see below, chapters 7 and 5 respectively.
4. For the question of policy towards re-unification, see below, chapter 6.
5. Lyons, *Ireland Since the Famine,* pp. 455-59.
6. In a speech at Ennis in 1924, cited in Longford and O'Neill, *Eamon de Valera,* p. 237.
7. This analogy is used by Ged Martin, 'The Irish Free State and the evolution of the Commonwealth, 1921-49' in Ronald Hyam and Ged Martin, *Reappraisals in British Imperial History* (London: Macmillan, 1975), p. 205.
8. David W. Harkness, *The Restless Dominion* (London: Macmillan, 1969), p. 44. This is a full account of Irish policy on dominion status from 1921 to 1931. For Ireland's contribution to the evolution of the Commonwealth, see Martin, op. cit.; W. K. Hancock, *Survey of British Commonwealth Affairs, Vol. 1: Problems of Nationality 1918-1936* (London: Oxford University Press, 1937), especially chapters 3 and 6; and Nicholas Mansergh, *Survey of British Commonwealth Affairs: Problems of External Policy 1931-1939* (London: Oxford University Press, 1952), especially chapters 1, 2 and 8. Concise accounts may be found in Conor Cruise O'Brien, 'Ireland in International Affairs' in Owen Dudley Edwards (ed.), *Conor Cruise O'Brien introduces Ireland* (London: Deutsch, 1969) and in Lyons, op. cit., pp. 504-10.

9. Dáil Debates: 53,207 (13 June 1934).
10. Cited in Lyons, op. cit., p. 508.
11. Cruise O'Brien, op. cit., p. 109.
12. Longford and O'Neill, op. cit., p. 274.
13. From a speech on 23 April 1933, quoted in ibid., p. 289.
14. The phrase is F. S. L. Lyons's in *Ireland Since the Famine*. See pp. 511-23 for a concise but detailed summary of de Valera's constitutional policy up to 1938. See also Longford and O'Neill op. cit., chapters 23-26.
15. See Hancock, op. cit., pp. 339-68.
16. For the economic consequences of the tariff war and the concurrent attitudes towards economic independence, see below, pp. 134-37.
17. Cabinet, 6/2, 12 March 1932.
18. For a concise survey of the role of the Irish situation committee, see D. W. Harkness, 'Mr. de Valera's Dominion: Irish Relations with Britain and the Commonwealth 1932-1938', *Journal of Commonwealth Political Studies*, VIII, 3 (1970), 206-28.
19. MacDonald played an important role at a critical stage in Anglo-Irish relations. This period has been examined in detail in a valuable but as yet unpublished thesis: see Deirdre McMahon, 'Malcolm MacDonald and Anglo-Irish Relations 1935-8', M.A. Thesis, University College, Dublin, 1975.
20. See below, p. 106.
21. See below, pp. 88, 107, 136-37.
    A general account of the negotiations is in Longford and O'Neill, op. cit., chapter 26, though this is open to criticism: see McMahon, op. cit., p. 284.
22. The policy of neutrality was also seen as desirable for other reasons: see below, chapters 5 and 6.
23. See John W. Spanier, *Games Nations Play* (London: Nelson, 1972), pp. 226-28.
24. See above, pp. 39, 56-57.
25. Dáil Debates: 21,1455 (16 November 1927).
26. The final compromise was 'United Kingdom Representative to Eire.' See Longford and O'Neill, op. cit., pp. 350-51. Throughout this period there had been an Irish high commissioner in London.
27. These are examined below, pp. 88-89.
28. See Joseph T. Carroll, *Ireland in the War Years* (Newton Abbot; David and Charles, 1975), p. 13.
29. ibid., pp. 101-07. For a detailed study of Irish-American relations during the war, see T. Ryle Dwyer, *Irish Neutrality and the USA 1939-47* (Dublin: Gill and Macmillan, 1977). One of the major themes of this work is summarised in T. Ryle Dwyer, 'American efforts to discredit de Valera during World War II', *Eire-Ireland*, VIII, 2 (Summer 1973), 20-33.
30. For detailed accounts of the American note affair, see Carroll, op. cit., chapters 8 and 9, and Dwyer, *Irish Neutrality and the USA 1939-47*, chapters 9 and 10.

31. See below, p. 112.
32. See Lyons, op. cit., pp. 563-70. In the long term, however, this policy may have had an adverse effect on partition. See below, pp. 112-13.
33. The Irish government had not participated in the Imperial conference of 1937, ostensibly because of the pressure of the Irish electoral campaign.
34. See below, pp. 109-12.
35. See Carroll, op. cit., pp. 163-66.
36. Dáil Debates: 77,592 (29 September 1939).
37. Policy-makers' assumptions about public attitudes towards Britain have generally been impressionistic and subjective. There are, however, some recent scientific findings. See Paul A. Pfretzschner and Donald M. Borock, 'Political Socialistation of the Irish Secondary School Student' in John Raven *et al., Political Culture in Ireland: The Views of Two Generations* (Dublin: Institute of Public Administration, 1976), pp. 110-15; and, for evidence of 'post-colonial attitudinal schizophrenia', see Michael MacGréil, *Prejudice and Tolerance in Ireland* (Dublin: College of Industrial Relations, 1977), pp. 362-75.
38. For details of Irish diplomatic representation up to 1973, see Keatinge, *The Formulation of Irish Foreign Policy,* pp. 110-15 and 121-24. More recent developments are described below, pp. 212-13.
39. Expenditure on this type of activity may also be justified on the grounds that the state should act as a patron of the cultural activities of its citizens; nevertheless, in the external context it is often as much a matter of promoting the national identity as the work of the individual artist.
40. See Patrick Keatinge, 'Ireland and the League of Nations', *Studies,* LIX, 234 (Summer 1970) 133-47.
41. See below, pp. 176-77.
42. Dáil Debates: 101,2448 (26 June 1946).
43. Dáil Debates: 159,143 (3 July 1956).
44. Keatinge, *The Formulation of Irish Foreign Policy,* pp. 32-34.
45. See Marshall R. Singer, *Weak States in a World of Powers* (New York: Free Press, 1972), p. 327.
46. Lester subsequently became the League's high commissioner for Danzig in 1934, Deputy Secretary General in 1937 and Acting Secretary General from 1940 to 1946. There is a detailed account of his career by Stephen Barcroft, 'The International Civil Servant: the League of Nations career of Seán Lester 1929-1946', unpublished PhD Thesis, Trinity College Dublin, 1972.
47. See also Brian Hillery and Patrick Lynch, *Ireland in the International Labour Organisation* (Dublin: Department of Labour, 1969) for details of Irish office-holding in the ILO.
48. See 'Irish Foreign Policy within the Context of the EEC: Text of Address by The Minister for Foreign Affairs, Dr Garret FitzGerald TD, to the Royal Irish Academy, 10th November 1975' (Dublin: Department of Foreign Affairs, n.d.).

49. Michael O'Kennedy in the Dáil, 27 November 1975. Dáil Debates: 286,364.
50. See Patrick Keatinge, 'Odd Man Out? Irish Neutrality and European Security', *International Affairs*, XLVIII, 3 (July 1972), 438-49.
51. For the ways in which modernisation has transformed foreign policy, see Edward L. Morse, *Foreign Policy and Interdependence in Gaullist France* (Princeton: Princeton University Press, 1973), chapter 1.
52. See FitzGerald, 'Irish Foreign Policy within the Context of the EEC', pp. 7-13.
53. ibid.
54. William Wallace and David Allen, 'Political Cooperation: Procedure as Substitute for Policy?' in William Wallace, Helen Wallace and Carole Webb, *Policy-making in the European Communities* (New York: Wiley, 1977), p. 243. The implications of the political co-operation procedures are examined below, pp. 165-169, 175, 189-90.

Chapter 5

1. This is reflected in the paucity of published material on Irish defence policy, outside the period of World War II. In attempting to provide a summary of defence policy, I have been assisted by H. M. Shehab, 'Irish Defence Policy 1922-1950', unpublished MLitt thesis, Trinity College Dublin, 1975, and for the period up to 1936 an unpublished paper by Nigel Cox on 'The Irish Free State, the League of Nations and Collective Security 1923-1936.'
2. See above, pp. 56-57.
3. Article 7 of the 1921 Treaty.
4. Article 6 of the 1921 Treaty. This article by implication precluded the construction of Irish naval vessels for any purpose beyond customs duties or fishery protection.
5. Article 8 of the 1921 Treaty. This was placed in the context of 'the principle of international limitation of armaments.'
6. For Document 2 see *Dáil Eireann: Private Sessions of Second Dáil, Appendix 18*, pp. 321-24.
7. *Dáil Eireann. Official Report: Debate on the Treaty between Great Britain and Ireland signed in London on 6 December 1921* (Dublin: 1922), pp. 37-38.
8. Macardle, *The Irish Republic*, pp. 892-93.
9. Jones, *Whitehall Diary*, p. 213.
10. This is to be found in a schedule entitled 'Defence policy', attached to the minutes of the cabinet meeting of 13 November 1925 (Cabinet, 2/225). Quotations relating to the 1925 defence policy are taken from this document.
11. For a history of the IRA see J. Bowyer Bell, *The Secret Army* (London: Anthony Blond, 1970).

12. Particularly the claim to revision of the boundary with Northern Ireland. See below, pp. 104-05.
13. W. T. Cosgrave later claimed that the major obstacle was the Irish inability to pay for the maintenance of the facilities, though this claim was denied by the de Valera government. See McMahon, op. cit., pp. 196-97. Irish intentions may be seen in 'Coastal defence — preliminary technical discussions with Admiralty representatives. Instructions to Irish representatives.' Schedule attached to the cabinet minutes of 22 April 1927 (Cabinet, 2/333).
14. Dáil Debates: 18,399 (8 February 1927).
15. Patrick McGilligan, then Minister for Industry and Commerce. See Dáil Debates: 18,671 (17 February 1927). For Irish attitudes to the League as a contribution to international order, see below, pp. 153-58.
16. Major Bryan Cooper: see Dáil Debates: 18,668 (17 February 1927).
17. Dáil Debates: 18,640 (17 February 1927).
18. Dáil Debates: 18,640-45 (17 February 1927). The defence document of 1925 was also ambiguous about neutrality, referring to it only in the context of co-operation with British forces 'in the defence of the Saorstát territory whether against actual hostilities or against violation of neutrality on the part of a common enemy.'
19. Dáil Debates: 18,656-57 (17 February 1927).
20. Dáil Debates; 21,1455 (16 November 1927).
21. Dáil Debates; 21,1456 (16 November 1927).
22. De Valera in the Dáil: see Dáil Debates: 50,1148 (7 February 1934).
23. Dáil Debates: 50,1136 (7 February 1934).
24. See Carroll, *Ireland in the War Years,* p. 67.
25. *The Irish Times,* 7 October 1935.
26. Cabinet minutes of 20 August 1935 (Cabinet, 7/252) and 22 October 1935 (Cabinet, 7/265).
27. Cited in Carroll, op. cit., p. 29.
28. Dáil Debates: 62,2660.
29. See above, p. 69.
30. McMahon, op. cit., pp. 96-97. The possibility of obtaining defence co-operation in exchange for some concession on partition was to be a recurrent feature of British, if not Irish, policy. See below, pp. 109-12.
31. The 1938 negotiations are summarised in Longford and O'Neill, op. cit., chapter 26. But McMahon, op. cit., offers a more detailed account.
32. McMahon, op. cit., pp. 221-25. Also, see below, pp. 107-09.
33. See Kevin B. Nowlan, 'On the Eve of the War' in Kevin B. Nowlan and T. Desmond Williams (eds.), *Ireland in the War Years and After 1939-1951* (Dublin: Gill and Macmillan, 1969), pp. 1-13.
34. Carroll, op. cit., p. 12.
35. See Carroll, op. cit., *passim*; Longford and O'Neill, op. cit., chapters 28-31; Nicholas Mansergh, *Survey of British Commonwealth Affairs: Problems of Wartime Co-operation and Post-War Change, 1939-1952* (London: Oxford University Press, 1958), chapter 6, and T. Desmond Williams, 'A Study of Neutrality', *The Leader,* January-April, 1953.
36. See below, p. 110.

37. Lord Cranborne, Secretary of State for the Dominions, 19 March 1941. Cited in Carroll, op. cit., p. 84. For the effect of economic pressure, see below, p. 137.
38. For the 'American note affair' of 1944, see above, pp. 72-73. The connection between neutrality and partition is examined below, pp. 109-12.
39. Carroll, op. cit., pp. 61-75. Although he accepted this assessment, Hitler, in a characteristic *non sequitur,* noted that 'the occupation of Ireland might lead to the end of the war.' Having come to this conclusion, he then proceeded to attack the Soviet Union!
40. ibid., pp. 81-82.
41. ibid., pp. 124-25.
42. Dwyer, *Irish Neutrality and the USA,* p. 174.
43. Carroll, op. cit., p. 53 and G. A. Hayes-McCoy, 'Irish Defence Policy, 1938-51' in Nowlan and Williams (eds.), op. cit., p. 40.
44. Carroll, op. cit., p. 117.
45. ibid., p. 30 and p. 37.
46. ibid., pp. 115-16.
47. ibid., p. 13.
48. For Anglo-Irish military co-operation, see ibid., pp. 41-44, 96-99, 117-18.
49. ibid., p. 109.
50. See Dr Thomas F. O'Higgins in the Dáil, Dáil Debates: 97,1450 (21 June 1945).
51. Dáil Debates: 99,2181 (7 March 1946).
52. Dáil Debates: 104,442 and 557-58 (28 and 29 January 1947).
53. See Cruise O'Brien in Edwards, op. cit., pp. 123-26. Also see below, p. 112.
54. Dáil Debates: 114,323-26 (23 February 1949).
55. Cruise O'Brien in Edwards, op. cit., p. 123 and p. 127.
56. Carroll, op. cit., p. 178.
57. Dáil Debates: 94,1448 (28 June 1944).
58. For a detailed analysis of the Irish army at this time, see John A. Jackson, 'The Irish Army and the development of the Constabulary Concept,' in Jacques van Doorn (ed.) *Armed Forces and Society* (The Hague: Mouton, 1968), pp. 109-26. For the army's participation in UN peace-keeping, see below, pp. 158-61.
59. For the 1969 crisis see below, pp. 115-16.
60. During the trials in September and October 1970, the Minister, James Gibbons, persistently referred to the unpreparedness of the army in 1969.
61. This idea was mooted in very general terms by the then opposition leader, Liam Cosgrave, and favourably received by the Minister for Defence, Jerry Cronin. It was seen as distinct from the traditional *bête noire* of conscription. See Dáil Debates: 258,676-77 and 847-48 (27 January and 3 February 1972).
62. See the articles by Basil Petersen and John Horgan in *The Irish Times,* 9 February 1972 and Joe McAnthony's article in *This Week,* Vol. 2, No. 51, 15 October 1971.
63. *The Irish Times,* 25 September 1974. For the Sunningdale agreement,

see below, pp. 120-21.
64. For this debate, see Dáil Debates: 193,1315-24.
65. Interview in *The Irish Press*, 2 December 1970.
66. In an open letter to *The Irish Times*, 19 September 1970.
67. Leon N. Lindberg and Stewart A. Scheingold, *Europe's Would-be Polity* (Englewood Cliffs: Prentice-Hall, 1970), p. 36, note 17.
68. The significance of European Community political consultations is examined below, pp. 165-169, 175, 189-90.
69. This attitude was reflected in an article FitzGerald wrote two months before he became Minister. See *The Irish Times*, 13 January 1973. For neutrality and international order, see below, pp. 166, 168-69.
70. Dáil Debates: 265,744 (9 May 1973).
71. *The Irish Times*, 3 July 1975.
72. See *The Irish Times*, 29 January 1977, for a report on a discussion paper issued by the Irish Council of the European Movement: and see *The Irish Times*, 9 May 1977, for the response of the anti-EEC group, the Irish Sovereignty Movement.
73. *The Future of Northern Ireland: a paper for discussion* (October 1972) London, H.M.S.O. 1972, p. 32.
74. 'Not for the first time in our history Ireland represents a potential Achilles heel of British defence', warned a pamphlet published by the right-wing Conservative ginger group, the Monday Club, in 1974. This theme had previously been pursued in another pamphlet entitled 'Ireland — Our Cuba?', published in 1970; one of the authors, John Biggs Davison, MP, has since re-iterated its conclusions: see *The Irish Times*, 19 May 1976.
75. See *The Military Balance 1977-1978* (London: The International Institute for Strategic Studies, 1977), p. 82.
76. Adam Roberts, *Nations in Arms: The Theory and Practice of Territorial Defence* (London: Chatto and Windus, 1976), p. 7.
77. See below, pp. 145-46.
78. I am grateful to David Greenwood of the University of Aberdeen for pointing out the security implications of Ireland's coastal interests. In the Autumn of 1977 the Irish government was hoping to obtain 75 per cent of increased expenditure on national fishery protection from the European Community.
79. Dáil Debates: 19,1345 (21 April 1927).

Chapter 6

1. Basil Chubb, *A Source Book of Irish Government* (Dublin: Institute of Public Administration, 1964), p. 215 and p. 222.
2. See above, pp. 40-41.
3. De Valera, quoted in a recent statement of the traditional nationalists' position: Kevin Boland, *'We won't stand (idly) by'* (Dublin: Kelly Kane, n.d.), p. 6. See also Boland's emphasis on the reunification of 'the National Territory' on p. 14.

4. *Bunreacht na hEireann,* Article 2.
5. Kenneth R. Minogue, *Nationalism* (London: Methuen, 1967), p. 64. Where convenience does *not* suggest its use it may be seen as 'the salt-water fallacy'.
6. Boland, op. cit., p. 9. To talk of 'two nations' is still considered a major political heresy. The permissible terms are 'communities' or 'traditions'.
7. Cruise O'Brien, *States of Ireland,* p. 185.
8. Dennis Kennedy, *The Irish Times,* 1 March 1972.
9. O'Farrell, *England and Ireland since 1800,* pp. 43-46.
10. Boland, op. cit., pp. 89-90.
11. Minutes of the Provisional Government, 20 January and 23 January 1922 (Government, 1/1).
12. From Article 12 of the 1921 Treaty, cited in Longford, op. cit., p. 290.
13. Lee, *The Modernisation of Irish Society,* p. 135.
14. The best account is Geoffrey J. Hand, 'MacNeill and the Boundary Commission' in Martin and Byrne, op. cit., pp. 201-75. See also Professor Hand's introduction to *Report of the Irish Boundary Commission 1925.* (Shannon: Irish University Press, 1969), pp. vii-xxii.
15. The phrase was used in the 1925 Agreement. See John Magee, *Northern Ireland: Crisis and Conflict* (London: Routledge and Kegan Paul, 1974), p. 91.
16. Eoin MacNeill, who had served on Irish delegations at Geneva, claimed he recommended taking the partition issue to the League, but to no ⁻ˑ³ avail. See Martin and Byrne, op. cit., pp. 272-73.
17. Dáil Debates: 46,192.
18. De Valera publicly renounced force before coming to office: see *The Irish Independent,* 28 October 1931. This was in line with his earlier renunciation of force on 22 August 1921: see *Private Sessions of Second Dáil: Minutes of Proceedings 18 August 1921 to 14 September 1921 and Report of Debates 14 December 1921 to 6 January 1922,* p. 29.
19. The northern government countered this ploy in 1934 by outlawing the nominations of declared abstentionists.
20. Harkness, 'Mr. de Valera's Dominion', p. 208.
21. Longford and O'Neill, *Eamon de Valera,* p. 310.
22. *Bunreacht na hEireann,* Articles 2 and 3.
23. Hoffman, *The State of War,* p. 132.
24. McMahon, 'Malcolm MacDonald and Anglo-Irish Relations, p. 99.
25. See Longford and O'Neill, op. cit., chapter 26, and McMahon, op. cit., *passim.*
26. McMahon, op. cit., pp. 175-76. There was a difficulty in dealing with this aspect of partition; it was sometimes felt that to emphasise it was to imply an acceptance of Britain's right to redress grievances (rather than her duty to do so), and this contradicted the claim to unity as of right. See Cruise O'Brien, *States of Ireland,* p. 139.
27. McMahon, op. cit., pp. 203-04.
28. ibid., p. 209.

29. ibid., pp. 220-30. The north-south civil servant contacts were also discontinued.
30. ibid., p. 148.
31. It seems not to have been universally shared in de Valera's cabinet; his Minister for Finance, Seán MacEntee, himself a northerner, thought that northern nationalists were 'impossible'. See ibid., p. 148.
32. Longford and O'Neill, op. cit., p. 310.
33. The phrase 'sore thumb' is generally associated with the anti-partition propaganda of the late nineteen-forties and early fifties. See Brian Inglis, *West Briton* (London: Faber, 1962), pp. 135-43.
34. The first example is taken from a speech de Valera made in the League of Nations Assembly on 21 September 1934; see Eamon de Valera, *Peace and War* (Dublin: Gill, 1944), p. 28. It contains a very brief reference to partition in Ireland. In September 1937 de Valera opposed the idea of partitioning Palestine, an intervention which the British saw as being mischievous: see McMahon, op. cit., p. 101.
35. Dwyer, *Irish Neutrality and the USA*, p. 12.
36. Reproduced in *The Irish Press*, 18 October 1938. For a full account see Denis Gwynn, *The History of Partition 1912-1925* (Dublin: Browne and Nolan, 1950), pp. 18-21.
37. Frank Gallagher, *The Indivisible Island* (London: Victor Gollancz, 1957), p. 305. Before this the idea of federalism had generally been neglected by Irish nationalists: see Mansergh, *The Irish Question*, pp. 323-24.
38. Dwyer, op. cit., p. 14.
39. Gwynn, op. cit., p. 30.
40. Some members of the Irish government and of the Department of External Affairs also saw de Valera's emphasis on propaganda as being counter-productive; see McMahon, op. cit., p. 230.
41. For the 1939 IRA campaign see Bell, *The Secret Army*, chapter 8.
42. Longford and O'Neill, op. cit., p. 353.
43. The best account is Carroll, *Ireland in the War Years*, chapter 3. See also Longford and O'Neill, op. cit., pp. 364-68.
44. See above, pp. 43-45.
45. Carroll, op. cit., p. 62. This tentative German approach in June 1940 is described on pp. 62-66.
46. The telegram ran as follows: 'Now is your chance. Now or never. "A Nation once again". Am very ready to meet you at any time.' See ibid., pp. 111-13.
47. Lyons, *Ireland Since the Famine*, p. 730.
48. Dwyer, op. cit., pp. 76-77.
49. For example, in November 1940 and March 1941: see ibid., pp. 89-90 and 109-11.
50. This point is developed by Cruise O'Brien in O. Dudley Edwards (ed.), *Conor Cruise O'Brien introduces Ireland*, pp. 118-27.
51. See above, pp. 72-73. The most detailed analysis of American policy is Dwyer, op. cit.
52. ibid., pp. 208-09.

53. See the ambiguous reference in Longford and O'iveill, op. cit., p. 430. There is no account of immediate post-war inter-governmental exchanges on partition, though British documents, recently released, may provide the basis for one: see *The Irish Times*, 3 January 1977.

54. See above, p. 92. The extent to which either Fine Gael or its coalition associates thought seriously in terms of a unity-NATO membership bargain is not clear.

55. See above, p. 73.

56. However, this was not a completely watertight pledge as the Westminster parliament could repeal the 1949 Act: see Lyons, op. cit., p. 738.

57. Dáil Debates: 115,813 (10 May 1949).

58. The anti-partition crusade after World War II awaits its historian. The feel of the period is conveyed in an observer's account of the Irish delegation at the Council of Europe in 1950: see Inglis, op. cit., pp. 135-43.

59. Longford and O'Neill, op. cit., pp. 442-43.

60. See Bell, op. cit., chapters 13-16.

61. On both sides the combination of these factors prevented a reconciliatory initiative in the UN which was considered as early as 1960. See Cruise O'Brien, *States of Ireland*, pp. 141-43.

62. From a speech at Tralee in July 1963: see Magee, op. cit., p. 109.

63. Functional co-operation had been by no means unknown before this, but Lemass presented it as an instrument of general reconciliation, rather than a series of *ad hoc* measures.

64. *Report of the Committee on the Constitution* (Dublin: Stationery Office, 1967, Pr. 9817), pp. 5-6.

65. For Boland's attempts to undermine constitutional revision, see Boland, op. cit., chapter 4.

66. A voluminous literature of uneven quality has developed on the Northern Ireland conflict. There is a useful select bibliography in Moody, op. cit. See also the bibliography in John Darby, *Conflict in Northern Ireland: the Development of a Polarised Community* (Dublin: Gill and Macmillan, 1976). The treatment of the Dublin government's role and policy is generally sketchy and unsystematic. However, there is some useful material in R. Ned Lebow's essay in G. Henderson, R. N. Lebow and J. G. Stoessinger, *Divided Nations in a Divided World* (New York: McKay, 1974), chapter 7.

67. This has been described as an expression of religious solidarity rather than nationalist feeling: see O'Farrell, *Ireland's English Question*, pp. 306-07.

68. 13 August 1969. See John Lynch, *Speeches and Statements on Irish Unity, Northern Ireland, Anglo-Irish Relations* (Dublin: Government Information Bureau, 1971), p. 3.

69. ibid., p. 67 (5 August 1971).

70. ibid., p. 13 and p. 75.

71. See Sunday Times Insight Team, *Ulster* (Harmondsworth: Penguin Books, 1972), chapter 11 and Lebow, op. cit., pp. 246-48.

72. Lynch, op. cit., p. 64.
73. The British case was based on Article 2 (7) of the UN Charter, though it is arguable that this does not preclude UN intervention. For a detailed analysis of the legal aspects of the internationalisation of the Northern Ireland conflict, see Roger H. Hull, *The Irish Triangle* (Princeton: Princeton University Press, 1976), pp. 237-55.
74. See Andrew Boyd, *Fifteen Men on a Powder Keg* (London: Methuen 1971), pp. 318-29.
75. Lynch, op. cit., p. 47, in a speech to the Fianna Fáil Ard Fheis (20 February 1971).
76. ibid., pp. 43-44.
77. ibid., p. 53.
78. ibid., p. 69.
79. The theory of international functionalism is usually applied to multi-lateral rather than bilateral situations. On functionalism in the UN, see Inis L. Claude, Jr., *Swords into Plowshares* (London: University of London Press, third edition, 1965), chapter 17: in the regional context, see Reginald J. Harrison, *Europe in Question* (London: Allen & Unwin, 1974), chapter 2.
80. For the exchange of telegrams of 19/20 August 1971, see Lynch, op. cit., pp. 77-81.
81. It seems that the Irish government had great difficulty in interpreting British intentions in the immediate aftermath of Bloody Sunday: see the report of an interview with Dr Hillery, *The Irish Times*, 13 November 1976.
82. See Lebow, op. cit., pp. 248-51 for instances of Irish attempts to internationalise the unity issue between 1969 and 1972.
83. These ideas were expressed in a very general form: see John M. Lynch, 'The Anglo-Irish problem', *Foreign Affairs*, 50, 4, July 1972, 601-17.
84. *The Future of Northern Ireland: a paper for discussion* (October 1972), H.M.S.O., London, 1972. See also 'The Irish Dimension', a special edition of *Administration*, 20, 4, Winter 1972.
85. *The Irish Times*, 17 March 1973. As early as September 1969 Fine Gael accepted that re-unification should depend on a majority vote in Northern Ireland.
86. Both had by this time published books on the northern problem, O'Brien's being regarded as particularly heretical by traditional nationalists. See Garret FitzGerald, *Towards a New Ireland* (London: Charles Knight, 1972) and Cruise O'Brien, *States of Ireland*.
87. For accounts of this conference and its aftermath, see Keith Kyle, 'Sunningdale and after: Britain, Ireland, and Ulster' in *The World Today*, 31, 11, November 1975, 439-50; and Rumpf and Hepburn, *Nationalism and Socialism in Twentieth-century Ireland*, pp. 208-18.
88. Clause 5 of the Sunningdale Communiqué, reproduced in Moody, op. cit., Appendix C, pp. 106-11.
89. The implications of the 'majority consent doctrine' are examined in Paul F. Power, 'Violence, Consent and the Northern Ireland Problem', *The Journal of Commonwealth and Comparative Politics*, XIV, 2, July

1976, esp. 130-35. The author concludes that the commitment to achieving a united Ireland has been 'severely diminished'.

90. For an account of the strike, see Robert Fisk, *The Point of No Return* (London: Deutsch, 1975).

91. John McClusker, MP, on the 4 July 1974, quoted in Kyle, op. cit., p. 443. For criticisms of the implementation of the Sunningdale agreement, see Donal Barrington, 'After Sunningdale', *Administration*, 24, 2, Summer 1976, 235-60.

92. For an examination of these possibilities, see Richard Rose, *Northern Ireland: a Time of Choice* (London: Macmillan, 1976) chapter 7.

93. See above, pp. 93-94.

94. In the three and a half years from 1 January 1973 to 12 May 1976 304 incursions by the British Army were reported to the Department of Foreign Affairs. 261 of these cases were taken up with the British, who expressed regret for 144; 19 were still under discussion, while there was disagreement about the facts in the remaining 117 cases. There were 22 Irish Army incursions into Northern Ireland during the same period. See Dáil Debates: 290,1323-33 (13 May 1976).

95. For an examination of some of the legal issues, see Hull, op. cit., esp. chapters 5 and 6.

96. See O'Brien's assessment, leaked to *The Irish Times*, 25 September 1974.

97. See the statement by the Minister for Defence, Patrick Donegan: *The Irish Press*, 11 September 1975.

98. The legal validity of Articles 2 and 3 is questioned in Hull, op. cit., chapter 3. The importance of the constitutional claim as a bargaining counter is also a controversial matter: see the exchange between John Hume of the SDLP and Conor Cruise O'Brien in *The Irish Times*, 28 January and 31 January 1977.

99. See *The Irish Times*, 28, 29 January 1977.

100. *The Irish Times*, 30 October 1975.

101. For Mr Lynch's views, see Dáil Debates: 300,226-27 (12 October 1977). There is a useful detailed analysis of Irish élite opinion in Al S. Cohan, 'The Question of a United Ireland', *International Affairs*, 53, 2, April 1977, 232-54.

102. According to a government estimate, from £500 million to £600 million between 1969 and 1975: see *The Irish Times*, 26 February 1976.

103. MacGréil, op. cit., esp. pp. 380-92. See also Pfretschner and Borock's study of school children's attitudes during a traumatic period in the northern conflict (1971-1972): Pfretschner *et al*, op. cit., pp. 112-13; and the more recent survey in *Magill*, October 1977.

104. MacGréil, op. cit., p. 384.

105. See Cohan, op. cit., p. 248; and MacGréil, op. cit., p. 452.

106. *The Irish Times*, 26 November 1974.

107. Loyalists have expressed reservations about the cross-border projects, ostensibly on the grounds that the 'people of Northern Ireland' ought to be consulted: see *The Irish Times*, 11 June 1976. The Irish government renewed its attempts to develop cross-border co-operation when

Mr Lynch met the British prime minister, Jim Callaghan, in September 1977: see *The Irish Times,* 29 September 1977.
108. Claude, op. cit., p. 367.
109. For Irish-American influence since 1922, and especially since 1969, see Lawrence J. McCaffrey, *The Irish Diaspora in America* (Bloomington: Indiana University Press, 1976), chapter 9.
110. Power, op. cit., p. 123.
111. This statement is reproduced in *The Irish Times,* 31 August 1977. For the Irish government its principal merit lay in its recognition that Dublin had a role to play, a point which is sometimes accepted with reluctance in London.
112. See Hull, op. cit., 255 and 265-71.

Chapter 7

1. Marxist writers of course stress the economic content of foreign policy almost to the exclusion of any other factor. Among non-Marxist writers recognition of the importance of economic foreign policy has not been helped by an increasing academic division of labour. For example, Conor Cruise O'Brien in his classical essay on 'Ireland in International Affairs' in O. Dudley Edwards (ed.), op. cit., ignores the economic aspect (which is included in a general survey of Irish economic developments in Patrick Lynch, 'The Economic Scene', ibid., pp. 71-82). International relations literature in general reflects this academic exclusivism: see Geoffrey Goodwin, 'Economics and International Politics' in Brian Porter (ed.), *International Politics 1919-1969* (London: Oxford University Press, 1972), chapter 11.
2. Arnold Wolfers, *Discord and Collaboration* (Baltimore: Johns Hopkins, 1962), p. 77.
3. See Tom Wilson, 'Economic Sovereignty' in John Vaizey (ed.), *Economic Sovereignty and Regional Policy* (Dublin: Gill and Macmillan, 1975), p. 8.
4. Alan A. Tait and John A. Bristow (eds.), *Ireland: Some Problems of a Developing Economy* (Dublin: Gill and Macmillan, 1972), p. vii.
5. James Meenan, *The Irish Economy since 1922* (Liverpool: Liverpool University Press, 1970), p. 280.
6. Kieran A. Kennedy and Brendan R. Dowling, *Economic Growth in Ireland: The Experience since 1947* (Dublin: Gill and Macmillan, 1975), p. 284.
7. See David Law, 'The Economic Problems of Ireland, Scotland and Wales' in Vaizey (ed.), op. cit., pp. 238-39.
8. Dermot McAleese, 'The Foreign Sector' in Norman J. Gibson and John E. Spencer (eds.), *Economic Activity in Ireland* (Dublin: Gill and Macmillan, 1977), pp. 115-16.

9. 'Openness' is used here to refer to 'the relative importance of commodity and financial flows across national boundaries to those occurring domestically': see T. K. Whitaker, 'Monetary Integration: Reflections on Irish Experience, *Quarterly Bulletin, Central Bank of Ireland,* Winter 1973, p. 68.
10. ibid., p. 69.
11. Comparative figures for the trade dependence of most existing states are in Singer, *Weak States in a World of Power,* pp. 229-47.
12. Anglo-Irish relations are in these respects comparable to those between the United States and Canada. See John Vaizey, 'First Choose your Theory' in Vaizey (ed.), op. cit., pp. 33-42, for a survey of the 'considerable degree of inter-penetration between the economies.'
13. For the *economic* costs of independence, see Law in Vaizey (ed.), op. cit., who argues that the problems Ireland shares with other peripheral regions in the British Isles 'have been aggravated by its independent status.' (p. 254). See also Dermot McAleese, 'Political Independence and Economic Performance – Ireland outside the United Kingdom' in E. T. Nevin (ed.), *The Economics of Devolution* (Birmingham: University of Aston Press, 1978).
14. See Law in Vaizey (ed.), op. cit., p. 247.
15. MacDonagh, op. cit., p. 125. For the problems of Irish agriculture at this time see Lyons, *Ireland Since the Famine,* pp. 602-06. A more detailed survey is in Raymond D. Crotty, *Irish Agricultural Production: its Volume and Structure* (Cork: University Press, Cork, 1966), chapter 5.
16. Lynch in O. Dudley Edwards (ed.), op. cit., p. 72.
17. See Fanning, *The Irish Department of Finance,* pp. 129-31.
18. T. K. Whitaker, 'From Protection to Free Trade – The Irish Experience' in *Administration,* 21, 4, Winter 1973, 407. See also T. K. Daniel, 'Griffith on his Noble Head: The Determinants of Cumann na nGaedheal Economic Policy, 1922-32', *Irish Economic and Social History,* III, 1976, 55-65. Rumpf and Hepburn, *Nationalism and Socialism,* pp. 24-25, maintain that the urge to acquire a 'respectable' image internationally can also be seen in the years prior to independence.
19. Whitaker 'From Protection to Free Trade', p. 411. For the application of selective protection, see Meenan, op. cit., pp. 139-41, and Fanning, op. cit., pp. 202-06.
20. For monetary policy, see Whitaker, 'Monetary Integration: Reflections on Irish Experience', *Quarterly Bulletin,* Winter 1973, 65-66; and Maurice Moynihan, *Currency and Central Banking in Ireland 1922-1960* (Dublin: Gill and Macmillan, 1975).
21. Wilson in Vaizey (ed.), op. cit., p. 13. For the rare occasions when exchange rate policy was reconsidered, see Moynihan, op. cit., chapters 8, 9 and 16.
22. In practice it was not altogether unambiguous, as, for example, in the case of Fianna Fáil attitudes towards the possible protection of a large *foreign-owned* firm, the Ford Motor Company in Cork. I am grateful to David Jacobson, who is writing a thesis on Ford's activities in Ireland, for bringing this point to my attention.

23. Longford and O'Neill, *Eamon de Valera*, p. 267.
24. Cited in Meenan, op. cit., p. 320.
25. See the remarks of one of his principal lieutenants, Seán Lemass, quoted at the beginning of this chapter.
26. See Kennedy and Dowling, op. cit., p. 332.
27. Meenan, op. cit., p. 142. See Fanning, op. cit., pp. 206-15 for the Irish government's response to the Depression.
28. See above, p. 68.
29. For a concise account of 'the economic war' see Lyons, op. cit., pp. 611-14.
30. Rumpf and Hepburn, op. cit., pp. 114-19, see the economic war as an inherent part of the strategy of self-sufficiency. Although tariffs would undoubtedly have been raised even had there been no dispute over annuities, it does not follow that this would have taken the form, or reached the extent, which occurred in the economic war.
31. For the concept of counter-dependence see Singer, op. cit., pp. 42-43.
32. Whitaker, 'From Protection to Free Trade', p. 409. Seán Lemass, as Minister for Industry and Commerce, overrode his departmental head's reservations on political grounds. For the politicisation of Anglo-Irish financial relations, see Fanning, op. cit., chapter 7.
33. Minutes of the cabinet meeting of 18 March 1932 (Cabinet, 6/5).
34. There is a concise assessment in Lyons, op. cit., pp. 619-22.
35. ibid., p. 620.
36. See McMahon, 'Malcolm MacDonald and Anglo-Irish Relations', pp. 94-95.
37. Keynes had caused a stir in Dublin in 1932 with his 'support' for self-sufficiency; his audience may have overlooked his reservations concerning the size of the Irish economy and its lack of natural resources. See Whitaker, 'From Protection to Free Trade', pp. 408-09.
38. For the Irish economy during World War II, see Lyons, op. cit., pp. 622-24 and Carroll, *Ireland in the War Years*, pp. 87-91.
39. Carroll, op. cit., p. 84. Details of British economic pressure are to be found in ibid., chapter 5.
40. McAleese in Gibson and Spencer (eds.), op. cit., p. 140.
41. Kennedy and Dowling, op. cit., pp. 81-82.
42. The phrase is from Dermot McAleese, 'Outward-looking policies, export performance and economic growth: the Irish experience' in Michael J. Artis and Alexander Nobay (eds.), *Essays in Economic Analysis* (London: Blackwell, forthcoming).
43. A major source for the post-war period is Kennedy and Dowling, op. cit., *passim*.
44. The claim has been made by Alan Matthews, 'Irish planning began with Marshall Aid', *The Irish Times*, 28 June 1973, and John A. Murphy, *Ireland in the Twentieth Century* (Dublin: Gill and Macmillan, 1975), pp. 123-24. It is questioned in Fanning, op. cit., pp. 405-06.
45. For details of the negotiations and implementation of Marshall Aid, see Fanning, op. cit., pp. 411-42.
46. ibid., pp. 386-91. Ireland did not join the IMF until 1957.
47. For the debate on the sterling crisis of 1949, see ibid., pp. 442-56.

48. Basil Chubb and Patrick Lynch, *Economic Development and Planning* (Dublin: Institute of Public Administration, 1969), p. 1.
49. Rumpf and Hepburn, op. cit., p. 119.
50. Kennedy and Dowling, op. cit., pp. 251-54.
51. For Lemass's own conversion, see Whitaker, 'From Protection to Free Trade', esp. pp. 413-19. See also Joseph Lee, 'Lemass and his two partnerships', *The Irish Times* (Supplement), 19 May 1976.
52. For the official judgement on protection see the *Programme for Economic Expansion*, November 1958 (Pr. 4796), pp. 37-38.
53. One of the latter, Kevin Boland (then Minister for Defence), subsequently claimed that Lemass's *volte face*, which he blamed on the civil service, was his first disillusionment with the Fianna Fáil party: see Boland, op. cit., pp. 26-28.
54. It was then (1957-8) that Ireland became institutionally integrated in the world economic system: see Fanning, op. cit., pp. 516-18.
55. For a concise account of these developments, see ibid., pp. 606-11.
56. See Dermot McAleese, 'Capital Inflow and Direct Foreign Investment in Ireland 1952 to 1970', *Journal of the Statistical and Social Inquiry Society of Ireland*, XXII, Part IV, 1971-72, 63-105.
57. The first World Bank loans were in 1969: see Fanning, op. cit., pp. 614-15.
58. McAleese, 'Capital Inflow and Direct Foreign Investment in Ireland', Table 5, p. 78.
59. Kennedy and Dowling, op. cit., p. 7.
60. For the period 1968-1972, see ibid., chapter 17.
61. ibid., pp. 275-77.
62. For a contemporary assessment see Dermot McAleese and John Martin, 'Ireland's Manufactured Exports to the EEC and the Common External Tariff', *Economic and Social Review*, 3, 4, July 1972, 615-31. McAleese's analysis of the prospects is further developed in 'Ireland in the Enlarged EEC: Economic Consequences and Prospects" in Vaizey (ed.), op. cit., pp. 133-62.
63. The anti-market case is contained in Anthony Coughlan, *The Common Market: Why Ireland should not join!* (Dublin: Common Market Study Group, 1970), Raymond Crotty, *Ireland and the Common Market: an Economic Analysis of the Effects of Membership* (Dublin: Common Market Study Group, 1971), and Raymond Crotty, *Irish Agriculture and the Common Market* (Dublin: Common Market Study group, n.d.).
64. See Keatinge, *The Formulation of Irish Foreign Policy*, pp. 288-91.
65. McAleese in Vaizey (ed.), op. cit., p. 149.
66. McAleese in Gibson and Spencer (eds.), op. cit., p. 144. For an assessment of the early years of EEC membership, see E. Moxon Browne, 'Ireland in the EEC', *The World Today*, 31, 10, October 1975, 424-32.
67. For Irish balance of payments figures since 1959, see McAleese in Gibson and Spencer (eds.), op. cit., p. 132.
68. See Whitaker, 'Monetary Integration: Reflections on Irish Experience', *Quarterly Bulletin*, Winter 1973, and for the debate in 1975, *European Monetary Union and the Sterling Link* (Dublin: Irish Council of the European Movement, 1975).

69. The effects of either a revaluation or devaluation of the Irish pound are problematic: see Kieran Kennedy in *The Irish Times*, 12 July 1977.
70. This is the view of Ciaran O Faircheallaigh in an unpublished thesis on 'The role of foreign investment in the Irish mining industry 1955-75', The Australian National University, Canberra.
71. The Resources Protection Group has succeeded from time to time in raising the issue of foreign ownership, and their attitude is also reflected in the policy of radical political groups.
72. Given the 200 mile economic zone, Ireland would rank as eighth in the world in terms of its ocean-to-land ratio, and ninth in the world in terms of its ocean-to-population ratio. I am grateful to David Greenwood of the University of Aberdeen for these calculations.
73. See above, p. 98.
74. This approach persisted in the negotiations which continued in the Autumn of 1977.
75. By the Autumn of 1977, both governments had agreed to submit the continental shelf issue to arbitration, but had not yet agreed on the form this was to take.
76. See FitzGerald, 'Irish Foreign Policy within the Context of the EEC', pp. 4-5
77. ibid., p. 22.
78. The Irish government has supported the application of Greece to join the Community, but there is undoubtedly concern over the cumulative effects of further enlargement: see *The Irish Times*, 8 and 9 September 1977.
79. See 'The Irish Economy – a New Strategy for Development' (Dublin: Radical Economists Group, 1976), Pamphlet No. 1, p. 12.

Chapter 8

1. The phrase is from Philip A. Reynolds, *An Introduction to International Relations* (London: Longman, 1971), p. 10.
2. Wolfers, *Discord and Collaboration*, pp. 73-74.
3. ibid.
4. Joseph Frankel, *National Interest* (London: Pall Mall, 1970), p. 53.
5. ibid., p. 134.
6. *Bunreacht na hEireann*, Article 29.1. The distinction between possession and milieu goals is also reflected in Irish parliamentary procedures, whereby public funds are formally allocated, and sometimes debated and voted on, separately, for 'External (or since 1971, Foreign) Affairs' on the one hand and 'International Co-operation' on the other.
7. For a discussion of this problem, see Hedley Bull, *The Anarchical Society: A Study of Order in World Politics* (London: Macmillan, 1977), chapter 4.

8.   See below, chapter 9.
9.   Bull, op. cit., p. 8.
10. ibid., p. 67.
11. ibid., pp. 16-20.
12. For a full analysis of order in the contemporary international system, see ibid., chapters 5-9.
13. *Bunreacht na hEireann*, Article 29.1 and 2.
14. See above, pp. 65-66. Another possession goal — unity — has also influenced Ireland's policies in international organisations: see above, chap. 6. On the evolution of Irish attitudes towards the League of Nations, see Keatinge, 'Ireland and the League of Nations'. I have been helped on the question of collective security by Nigel Cox's unpublished paper, 'The Irish Free State, the League of Nations and Collective Security (1923-1936)'.
15. This report, dated 21 October 1926, is in the papers of Desmond Fitzgerald.
16. Dáil Debates: 1,391-92 (18 September 1922).
17. Dáil Debates: 5,423 (31 October 1923).
18. See above, p. 85. Of course Ireland was by no means unique in this attitude towards collective security, an arrangement which was logicially inconsistent and which rested on prerequisites which did not then exist: see Claude, op. cit., chapter 12.
19. The Welsh equivalent had 36,000 members. For details of the Irish League of Nations Society, see its periodical *Concord,* published from 1927.
20. Conor Hogan, TD, Dáil Debates: 16,355-56 (3 June 1926).
21. Dáil Debates: 28,279 (21 February 1929).
22. Dáil Debates: 39,1146-7 and 1275.
23. See Longford and O'Neill, *Eamon de Valera,* pp. 335-37. The speech is to be found in de Valera, *Peace and War,* pp. 5-14.
24. See Barcroft, *The International Civil Servant,* pp. 39-45.
25. ibid., pp. 45-65.
26. ibid., p. 6.
27. Dáil Debates: 56,2230 and 2210 (4 June 1935).
28. See below, pp. 176-77.
29. See his speeches in a broadcast to the USA (12 September 1935) and in the League Assembly (16 September 1935): de Valera, op. cit., pp. 39-48.
30. See *The Irish Times,* 28 September 1935, for a report of a meeting at which one of the speakers was Seán MacBride, later to be Minister for External Affairs (1948-1951) and whose work for the International Commission of Jurists and the United Nations was to win him the Nobel Prize for Peace in 1974.
31. See below, p. 177.
32. For de Valera's attitude as the sanctions policy developed, see his speech in the Dáil on 6 November 1935 (Dáil Debates: 59,482-86 and 533-39).
33. Dáil Debates: 62,2655.

34. See below, pp. 177-78.
35. McMahon, op. cit., p. 211. This paragraph follows Deirdre McMahon's account of Irish policy during the 1938 crisis: see pp. 208-25.
36. Dáil Debates: 62,2655 (18 June 1936).
37. Dáil Debates: 75,1467.
38. In a private conversation with the American representative in Dublin: see Dwyer, *Irish Neutrality and the USA*, pp. 22-23.
39. From 1940 Seán Lester was Acting Secretary-General of the League and the day before it was wound up he was nominated as its third and last Secretary-General; this was the beginning of the precedent, subsequently followed in the United Nations, of selecting Secretaries-General outside the ranks of the great powers. It is not clear whether Lester's position influenced de Valera's support for the moribund League, which after 1940 was little more than a collection of archives and a few disillusioned officials.
40. The definition is from Larry L. Fabian, *Soldiers without Enemies* (Washington D.C.: The Brookings Institution, 1971), p. 16. The assumptions underlying peace-keeping of this sort were subsequently rationalised as the 'theory' of preventive diplomacy. See Claude, *Swords into Plowshares*, chapter 14. For a detailed analysis of UN peace-keeping see Alan James, *The Politics of Peacekeeping* (London: Chatto and Windus, 1969).
41. Fabian, op. cit., p. 88. The term 'middle power' must be used with caution; it can also refer to the capabilities of the state, in which sense Ireland is clearly a small power.
42. ibid., p. 25 and see Appendix B, pp. 266-68.
43. ibid., p. 158. ONUC and UNFICYP refer to the Congo and Cyprus peace-keeping operations respectively.
44. For a detailed analysis of Irish participation in the Congo operation, see Nina Heathcote, 'Ireland and the United Nations Operation in the Congo', *International Relations*, III, 11, May 1971, 880-902.
45. Dr Cruise O'Brien's controversial struggle against great power interests in Katanga is recounted in *To Katanga and Back* (London: Hutchinson, 1962).
46. In military terms the recall may have been counter-productive, since service overseas has proved to be a valuable form of training which does more for the morale of troops than patrolling the border.
47. Fabian, op. cit., p. 160.
48. ibid., p. 161. A by-product of Ireland's position on financing peace-keeping operations has been a refusal to commit permanent 'stand-by forces' to the UN. Fabian argues that this has not reduced their efficiency significantly (p. 130) and that standby forces are in any case likely to be the exception rather than the rule (p. 253).
49. See the selection of speeches entitled *Ireland at the United Nations*, published annually by the Department of Foreign (before 1971, External) Affairs since 1957, for instances of Irish policy on this and other major topics of Irish UN policy.
50. For attitudes to the Congo operation, see Heathcote, op. cit., *passim*.

51. Dáil Debates: 194,1390 (5 April 1962).
52. See Claude, op. cit., chapter 13.
53. *League of Nations Tenth Assembly: Report of the Irish Delegates*, P. No. 146 (Dublin: Stationery Office, 1930), pp. 77-79.
54. Dáil Debates: 39,1270. On 4 May 1931 a cabinet committee was formed to prepare for the following year's conference. It consisted of the President of the Executive Council (William T. Cosgrave), the Vice-President (Ernest Blythe), the Minister for Defence (Desmond FitzGerald) and McGilligan himself: Cabinet, 5/60.
55. Barcroft, op. cit., pp. 22-23.
56. See the detailed account of the Nuclear Proliferation Treaty, Georges Fischer, *The Non-Proliferation of Nuclear Weapons* (London: Europa, 1971). Fischer refers to the 'Irish resolution' on p. 20 but offers no comment on its significance.
57. *Ireland at the United Nations: Text of the Main Speeches 1971* (Dublin: Browne and Nolan, n.d.), p. 57.
58. ibid., p. 70. See also Patrick Keatinge, '[The] Study of International Relations in Ireland', *Leargas: Public Affairs*, 4, 5, January 1972, 5-7.
59. Claude, op. cit., p. 344. Of course, in practice the distinction between 'political' and 'functional' is blurred, and not only for the Marxist; see, for example, the Irish Free State's use of a functional organisation — the International Labour Organisation — to 'assert the political independence of the State': Brian Hillery and Patrick Lynch, *Ireland in the International Labour Organisation* (Dublin: Department of Labour, 1969), p. 20.
60. The phrase is C. K. Webster's, cited by Geoffrey Goodwin in Porter (ed.), *International Politics*, p. 244. For discussion of international functionalism see Claude, op. cit., chapter 17 and Harrison, *Europe in Question*, chapter 2. For the limitations of the functional approach in the context of north-south relations in Ireland, see above, pp. 107, 114, 117-18, 120-21, 124-25.
61. See above, pp. 138-39.
62. The Minister for Foreign Affairs, Dr Hillery, in the Dáil, 18 April 1972 (Dáil Debates: 260,386-87).
63. See below, pp. 187-88.
64. Claude, op. cit., chapter 6.
65. In an address to the Irish United Nations Association, 21 April 1967: *Ireland at the United Nations 1967* (Dublin: Browne and Nolan, n.d.), p. 81.
66. For an analysis of this development see William Wallace and David Allen, 'Political Co-operation: Procedure as Substitute for Policy?' in W. Wallace, C. Webb and H. Wallace (eds.), op. cit.
67. See Brian J. O'Connor, *Ireland and the United Nations* (Dublin: Tuairim Pamphlet, 1961), pp. 9-10.
68. See the Minister for Foreign Affairs, Garret FitzGerald, in the Dáil on 28 June 1975 (Dáil Debates: 266,1401).
69. Wallace and Allen in Wallace *et al* (eds.), op. cit., pp. 241-42.
70. ibid., p. 246, n. 25. For detailed analyses of the voting of the Nine at the UN, see Beate Lindeman, 'Europe and the Third World: the Nine

at the United Nations', *The World Today*, 32, 7, July 1976; and Leon Hurwitz, 'The EEC and Decolonization: the Voting Behaviour of the Nine in the UN General Assembly', *Political Studies*, XXIV, 4, December 1976, 435-47.
71. For a brief examination of the implications of 'positive' neutrality see Patrick Keatinge in *The Irish Times*, 12 July 1972.
72. See Garret FitzGerald in the Dáil. Dáil Debates; 265,744 (9 May 1973).
73. *The Irish Times*, 3 July 1975.
74. Dáil Debates: 265,753 (9 May 1973).
75. FitzGerald, 'Irish Foreign Policy within the Context of the EEC', p. 16.

Chapter 9

1. Bull, *The Anarchical Society*, p. 91.
2. For definitions of the usage of 'justice' in international politics see ibid., esp. pp. 78-86.
3. Desmond FitzGerald, Minister for External Affairs, in the Seanad, 19 April 1923 (Seanad Debates: 1,971). The idea of a national mission in international relations is associated with Mazzini, who dismissed Irish nationality largely because he could not identify a world mission for Ireland! See Mansergh, *The Irish Question*, pp. 95-102.
4. Liam de Paor, 'The GPO Tradition' in *The Irish Times*, 9 March 1976. See also above, chapters 2 and 3.
5. See Herbert Butterfield, 'Morality and an International Order' in Porter (ed.), *International Politics*, p. 348.
6. See above, p. 63.
7. Dáil Debates: 11,1448-49 and 1462 (13 May 1925).
8. For Cosgrave's 'three principles' enunciated in the Dáil on 3 July 1956, see Dáil Debates: 159,138-46.
9. *Ireland at the United Nations 1960* (Dublin: Browne and Nolan, n.d.), p. 13. This speech is also a good example of the emphasis on 'small states'.
10. O'Connor, *Ireland and the United Nations*, pp. 10-11. There are some interesting parallels between the Tibet-China relationship and the Ireland-Britain relationship: see Coral Bell, 'The Foreign Policy of China' in Frederick S. Northedge (ed.), *The Foreign Policies of the Powers* (London: Faber and Faber, 1968), p. 118.
11. See Cruise O'Brien in Edwards, *Conor Cruise O'Brien introduces Ireland*, pp. 127-34.
12. For example, there was opposition on racial grounds to Irish participation in the Congo peace-keeping operation: see Heathcote, 'Ireland and the United Nations Operation in the Congo', pp. 882-83 and 887-88.
13. See the privately published pamphlets by Garreth Byrne, *The Afro-Irish Connection* (1974), and *Sources and Themes for Afro-Irish Studies* (1974).

14. See Kader Asmal, *Irish opposition to Apartheid,* UN Department of Political and Security Council Affairs: Unit on Apartheid, Notes and Documents, no. 3/71, February 1971.
15. ibid., pp. 8-9.
16. Seán F. Lemass, 'Small States in International Organizations' in August Schou and Arne O. Brundtland, *Small States in International Relations* (Uppsala: Almqvist and Wiksell, 1971), p. 118.
17. Dáil Debates: 260,400 (18 April 1972).
18. Dáil Debates: 265,750 (9 May 1973).
19. Dáil Debates: 268,1202 (1 November 1973).
20. Dáil Debates: 294,633-37 (24 November 1976), and *The Irish Times,* 15 November 1976. For the effects of European Community political co-operation, see below, pp. 189-90.
21. See *The Irish Times,* 25, 27 August 1977.
22. For example, policies towards aid-trade relations and human rights, which are examined separately below, pp. 181-88.
23. A notable example in the nineteenth century was its support for the Papal States in 1860: see O'Farrell, *Ireland's English Question,* p. 87.
24. This thesis has been advanced in ibid., see especially pp. 215, 235, 237, 279-81, 296-99.
25. From a Dáil motion on 21 November 1946, condemning religious persecution in central and eastern Europe: see Dáil Debates: 103,1401.
26. See above, pp. 50, 53.
27. See for example, Dáil Debates: 48,2132-46 (11 July 1933) and Dáil Debates: 53,218-26 (13 June 1934).
28. The notion of Ireland 'guaranteeing' the position of the Christian religion in the USSR had been written into the abortive drafty treaty of 1920: see above, p. 50. In 1934 it went a long way to appeasing catholic opinion: see Cruise O'Brien in Edwards (ed.), op. cit., p. 112.
29. For attitudes towards Italy, see ibid., pp. 113-15.
30. The speaker was William Kent. See Dáil Debates: 59,530 (6 November 1935). Mussolini was also referred to by a colleague as 'the Abraham Lincoln of Africa'. In the Seanad a notable advocate of this position was the literary figure, Oliver St. John Gogarty: see Seanad Debates: 20,1119-22 (13 November 1935).
31. See Cruise O'Brien in Edwards (ed.), op. cit., p. 116-17. For a detailed account of this issue, see J. Bowyer Bell, 'Ireland and the Spanish Civil War 1936-1939' in *Studia Hibernica,* 7, 1969.
32. See James Dillon, Dáil Debates: 65,695 (19 February 1937).
33. In a sense catholicism was in conflict with the anti-imperialist tradition in Irish politics: O'Duffy's men were faced in Spain by their countrymen fighting on the Republican side, many of whom were IRA members.
34. Among them was the former Minister for External Affairs, Desmond FitzGerald: see Cruise O'Brien in Edwards (ed.), op. cit., p. 117.
35. Carroll, *Ireland in the War Years,* p. 115.
36. ibid., pp. 93-94 and 136-38.
37. ibid., p. 136.

38. Dáil Debates: 97,2601 (17 July 1945).
39. Deputy Patrick Cogan, Dáil Debates: 102,1336 (24 July 1946). He appears to have been speaking to only 21 deputies, but he was by no means alone in expressing explicitly religious attitudes.
40. Dáil Debates: 103,1322-1402.
41. See above, p. 112.
    A cynic might observe that it was not so much a downgrading of religious values as a choice between a world made safe for Christianity and a piece of Ireland made safe from protestantism. Sectarianism, like charity, begins at home.
42. Dáil Debates: 159,144 (3 July 1956).
43. See for example, Patrick McGilligan, Dáil Debates: 176,605-24 (7 July 1959).
44. Dáil Debates: 260,413 (18 April 1972). The British government also showed uneasiness about the establishment of a Soviet Embassy in Dublin, mainly on security grounds.
45. Bull, op. cit., p. 88.
46. James K. Spicer, *A Samaritan State? External Aid in Canada's Foreign Policy* (Toronto: University of Toronto Press, 1966), p. 11.
47. See below, pp. 185-86. The only economic unit of sufficient size and with sufficient domestic ramifications to influence Irish policy would seem to be the Guinness subsidiary in Nigeria.
48. In other states the missionary tradition is also important (e.g. see Spicer, op. cit., p. 6 for the case of Canada). But in few does it loom so large, alongside economic and political links with Third World countries, as it does in Ireland.
49. See *Development Assistance: Efforts and Policies of the Members of the Development Assistance Committee: 1971 Review* (Paris: OECD, 1971), pp. 144-45, Table 2.
50. See the memorandum on 'Personal Service in Developing Countries', drawn up by representatives of several interested groups and published in *The Irish Times,* 11 September 1971. The figure of 1 per cent for official aid may be inflated. In 1972/73 official aid through multilateral obligations was only 0.035 per cent of GNP: see FitzGerald, 'Irish Foreign Policy within the Context of the EEC', p. 19.
51. *The Irish Times,* 11 September 1971.
52. Dáil Debates: 241,1899 (28 October 1969).
53. See the speech of the Taoiseach, Jack Lynch, on the eve of the 1972 Referendum, *The Irish Press,* 10 May 1972.
54. For the first detailed analysis of Irish aid, see Mary Sutton, *Irish Government Aid to the Third World: Review and Assessment* (Dublin: Trócaire and the Irish Commission for Justice and Peace, 1977). The author is very critical of the government's ambiguity in its statements of aid targets and an apparent diminution of its commitment from 1975 on. Development aid structures and programmes are also reviewed in 'Ireland and the Third World', *The Irish Times (Supplement),* 22 June, 1977.

55. This was obvious as soon as he entered the Dáil in 1969: see Dáil Debates, 241,2172 (29 October 1969) and 242,51-63 (4 November 1969).
56. Speech at Lomé, 28 March 1975.
57. See his speeches at the UN Special Session, 19 April 1974 and 4 September 1975: also his comments on the role of Europe at the Conference on Security and Co-operation in Europe, at Helsinki, 5 July 1973.
58. Links with Zambia started in 1963, and since that time small groups of Zambian administrators were trained at the Institute of Public Administration in Dublin. To a lesser extent, military training was provided by the Irish Army.
59. Gorta, the Irish National Committee of the United Nations Freedom from Hunger Campaign, was set up in 1965. It emphasises self-help projects in the agricultural sector and has close links with the Department of Agriculture and the Irish Farmers' Association. Concern — originally Africa Concern — was established some years later, during the Nigerian civil war. It now stresses disaster relief as a means of creating aid programmes. It is a private, non-denominational organisation.
60. The Irish Commission for Justice and Peace has a promotional and educational role, largely in the field of development aid. It is a major source of policy proposals, and carries out a continuous review of existing policies.
61. In 1977 the latter was re-formed as the Confederation of Non-Governmental Organisations on Overseas Development.
62. APSO's origins lay in the private initiative referred to above, note 50. For details of APSO's operations see *Chairman's Report to the First Annual General Meeting*, 3 July 1975.
63. For the debate on structures, see *APSO: Chairman's Report to the Second Annual General Meeting*, 20 May 1976, pp. 8-10; *APSO: Chairman's Report to the Third Annual General Meeting*, 24 May 1977, pp. 12-15; and the interview with Garret FitzGerald in *The Irish Times (Supplement)*, 22 June 1977.
64. See Louise Leonard, 'The EEC's Trade Relationships with Less-Developed Countries and their Possible Impact on Ireland', minor thesis for M.Econ.Sc. (Joint UCD/TCD course in European Studies), July 1976.
65. For attitudes towards the 1976 UNCTAD Conference, see the debate in the Seanad on 24 June 1976 (Seanad Debates: 84,619-76).
66. The first speaker was Senator Michael D. Higgins (Seanad Debates: 84,674); the second was the Minister for Foreign Affairs, Garret FitzGerald (Seanad Debates: 84,654).
67. The Fianna Fáil party, while in opposition, took the line that aid expenditure should be a subject of bipartisan agreement. Thus the accession of a Fianna Fáil government in 1977 did not see any fundamental change in policy. For the views of the new Minister for Foreign Affairs, Michael O'Kennedy, see *The Irish Times (Supplement)*, 22 June 1977 and *The Irish Times*, 6 September 1977.
68. Bull, op. cit., p. 90.

69. See above, p. 108.
70. This was reflected in the Democratic Programme of the First Dáil in 1919: see Lyons, *Ireland Since the Famine*, p. 402. For Ireland in the ILO, see Hillery and Lynch, *Ireland in the International Labour Organisation*.
71. See above, p. 118. The Lawless case arose out of a challenge that the internment of IRA suspects in 1957 violated Articles 5 and 6 of the European Convention; the European Court of Human Rights delivered judgement in 1961. See John M. Kelly, *Fundamental Rights in the Irish Law and Constitution*, (Dublin; Allen Figgis, second edition, 1967), pp. 85-88; and Arthur H. Robertson, *Human Rights in Europe*, (Manchester: Manchester University Press, second edition, 1977), pp. 51-53, 111-14, 212-21.
72. See *The Irish Times*, 3 September 1976.
73. In an address to the Irish United Nations Association, 24 October 1971: see *The Irish Times*, 25 October 1971.
74. *The Irish Times*, 15 July 1976. An earlier body, with a specific interest in the treatment of political prisoners, is the Irish branch of Amnesty International. In 1977 Amnesty International made a critical report of the treatment of Irish political prisoners.
75. Eoin MacNeill, 'Ireland's place among the nations', *New Ireland*, 23 February 1918.
76. The first quotation is from a memo by George Gavan Duffy on 20 June 1922, cited in Harkness, op. cit., p. 32. The concise expression of *Realpolitik* was made by a backbencher, Frank Sherwin, who claimed to have 'studied diplomacy from Richelieu and Metternich and all the rest.' See Dáil Debates: 176,569 (2 July 1959).
77. Henry Dockrell, TD, Dáil Debates: 69,2269 (14 December 1937).
78. Bull, op. cit., p. 94.
79. Lemass in Schou and Brundtland, op. cit., p. 117.
80. For criticism of the government and for Garret FitzGerald's defence of his policy, see Dáil Debates: 286,384-88 and 508-12 (27 November 1975).
81. See FitzGerald's speech in the Seanad, 31 March 1976 (Seanad Debates: 83,1470-72). For evidence of Ireland's 'deviance' among the Nine, see Hurwitz, op. cit., esp. p. 441; and Lindeman, op. cit., pp. 265-66. With regard to the north-south dialogue, there is also evidence of Ireland, along with the Netherlands and Denmark, following a more 'progressive' line than the larger European Community states: see *The Irish Times*, 6 April 1977.
82. Seanad Debates: 83, 1470.

Chapter 10

1. Dr Patrick Hillery, Minister for Foreign Affairs, in the Dáil, 18 April 1972 (Dáil Debates: 260,385).
2. Morse, *Foreign Policy and Interdependence in Gaullist France*, p. 14.
3. See, for example, Reynolds, op. cit., chapter 3.
4. Kalevi J. Holsti, *International Politics* (Englewood Cliffs: Prentice-Hall, Third edition, 1977), p. 109. The concept of orientation is examined in ibid., pp. 107-30.
5. See Keatinge, *The Formulation of Irish Foreign Policy*, pp. 218-21.
6. Holsti, op. cit., pp. 112-13.
7. See above, p. 47.
8. Strictly speaking, 'neutrality' refers to a legal status: see Holsti, op. cit., pp. 113-14.
9. Dáil Debates: 265,743 (9 May 1973).
10. *The Irish Times*, 13 October 1975.
11. For an example of 'orientation' used in this way see Peter Hansen, 'Adaptive Behavior of Small States: the Case of Denmark and the European Community' in Patrick J. McGowan (ed.), *Sage International Yearbook of Foreign Policy Studies*, Vol. II (Beverly Hills: Sage, 1974).
12. Dáil Debates: 260,385.
13. Holsti, op. cit., p. 130. National roles are examined in ibid., pp. 130-36.
14. In Holsti's sample the average number of roles per state was 4.6, somewhat less than the five or six identified for Ireland above. However, not all roles involve equal commitment of resources or activity; Holsti's list is ranked roughly according to the likely level of activity, and the roles Ireland plays were ranked between 8 and 13 out of the total of 16, 16 being the least demanding role. This gives a very crude idea of the comparative level of involvement in international affairs; for anything beyond this, an updated and refined comparative analysis would be necessary.
15. Frederick S. Northedge, 'The Nature of Foreign Policy' in Northedge (ed.), *The Foreign Policies of the Powers*, p. 16.
16. See above, pp. 173, 179.
17. Dáil Debates: 260,390 (18 April 1972). This type of quasi-geographical formulation of areas of interest is not uncommon; the British Duncan Report on overseas representation, published in 1969, included a similar notion.
18. Dáil Debates: 275,895 (5 November 1974). Of course, strictly speaking, Brian Lenihan was Hillery's successor, but the general election of 1973 deprived him of an opportunity to elaborate a 'foreign policy philosophy'.
19. Dáil Debates: 260,385.
20. Morse, op. cit., p. 7.
21. ibid., pp. 32-35.

Chapter 11

1. See Graham T. Allison, *Essence of Decision: Explaining the Cuban Missile Crisis* (Boston: Little, Brown, 1971).
2. Allison's alternative models are the 'organisational process model' and the 'bureaucratic politics model', focusing respectively on the administrative structure and internal politics of the government.
3. For a detailed analysis of institutions associated with foreign policy, see, Keatinge, *The Formulation of Irish Foreign Policy*.
4. This was reflected in the opposition to a separate Department of External Affairs: see ibid., pp. 107-10.
5. ibid., pp. 52-54.
6. An example of this pattern of work emerges from the minutes of the Executive Council for 4 and 12 February 1924 (Cabinet, 2/48 and Cabinet, 2/50). In the course of negotiating with the British government on the establishment of the Boundary Commission, the task of drafting a reply was given to the Minister for Finance, Ernest Blythe (a northerner), but *all* members of the Executive Council were requested to provide memoranda 'for consideration in conjunction with the draft reply'. The subsequent draft was assigned to the Minister for Education, Eoin MacNeill (another northerner).
7. Hand, in Martin and Byrne (eds.), *The Scholar Revolutionary*, p. 273.
8. Keatinge, op. cit., pp. 136-41.
9. Hand, op. cit., p. 265.
10. Harkness, *Restless Dominion,* p. 147.
11. The weakness of the Irish parliamentary system with regard to foreign policy is examined in Keatinge, op. cit., chapters 7 and 8.
12. McMahon, op. cit., pp. 51-53. However, it is probable that de Valera's relationship with his envoys was not close, apart from those in London and Washington.
13. ibid., pp. 120-21, 143, 146-48.
14. Fanning, op. cit., pp. 276-91.
15. McMahon, op. cit., p. 84, note.
16. Minutes of the cabinet, 22 December 1936 (Cabinet, 7/381).
17. Keatinge, op. cit., p. 235, and Longford and O'Neill, op. cit., p. 371.
18. Carroll doubts that de Valera confided details to Ministers, 'some of whose wives were notoriously indiscreet and whose telephones had to be tapped.' Even Frank Aiken, who was close to de Valera, was probably not always fully informed because he was believed to be pro-German: Carroll, *Ireland in the War Years,* pp. 174-75.
19. See, for example, Carroll, op. cit., pp. 64 and 175, and Longford and O'Neill, op. cit., p. 412. As far as military policy was concerned, de Valera's personal supervision was also evident in a close working relationship with the Chief-of-Staff, General Dan McKenna.
20. Longford and O'Neill, op. cit., p. 406.
21. Minutes of the cabinet, 6 March 1944 (Government Cabinet, 3/50A).
22. Henry A. Kissinger, 'Domestic Structure and Foreign Policy' in James N. Rosenau (ed.), *International Politics and Foreign Policy* (New York: The Free Press, 1969), p. 268.

23. See Fanning, op. cit., chapter 10.
24. This is the opinion of one of the participants, the Secretary of the Department of Finance, T. K. Whitaker, who describes the Department of External Affairs as one of 'the four main economic departments'. See Whitaker, 'From protection to free trade', p. 417.
25. The growth of the Department of Foreign Affairs between 1967 and 1972 may be seen in Keatinge, op. cit., pp. 310-11, figures 2 and 3. I am grateful to Stephen Barcroft and the Department of Foreign Affairs for providing more recent information on the department's development. The figures cited here do not include either executive grade officials or service personnel – clerical staff, messengers and cleaners – whose numbers have also risen correspondingly.
26. For the department's structure, see Appendix 1.
27. This division is not quite so heterogeneous as the title implies; much of the information work has been connected with policy towards Northern Ireland. In the Autumn of 1977 there was speculation that all or part of the Anglo-Irish section was to be transferred to the Department of the Taoiseach: see *Magill*, October 1977.
28. In the Summer of 1977 the desk system operated on the following basis:

    Desk No. 1: The UN : Africa
    Desk No. 2: Asia : Australia : Latin America
    Desk No. 3: Eastern Europe; follow-up to the Conference on Security and Co-operation in Europe : Disarmament : Western Europe other than the European Community
    Desk No. 4: Southern Europe ; Mediterranean : USA and Canada
    Desk No. 5: Middle East and North Africa
    Desk No. 6: European Political Co-operation : general political questions.

29. For a full list of overseas representation, see Appendix 2.
30. For a full description, see Brigid Burns and Trevor C. Salmon, 'Policy-Making Co-operation in Ireland on European Community Issues', *Journal of Common Market Studies*, XV, 4, June 1977, 272-87.
31. Officially the home department officials are given diplomatic rank and are regarded as being seconded to the Department of Foreign Affairs. Their career prospects and departmental loyalties are, however, generally focused on their original departments; as one non-diplomat put it, they are 'on loan'.
32. For the Irish context up to 1973, see Keatinge, op. cit., pp. 128-31. The varying practices of the original six EEC states are examined in Helen Wallace, *National Governments and the European Communities* (London: Chatham House/PEP, 1973).
33. See Maurice A. East, 'Size and Foreign Policy Behavior: a Test of Two Models', *World Politics*, XXV, 4, July 1973, 558-59.
34. See Allen and Wallace, in Wallace *et al* (eds.), *Policy-making in the European Communities*, p. 237.
35. For the deficiencies of the Irish 'foreign policy community', see below, pp. 221-22.

36. See Charles Pentland, *International Theory and European Integration* (London: Faber, 1973), p. 220.

37. See Robert O. Keohane and Joseph S. Nye, 'Transgovernmental Relations and International Organisations', *World Politics*, XXVII, 1, October 1974, 39-62.

38. H. Wallace, op. cit., chapter 3.

39. Instructions from Dublin may on occasion still give flexibility to negotiators at Brussels. However, it seems that the time has passed when, as one official put it, instructions at some international conferences consisted of the phrase 'do the best you can', or in a more dynamic version, 'kick to touch'.

40. An increasing interdependence between 'economic' and 'political' issues, e.g. in the Euro-Arab dialogue, may make this separation more difficult in the future. At the European Community level there has already been a blurring of the distinction between the community's economic policies and the harmonisation of 'foreign policies' in the political co-operation process: see Allen and Wallace, op. cit., pp. 243-44.

41. See Helen Wallace, 'Holding the ring: the EEC Presidency', *The World Today*, 31, 8, August 1975.

42. Burns and Salmon, op. cit., p. 287.

43. In conjunction with the possibility of more direct supervision of Northern Ireland affairs by the Taoiseach (see above, note 27), such a development would make the latter's department a much more important element in the foreign policy process.

44. Basil Chubb, *Cabinet Government in Ireland* (Dublin: Institute of Public Administration, 1974), pp. 50-51.

45. See Keatinge, op. cit., Part III, *passim.*

46. During the Dáil of 1973-77 the Joint Committee consisted of twenty-six members, including the ten members of the European Parliament, and was chaired by a leading opposition deputy, Charles Haughey. For details of its activities, see *Fifty-fifth Report of the Joint Committee on the Secondary Legislation of the European Communities (Functions and Work of Joint Committee)*, 23 March 1977, Prl. 6169.

47. For the early difficulties of the Joint Committee see Mary T.W. Robinson, 'The Role of the Irish Parliament', *Administration*, 22, 1, Spring 1974.

48. Between April 1975 and 23 March 1977 the Joint Committee produced fifty reports.

49. The extent of public control in Denmark reflects the controversy surrounding membership of the European Community as well as the more flexible parliamentary organisation employed there. See John Fitzmaurice, 'National Parliaments and European policy-making: the case of Denmark', *Parliamentary Affairs*, Vol. XXIX, 3, Summer 1976, 281-292.

50. A brief summary of the major developments in political co-operation has been included in the government's half-yearly reports but, as can be seen above, the latter are not always examined in detail. The Joint Committee's original terms of reference also precluded it from dealing

with the Commission's outline proposals: see *Fifty-fifth Report of the Joint Committee*, p. 11.

51. See Keatinge, op. cit., chapter 7.

52. There has been increased teaching in international studies in Dublin, Cork, Galway and Limerick, without any additional staff being appointed. In 1976 the two Dublin universities, Trinity College and University College, announced a joint one-year postgraduate course in European Studies, and on an all-Ireland basis an Irish Association for European Studies was established. Both these innovations were 'primed' by financial aid from the European Community Commission, but they do not have the resources for a full-time research programme. The Economic and Social Research Institute, which does operate a full-time research programme, envisages undertaking some foreign policy research from 1976 to 1980, mainly under the heading 'External Trade and Capital Flows: see *The ESRI Research Plan 1976-80 and Background Analysis* (Dublin: Economic and Social Research Institute, 1976). But this is only one of ten categories of research which are planned; nor does it cover more than a part of the foreign policy field.

Chapter 12

1. For the major developments in international relations, see Geoffrey Barraclough, *An Introduction to Contemporary History* (Harmondsworth: Pelican, 1967), Frederick S. Northedge and Michael J. Grieve, *A Hundred Years of International Relations* (London: Duckworth, 1971), and Brian Porter (ed.), *International Politics*.

2. Bull, op. cit., p. 320. See also Robert W. Cox, 'On Thinking about Future World Order', *World Politics*, XXVIII, 2, January 1976, 175-196. For a useful summary of West European attempts to establish predictive systems, and proposals for developing these on a European Community basis, see Wayland Kennet, *The Futures of Europe* (London: Cambridge University Press, 1976).

3. See Donald J. Puchala and Stuart I. Fagan, 'International Politics in the 1970s: the Search for a Perspective', *International Organization*, 28, 2, Spring 1974, 247-66.

4. See ibid.

5. In 1976 the Minister for Foreign Affairs, Garret FitzGerald, was reported to have admitted that 'uniting Europe could be the task of a new generation of politicians, possibly in the closing years of this century': *The Irish Times*, 8 September 1976.

6. See, for example, Rose, op. cit., pp. 156-57. Economic implications are examined in Norman Gibson, 'Some Economic Implications of the Various "Solutions" to the Northern Ireland Problem', in Vaizey (ed.), *Economic Sovereignty and Regional Policy*, pp. 212-14.

7. By elements of the Scottish Nationalist Party: see *The Irish Times*, 31 May 1976.

8. A recent innovation in the Department of Foreign Affairs has been the establishment of a Planning Section, which consists of only one official and, being located in the department's Administrative Division, is directed towards financial and administrative planning rather than policy planning in the broader sense.
9. This may be given added direction by the Department of Economic Planning and Development, established in 1977.

APPENDIX 1: DEPARTMENT OF EXTERNAL/FOREIGN AFFAIRS: HEADQUARTERS ORGANISATION 1967-77

June 1967

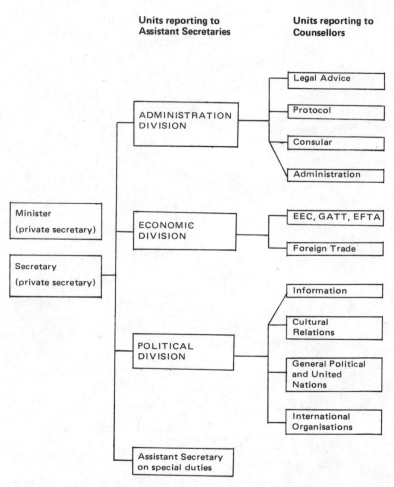

Sources: Directory of State Services 1967 and 1977, and information supplied by the Department of Foreign Affairs.

June 1977

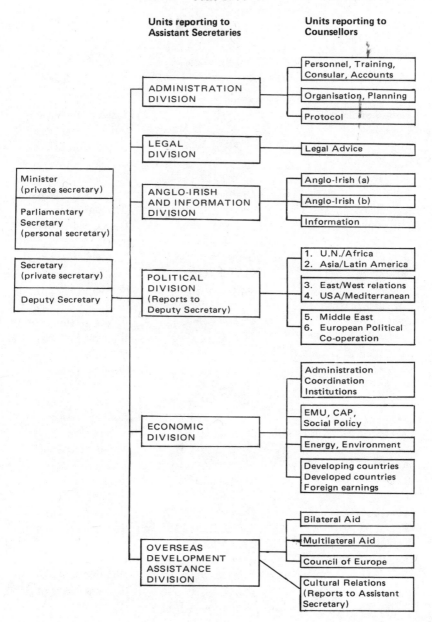

Units reporting to Assistant Secretaries

Units reporting to Counsellors

Minister (private secretary)

Parliamentary Secretary (personal secretary)

Secretary (private secretary)

Deputy Secretary

ADMINISTRATION DIVISION
- Personnel, Training, Consular, Accounts
- Organisation, Planning
- Protocol

LEGAL DIVISION
- Legal Advice

ANGLO-IRISH AND INFORMATION DIVISION
- Anglo-Irish (a)
- Anglo-Irish (b)
- Information

POLITICAL DIVISION (Reports to Deputy Secretary)
- 1. U.N./Africa
- 2. Asia/Latin America
- 3. East/West relations
- 4. USA/Mediterranean
- 5. Middle East
- 6. European Political Co-operation

ECONOMIC DIVISION
- Administration Coordination Institutions
- EMU, CAP, Social Policy
- Energy, Environment
- Developing countries Developed countries Foreign earnings

OVERSEAS DEVELOPMENT ASSISTANCE DIVISION
- Bilateral Aid
- Multilateral Aid
- Council of Europe
- Cultural Relations (Reports to Assistant Secretary)

APPENDIX 2: COUNTRIES WITH WHICH IRELAND MAINTAINS DIPLOMATIC RELATIONS

	Date of establishment of diplomatic relations	Level of recognition in December 1977
Great Britain	January 1923	Resident Embassy
United States of America	October 1924	Resident Embassy and 4 Consul-Generals (New York, Boston, Chicago, San Francisco)
Holy See	June 1929	Resident Embassy
France	October 1929	Resident Embassy
Germany	October 1929	Resident Embassy
(Federal Republic	11 June 1951)	and Consul-General (Hamburg)
Belgium	September 1932	Resident Embassy
Spain	April 1935	Resident Embassy
Italy	April 1938	Resident Embassy
Canada	April 1939	Resident Embassy
Switzerland	October 1940	Resident Embassy
Portugal	November 1941	Resident Embassy
Netherlands	October 1945	Resident Embassy
Sweden	March 1946	Resident Embassy
Australia	April 1946	Resident Embassy
Argentina	August 1947	Resident Embassy
India	January 1949	Resident Embassy
Norway	April 1950	Non-Resident
Iceland	June 1951	Non-Resident
Austria	May 1951	Resident Embassy
Turkey	October 1951	Non-Resident
Nigeria	July 1960	Resident Embassy
Luxembourg	December 1961	Resident Embassy
Denmark	January 1962	Resident Embassy
Finland	March 1962	Non-Resident
Malaysia	July 1962	Non-Resident
New Zealand	October 1965	Non-Resident
Japan	March 1973	Resident Embassy
Soviet Union	September 1973	Resident Embassy

	Date of establishment of diplomatic relations	Level of recognition in December 1977
Lebanon	January 1974	Resident Embassy
Bahrain	September 1974	Non-Resident
Qatar	September 1974	Non-Resident
Saudi Arabia	September 1974	Non-Resident
Kuwait	October 1974	Non-Resident
United Arab Emirates	October 1974	Non-Resident
Singapore	December 1974	Non-Resident
Egypt	December 1974	Resident Embassy
Israel	December 1974	Non-Resident
Algeria	January 1975	Non-Resident
Morocco	January 1975	Non-Resident
Tunisia	January 1975	Non-Resident
Greece	January 1975	Resident Embassy
Thailand	January 1975	Non-Resident
Brazil	September 1975	Non-Resident
Czechoslovakia	December 1975	Non-Resident
Iran	February 1976	Resident Embassy
Mexico	August 1976	Non-Resident
Hungary	October 1976	Non-Resident
Poland	October 1976	Non-Resident
Yugoslavia	April 1977	Non-Resident
Libya	July 1977	Non-Resident

SELECT BIBLIOGRAPHY

BOOKS

BELL, J. Bowyer. *The Secret Army*. London, Anthony Blond, 1970.

BOLAND, Kevin. *We won't stand (idly) by*. Dublin, Kelly Kane, n.d.

CARROLL, Joseph T. *Ireland in the War Years*. Newton Abbot, David and Charles, 1975.

CHUBB, Basil. *The Government and Politics of Ireland*. London, Oxford University Press, 1970.

DARBY, John. *Conflict in Northern Ireland: the Development of a Polarised Community*. Dublin, Gill and Macmillan, 1976.

Department of External (from 1971 Foreign) Affairs. *Ireland at the United Nations*. Dublin, Department of External/Foreign Affairs, 1957—

DWYER, T. Ryle. *Irish Neutrality and the USA 1939-47*. Dublin, Gill and Macmillan, 1977.

EDWARDS, Ruth Dudley. *An Atlas of Irish History*. London, Methuen, 1973.

FABIAN, Larry L. *Soldiers without Enemies*. Washington DC, The Brookings Institution, 1971.

FANNING, Ronan. *The Irish Department of Finance 1922-58*. Dublin, Institute of Public Administration, 1978.

FARRELL, Brian. *The Founding of Dáil Eireann*. Dublin, Gill and Macmillan, 1971.

FITZGERALD, Garret. *Towards a New Ireland*. London, Charles Knight, 1972.

HANCOCK, W. K. *Survey of British Commonwealth Affairs. Vol. I. Problems of Nationality 1918-1936*. London, Oxford University Press, 1937.

HAND, Geoffrey J. 'MacNeill and the Boundary Commission' in F. X. Martin and F. J. Byrne (eds.). *The Scholar Revolutionary, Eoin MacNeill, 1867-1945, and the Making of the New Ireland*. Shannon, Irish University Press, 1973.

HARKNESS, David W. *The Restless Dominion*. London, Macmillan, 1969.

HILLERY, Brian and LYNCH, Patrick. *Ireland in the International Labour Organisation*. Dublin, Department of Labour, 1969.

HULL, Roger H. *The Irish Triangle*. Princeton, Princeton University Press, 1976.

Irish Council of the European Movement. *European Monetary Union and the Sterling Link*. Dublin, Irish Council of the European Movement, 1975.

JACKSON, John A. 'The Irish Army and the Development of the Constabulary Concept' in Jacques van Doorn (ed.) *Armed Forces and Society*. The Hague, Mouton, 1968.

JONES, Thomas. *Whitehall Diary, Vol. III: Ireland 1918-1925*. K. Middlemas (ed.) London, Oxford University Press, 1971.

KEATINGE, Patrick. *The Formulation of Irish Foreign Policy*. Dublin, Institute of Public Administration, 1973.

KEE, Robert. *The Green Flag: A History of Irish Nationalism*. London, Weidenfeld and Nicolson, 1972.

KENNEDY, Kieran A. and DOWLING, Brendan R. *Economic Growth in Ireland: the Experience since 1947.* Dublin, Gill and Macmillan, 1975.

LEBOW, R. Ned. 'Ireland' in G. Henderson, R. N. Lebow and J. G. Stoessinger (eds.). *Divided Nations in a Divided World.* New York, McKay, 1974.

LEMASS, Seán F. 'Small States in International Organizations' in August Schou and Arne O. Brundtland. *Small States in International Relations.* Uppsala, Almqvist and Wiksell, 1971.

LYNCH, John. *Speeches and Statements on Irish Unity, Northern Ireland, Anglo-Irish Relations.* Dublin, Government Information Bureau, 1971.

LYONS, F. S. L. *Ireland Since the Famine.* London, Fontana, revised edition, 1973.

McALEESE, Dermot. 'Outward-looking policies, export performance and economic growth: the Irish experience' in Michael J. Artis and Alexander Nobay (eds.), *Essays in Economic Analysis.* Oxford, Blackwell, 1978.

McALEESE, Dermot. 'Political Independence and Economic Performance – Ireland outside the United Kingdom' in E. T. Nevin (ed.). *The Economics of Devolution.* Birmingham, University of Aston Press, 1978.

McALEESE, Dermot. 'The Foreign Sector' in Norman J. Gibson and John E. Spencer (eds.). *Economic Activity in Ireland.* Dublin, Gill and Macmillan, 1977.

MACARDLE, Dorothy. *The Irish Republic.* London, Corgi edition, 1968.

McCAFFREY, Lawrence J. *The Irish Diaspora in America.* Bloomington, Indiana University Press, 1976.

MacDONAGH, Oliver. *Ireland: The Union and its Aftermath.* London, Allen and Unwin, 1977.

MacGREIL, Michael. *Prejudice and Tolerance in Ireland.* Dublin, College of Industrial Relations, 1977.

MANSERGH, Nicholas. *Survey of British Commonwealth Affairs: Problems of External Policy 1931-1939.* London, Oxford University Press, 1952.

MANSERGH, Nicholas. *Survey of British Commonwealth Affairs: Problems of Wartime Co-operation and Post-war Change 1939-1952.* London, Oxford University Press, 1958.

MANSERGH, Nicholas. *The Irish Question 1840-1921.* London, Allen and Unwin, third revised edition, 1975.

MEENAN, James. *The Irish Economy since 1922.* Liverpool, Liverpool University Press, 1970.

MOODY, T. W. *The Ulster Question 1603-1973.* Cork, Mercier, 1974.

MURPHY, John A. *Ireland in the Twentieth Century.* Dublin, Gill and Macmillan, 1975.

NOWLAN, Kevin B. and WILLIAMS, Desmond T. (eds.). *Ireland in the War Years and After 1939-1951.* Dublin, Gill and Macmillan, 1969.

O'BRIEN, Conor Cruise. 'Ireland in International Affairs' in Owen Dudley Edwards (ed.). *Conor Cruise O'Brien introduces Ireland.* London, Deutsch, 1969.

O'BRIEN, Conor Cruise. *States of Ireland.* London, Panther, revised edition, 1974.

O'FARRELL, Patrick. *Ireland's English Question: Anglo-Irish Relations*

1534-1970. London, Batsford, 1971.
O'FARRELL, Patrick. *England and Ireland Since 1800.* London, Oxford University Press, 1975.
PAKENHAM, Frank A. (Lord Longford). *Peace by Ordeal.* London, Sidgwick and Jackson, revised edition, 1972.
PAKENHAM, Frank A. (Lord Longford) and O'NEILL, Thomas P. *Eamon de Valera.* London, Arrow, revised edition, 1974.
PFRETZSCHNER, Paul A. and BOROCK, Donald M. 'Political Socialisation of the Irish Secondary School Student' in John Raven *et. al. Political Culture in Ireland: The Views of Two Generations.* Dublin, Institute of Public Administration, 1976.
ROSE, Richard. *Northern Ireland: a Time of Choice.* London, Macmillan, 1976.
RUMPF, E. and HEPBURN, A. C. *Nationalism and Socialism in Twentieth-century Ireland.* Liverpool, Liverpool University Press, 1977.
SUTTON, Mary. *Irish Government Aid to the Third World – Review and Assessment.* Irish Commission for Justice and Peace: Dublin, 1977.
VAIZEY, John (ed.). *Economic Sovereignty and Regional Policy.* Dublin, Gill and Macmillan, 1975.
WALLACE, William and ALLEN, David. 'Political Cooperation: Procedure as Substitute for Policy?' in William Wallace, Helen Wallace and Carole Webb, *Policy-making in the European Communities.* New York, Wiley, 1977.
WARD, Alan J. *Ireland and Anglo-American Relations 1899-1921.* London, Weidenfeld and Nicolson, 1969.

ARTICLES AND PAMPHLETS

ASMAL, Kader. 'Irish opposition to Apartheid.' UN Department of Political and Security Council Affairs: Unit on Apartheid, notes and documents No. 3/71, February 1971.
BELL, J. Bowyer. 'Ireland and the Spanish Civil War 1936-1939'. *Studia Hibernica,* No. 7, 1969.
BURNS, Brigid and SALMON, Trevor C. 'Policy-Making Coordination in Ireland on European Community Issues'. *Journal of Common Market Studies,* vol XV, No. 4, June 1977.
COHAN, Al S. 'The Question of a United Ireland'. *International Affairs,* Vol. 53, No. 2, April 1977.
DANIEL, T. K. 'Griffith on his Noble Head: The Determinants of Cumann na nGaedheal Economic Policy 1922-32'. *Irish Economic and Social History,* Vol. III, 1976.
DWYER, T. Ryle. 'American efforts to discredit de Valera during World War II', *Eire-Ireland,* Vol. VIII, No. 2, Summer 1973.

FITZGERALD, Garret. 'Irish Foreign Policy within the Context of the EEC: Text of Address by The Minister for Foreign Affairs, Dr. Garret FitzGerald TD to the Royal Irish Academy, 10th November 1975'. Dublin, Department of Foreign Affairs, n.d.

HARKNESS, David W. 'Mr. de Valera's Dominion: Irish Relations with Britain and the Commonwealth 1932-1938'. *Journal of Commonwealth Political Studies*, Vol. VIII, No. 3, 1970.

HEATHCOTE, Nina. 'Ireland and the United Nations Operation in the Congo'. *International Relations*, Vol. III, No. 11, May 1971.

HURWITZ, Leon. 'The EEC and Decolonization: the Voting Behaviour of the Nine in the UN General Assembly'. *Political Studies*, Vol. XXIV, No. 4, December 1976.

KEATINGE, Patrick. 'Ireland and the League of Nations'. *Studies*, Vol. LIX, No. 234, Summer 1970.

KYLE, Keith. 'Sunningdale and after: Britain, Ireland and Ulster.' *The World Today*, Vol. 31, No. 11, November 1975.

LINDEMAN, Beate. 'Europe and the Third World: the Nine at the United Nations'. *The World Today*, Vol. 32, No. 7, July 1976.

LYNCH, John M. 'The Anglo-Irish problem'. *Foreign Affairs*, Vol. 50, No. 4, July 1972.

McALEESE, Dermot. 'Capital Inflow and Direct Foreign Investment in Ireland 1952 to 1970'. *Journal of the Statistical and Social Inquiry Society of Ireland*, Vol. XXII, Part IV, 1971-72.

McALEESE, Dermot and MARTIN, John. 'Ireland's Manufactured Exports to the EEC and the Common External Tariff'. *Economic and Social Review*, Vol. 3, No. 4, July 1972.

MOXON BROWNE, E. 'Ireland in the EEC'. *The World Today*, Vol. 31, No. 10, October 1975.

O'CONNOR, Brian J. 'Ireland and the United Nations'. Dublin, Tuairim, 1961.

POWER, Paul F. 'Violence, Consent and the Northern Ireland Problem'. *The Journal of Commonwealth and Comparative Politics*, Vol. XIV, No. 2, July 1976.

WHEELER, Marcus. 'Soviet Interest in Ireland'. *Survey*, No. 3 (96), Summer 1975.

WHITAKER, T. K. 'From Protection to Free Trade – The Irish Experience'. *Administration*, Vol. 21, No. 4, Winter 1973.

WHITAKER, T. K. 'Monetary Integration: Reflections on Irish Experience'. *Quarterly Bulletin, Central Bank of Ireland*, Winter 1973.

WILLIAMS, Desmond T. 'A Study of Neutrality'. *The Leader*, January-April 1953.

Aberdeen, University of 243(n78), 253(n72)
Act of Union (1800) 16-17, 24, 232(n9)
Africa 20, 38, 161, 173, 224, 264(n28), App. 1.
Agency for Personal Service Overseas (APSO) 185, 260(n62)
Agriculture, Department of 209, 214, 217, 219, 260(n59)
Aid see Development aid
Aiken, Frank 2, 76, 87, 160, 161-163, 166, 167, 173-174, 179, 200-201, 209, 214, 263(n18)
Air Corps see Defence Forces
Algeria 174, 212, App. 2
Aliens Act (1935) 68
Alliance Party 120
Allison, Graham T. 263(n2)
America 11(epigram), 41, 42(epigram)
Amnesty International 261(n74)
Andrews, David 211
Anglo-Irish agreements (1938) 70-71, 136-137, 241(n31); and defence 87-88; and interactions between issue-areas 194; and Irish unity 107, 108
Anglo-Irish Free Trade Area (AIFTA) 141
Anglo-Irish relations: and anti-imperialism 171-174; attitudes towards Britain in World War II 178; constitutional revision (1922-49) 63-73, 201, 206-207; and decline of Britain 224; and Department of Foreign Affairs 213, App. 1; economic dependence 130-131, 139, 146-147, 148, 250(n12); economic relations 131-137, 141; exchange of representatives 71; as framework for Irish foreign policy 200; historical development before 1922 10-58; interactions between issue-areas 194-196; and international order 156-157; and Irish defence policy 82-91, 93-94, 97; and Irish orientations 198; and Irish unity 100-125, 243-249; and policy-making 204-208, 210, 212, App. 1; prospects for 228-230; and Soviet-Irish relations 259(n44); and World War II 70-73, 87-91, 137
Anglo-Irish Treaty (1921) 18, 21, 162; attitudes towards 61-62, 237(n54); defence provisions 82-83, 240(n3, n4,n5); historical context 9-10; interactions between issue-areas 194; negotiations with British government 46, 53-58, 109; and Northern Ireland 102-104, 105; registration with League of Nations 65-66; revision of 63-70, 85, 87-88, 135; signed and ratified 58
Anti-communism 178-181
Anti-imperialism 171-176, 258(n33)
Aontacht Éireann Gloss., 116
Argentine App. 2
Arms control see Disarmament
Army see Defence Forces
Articles of Agreement for a Treaty between Great Britain and Ireland see Anglo-Irish Treaty (1921)
Asia 224, 264(n28), App. 1
Asquith, Henry Herbert 43
Athens 213
Attlee, Clement 90
Aughrim, Battle of 11
Australia 18, 28, 29, 64, 112, 264(n28), App. 1, App. 2
Austria 98, 213, App. 2
Austro-Hungarian Empire 36-37, 58

Bahrein 212, App. 2
Balfour Declaration (1926) 66
Bandung 174
Banking Commission (1926) 127 (epigram), 133
Bantry Bay 12
Barcroft, Stephen 264(n25)
Barry, Michael Joseph 35
Baxter, Patrick F. 81(epigram)
Belfast 15, 104, 105, 112, 118, 229
Belgium 39, 130, 147 (table 4), 161
Belton, Patrick 177
Berehaven 85
Berne 48

Betjeman, John 178
Biggs-Davison, John 243(n74)
Birkenhead, Lord 55
Blaney, Neil 116
Blue Shirts 177
Blythe, Ernest 98, 153, 205, 256(n54), 263(n6)
Boer War 30, 38
Boland, Frederick H. 77, 205, 208
Boland, Kevin 114, 116, 121, 243(n3), 246(n65), 252(n53)
Bolivia 155
Bord Fáilte Gloss., 140
Boundary Commission 56, 103-104, 106, 204, 205, 263(n6)
Boyne, Battle of 11
Brazil 212, App. 2
Brennan, Robert 208
British Army 248(n94)
British Commonwealth 57, 58, 78, 87, 92, 106, 112, 165, 172, 197, 198, 229, 237(n8); de Valera's attitude towards 67-68; as diplomatic forum 65; dominions support Ireland 66, 70, 73, 76; Ireland withdraws 73; and public opinion 67; significance of membership 75; see also External association
British Empire 27, 33, 43, 172
British Isles 10, 16, 63, 69, 81 (epigram), 82, 85, 89, 97, 103-104, 129, 131, 146, 196, 198, 225, 228-229, 250(n13)
Browne, Noel 161
Brugha, Cathal 51
Brussels 168, 195, 196, 210, 211, 214, 217, 218, 219, 221, 227, 265(n39)
Bull, Hedley 223(epigram)
Bunreacht na hÉireann see Constitution of Ireland (1937)
Butt, Isaac 32-33, 34

Cabinet: and policy-making 204-208, 219-220, 263(n6)
Callaghan, Jim 248(n107)
Canada 18, 27, 64, 66, 98, 146(Table 3), 158, 159, 168, 181, 198, 250(n12), 259(n47), 264(n28) App. 1, App. 2
Caracas 145
Carrickfergus 11
Carroll, Lewis 59(epigram)
Carson, Sir Edward 44
Carter, Jimmy 125

Casement, Sir Roger 12, 38-39, 42, 45-46, 47, 51, 52, 57, 71, 235 (n8)
Catholic Church 117, 176, 179; see also Religious divisions; Religious values
Central Bank 136
Central Bank Act (1971) 144
Chamberlain, Joseph 28, 34
Chamberlain, Neville 70, 88, 107, 108, 157
Childers, Erskine 51, 56, 58, 83, 236(n37)
China 76, 163, 174, 180, 225, 257(n10)
Churchill, Winston Spencer 67, 71, 73, 89, 90, 110, 111, 113
Civil rights, in Northern Ireland 115
Civil war (1922-23) 9, 58, 83, 86, 93, 104, 132, 162, 172, 176
Clan na Gael (United Brotherhood) Gloss., 28, 29, 30, 45
Clann na Poblachta Gloss., 73, 92
Clarke, Thomas 30, 45
Cobh 12, 85
Cohalan, Daniel 48
Cogan, Patrick 259(n39)
Cold war 75, 91, 158
Collective security 85, 87, 153-156, 158, 223, 254(n18)
Collins, Michael 51, 52, 58, 62, 103, 104
Columbia 155
Committee on the Constitution 114
Common Agricultural Policy (CAP) see European Community
Common Market Defence Campaign 143
Commonwealth see British Commonwealth
Concern 184, 260(n59)
Confederation of Non-Governmental Organisations on Overseas Development 260(n61)
Conference on Security and Co-operation in Europe 95, 167, 187-188, 260(n57), 264(n28), App. 1
Congo 159, 161, 255(n43,n44,n50), 257(n12)
Connolly, James 30, 38, 234(n56), 235(n75)
Conscription 44, 46, 47, 89, 111
Conservative Party 29, 41, 42, 243(n74)
Constitution of the Irish Free State (1922) 83, 154
Constitution of Ireland (1937) 61(epi-

gram), 70, 101, 106-107, 114, 116, 117, 119, 120, 123, 151, 152-153, 248(n98)
Constitutional Convention (Northern Ireland, 1975) 122
Control of Manufactures Act (1932) 135-136, 140
Coogan, Eamonn 81(epigram), 92
Cooper, Bryan 241(n16)
Córas Tráchtála Teo (CTT) Gloss., 138, 144, 175
Cork 250(n22), 266(n52)
Cosgrave, Liam 76, 120, 123, 173, 179, 200, 242,(n61), 257(n8)
Cosgrave, William T. 64, 67, 68, 104, 109, 131-134, 135, 136, 172, 205, 241(n13), 256(n54)
Costello, John A. 73, 112
Council of Europe 113, 119, 166, 187, 188, 246(n58)
Council of Ireland 103, 120-121
Craig, Sir James (later Lord Craigavon) 55, 103, 110
Craigavon, Lord see Craig, Sir James
Cranborne, Lord 111, 137, 242(n37)
Cromwell, Oliver 14
Cronin, Jerry 242(n61)
Cross-border co-operation see Functional co-operation: and north-south relations in Ireland
Crown, as symbol of allegiance 57-58, 63, 67, 68, 69, 73
Cuba 50, 52, 243(n74)
Cultural diplomacy 74-75, 239(n39)
Cumann na nGaedheal Gloss., 67
Currency Act (1927) 133
Cyprus 159, 160
Czechoslovakia 88, 157, 212, App. 2

Dáil Éireann (1912-22) Gloss., 9(epigram), 47-54, 58, 261(n70)
Dáil Éireann (1922-   ): all-party Committee on Irish Relations 123; and decisions on war 83, 86; procedures and foreign policy 253(n6); see also Policy-making: public control
Danzig 77, 155, 239(n46)
Davis, Richard 236(n29)
Davis, Thomas 25, 35, 36
Declaration of Independence (1919) 47
Defence Conference 208
Defence Forces: Air Corps 84, 90, 92; Army: and civil-military relations

83-84, 86, 93; and Northern Ireland 93-94, 115, 248(n94); origins 83; role before World War II 84-87; role in World War II 90; role after World War II 91-93, 242(n58), 260(n58); Navy 84, 90, 92
Defence Forces (Temporary Provisions) Bill (1927) 85
Defence policy see Security
Democratic Party 50
Democratic Programme (1919) 47
Denmark 79, 80, 96, 141, 147(Table 4), 158, 168, 169, 175, 198, 221, 265(n49), App. 2
Derry 118
De Valera, Eamon 49, 76, 94, 113, 203(epigram), 231(n1), 236(n36), 236(n42), 241(n13), 243(n3), 245(n31); and constitutional revision 64, 67, 68-70, 238(n14); and Dáil Éireann (1919-1922) 50-54, 236(n33); and defence policy 83, 86-91; and the economic war 135; and external association 57-58, 63; and Irish unity 105-113, 116, 245(n34,n40); and the League of Nations 76-77, 154-158, 176-178, 187, 254(n32); and neutrality 71-74, 83, 86-91, 92; and policy-making 206-209, 263(n12,n18,n19); and religious values 176-178; and self-sufficiency 134
Development aid 181-186, 226, 259(n54)
Development Aid Committee (DAC) 182
Development Co-operation Organisation (DEVCO) 185
Devoy, John 27, 28, 45, 46, 48
Dillon, James 91, 92, 161, 178, 179, 208
Dillon, John 28, 33, 34, 235(n17)
Diplomatic service 213
Direct rule in Northern Ireland 119
Disarmament 161-164, 226, 264(n28), App. 1
Disarmament Conference (1932) 162
Dockrell, Henry 261(n77)
Domestic autonomy see Home Rule
Dominion status 20, 35, 46, 57, 64-65
Dominions Office 65, 107, 108
Donegan, Patrick 220
Downing Street Declaration (1969) 117
Draft Treaty A 57

Dublin 15, 44, 46, 58, 72, 83, 90, 96, 102, 103, 104, 105, 106, 108, 114, 118, 121, 123, 159, 196, 211, 214, 218, 229, 259(n44), 260(n58), 265(n39), 266(n52)
Duffy, George Gavan 153, 170(epigram), 261(n76)
Dulanty, John W. 88, 206, 207, 208

Economic depression, effect on Ireland 134-135, 251(n27)
Economic Planning and Development, Department of 267(n9)
Economic policy: and foreign policy (1922-77) 131-148; foreign investment 135-136, 138, 141, 145; and global issues 226; and monetary policy 133-134, 136, 139, 144-145, 250(n20,n21), 251(n47), 253(n69); and policy-making 209-210; and protection 34, 37, 46, 55, 128, 133, 134-135, 139-141, 250(n19,n22), 251(n30), 252(n52); resources 145-146; role of government 128, 132-133, 138-139; see also Economy; Maritime interests; Prosperity; Trade
Economic recession, effect on Ireland 144-145
Economic and Social Research Institute (ESRI) 266(n52)
Economic war (1932-38) 68, 135, 156, 251(n29,n30)
Economy: dependence on Great Britain 130-131; level of development 128-129; openness 129-130, 250(n9); size 128-129
Edward VIII, King 69
EEC see European Community
Egypt 213, App. 2
Election: (1918) 47; (1923) 64; (1932) 67-68; (1933) 68; (1948) 73, 92, 112; (1957) 131; (1973) 120; (1977) 123
Electricity Supply Board (ESB) 132
Emigration 17-20, 136, 232(n13)
Engels, Friedrich 234(n50)
England 11(epigram), 27, 34, 35, 44, 45, 46, 89, 229
Ennis 237(n6)
Ethiopia 87, 156, 177, 207
Europe 11(epigram), 18, 40, 42(epigram), 43, 44, 45, 49, 57, 84, 87, 89, 141, 145, 167

European Community 2, 179, 180, 198, 199, 200, 202, 225, 229, 230, 264(n28,n32), 265(n49), 266(n2); Commission 79, 219, 265(n50), 266(n52); Committee of Permanent Representatives (COREPER) 218; Common Agricultural Policy (CAP) 142-143, 144, 148, 217; Council of Ministers 77, 79, 80, 124; and development aid 183-184; effects on economy 144, 252(n66); European Council 218; and European defence 228; European Parliament 79, 227, 265(n46); fishery policy 98, 145-146, 243(n78); further enlargement 228, 253(n78); and interactions between issue-areas in Irish foreign policy 195-196; Ireland's Permanent Representation 214-215, 217-218; Irish attitudes towards economic policies 147-148; Irish attitudes towards political evolution 79-80, 253(n78), 266(n5); Irish attitude towards possible British withdrawal 146-147; Irish debate on membership 142-144; and Irish economic policy (1958-63) 140-141; Irish leadership in 77, 79, 80; and Irish neutrality 78, 94-98; and Irish policy in the United Nations 161, 165-168, 256(n70), 261(n81); and Irish policy-making 209-221; and Irish Referendum (1972) 78; Irish trade dependence in 147; and Northern Ireland 117, 123, 124; as a political system 78; and prospects for Irish foreign policy 226-228; Regional Fund and policy 79, 124, 143, 144, 148; scrutiny by Joint Committee of Dáil and Seanad 220-221, 265(n46,n47,n48,n50); and South Africa 175; and trade with the Third World 185-186; see also European political co-operation
European Convention on Human Rights and Fundamental Freedoms 122, 187
European Court of Human Rights 118, 187
European Free Trade Area (EFTA) 140
European Parliament see European Community: European Parliament

European political co-operation 80, 164, 165-169, 230, 256(n70), 261(n81), 264(n28), 265(n40), App. 1; and international justice 189-190; and Irish neutrality 95, 168-169, 256(n70); and Irish policy-making 212, 215-216, 221, 265(n50)
Evening Standard 108
Executive Authority (External Relations) Act (1936) 69, 73
External Affairs, Department of 1, 162, 245(n40), App. 1; and the League of Nations 155; and Marshall Aid 138; and policy-making 205-210, 263(n4), 264(n24); see also Foreign Affairs, Department of
External association 57-58, 63; implemented 69-70; and Irish unity 73; 106-107, 112-113, 246(n53); repealed 73

Fabian, Larry L. 158, 159, 255(n48)
Famine 15, 17-18, 25, 35
Far East 20
Faulkner, Brian 118
Federalism: and the British Isles 27, 32, 34, 35, 228-229; and the European Community 79, 96, 227; and Irish unity 109, 245(n37)
Feetham, Richard 104
Fenians see Irish Republican Brotherhood (IRB)
Fianna Fáil 67, 92, 94, 100, 106, 108, 114, 116, 121, 123, 134, 135, 140, 142, 154, 173, 179, 180, 247(n75), 250(n22), 252(n53), 260(n67)
Finance, Department of 132-133, 138-139, 160, 206, 207, 209, 210, 214, 217, 218, 219, 264(n24)
Fine Gael 89, 91, 93, 100, 120, 123, 142, 156, 177, 180, 219, 246(n54), 247(n85)
Finland 98, 158, App. 2
First Programme for Economic Expansion 139-140
Fischer, Georges 256(n56)
Fisher, Joseph R. 104
Fisheries, Department of 219-220
Fishery policy   see European Community: fishery policy
FitzGerald, Desmond 65, 85, 86, 170(epigram), 173, 256(n54), 257(n3), 258(n34)

FitzGerald, Garret 77, 96, 120, 123, 149(epigram), 168, 175, 184-185, 197, 200, 201, 220, 243(n69), 256(n68), 257(n72), 260(n60), 261(n80), 266(n5)
Ford Motor Company 250(n22)
Foreign Affairs, Department of 2, 248(n94); and cultural diplomacy 75; and development aid 184, App. 1; expansion (1967-77) 210-213, App. 1; headquarters organisation 211-212, 264(n26,n27,n28), App. 1; and policy-making 210-218; and policy-planning 230, 267(n8); representation overseas 212-213, 214-215, 264(n29,n31), App. 2; see also External Affairs, Department of
Foreign Office 38
Foreign policy: definition 3, 193-194; design 193-202; and freedom of choice 200-202; usage of the term 1-3, 209; see also Images; Issue-areas; Orientations; Priorities; Policy-making; Roles; Values
France 11-12, 16, 18, 24, 25-26, 41, 72, 96, 147(Table 4), 156, 161, 163, 168, 174, 235(n5), App. 2
Franco, Francisco 177, 189

Gaelic Athletic Association (GAA) 30
Gaelic League 30
Gallagher, Frank 208
Galway 266(n52)
Gaulle, Charles de 94
General Act for the Settlement of International Disputes 155
General Agreement on Tariffs and Trade (GATT) 141, 165
Geneva 153, 204, 205, 244(n16)
Geographical location of Ireland 10, 11(epigram), 13, 32, 39, 189, 224
Germany 12, 37, 38-39, 42, 45-46, 57, 70, 87, 88, 89-90, 110, 141, 147(Table 4), 154, 167, 178, 235(n8), 245(n45), App. 2
Gibbons, James 242(n60)
Gibralter 29
Gibson, Norman 130(Table 2), 146 (Table 3)
Gladstone, William E. 28
Gogarty, Oliver St. John 258(n30)
Gorey, Denis J. 231(n1)
Gorta Gloss., 184, 260(n59)

Government of Ireland Act (1920) 55, 100, 102-103
Grattan, Henry 16
Grattan's Parliament 16, 24, 25
Gray, David 72, 111
Great Britain 3, 81(epigram), 159, 161; control over Ireland 16-17; economic interests in Ireland 13-15; Irish attitudes towards 74; proximity to Ireland 10; strategic interests in Ireland 10-13; see also Anglo-Irish agreements (1938); Anglo-Irish relations; Anglo-Irish Treaty (1921); British Army; British Commonwealth; British Empire; British Isles
Greece 96, 212, 228, 253(n78), App. 2
Greenwood, David 243(n78), 253(n72)
Griffith, Arthur 30, 36-38, 39, 48, 51, 52, 53, 54, 58, 128, 234(n51,n54)
Guinness 259(n47)

Hague, the 166
Haughey, Charles J. 116, 265(n46)
Health, Department of 214
Hearne, John J. 205
Heath, Edward 118, 142
Helsinki 95, 167, 260(n57)
Hempel, Eduard 91
Higgins, Michael D. 260(n66)
Hillery, Patrick J. 1(epigram), 94, 117, 119, 175, 183, 193(epigram), 198, 200, 210, 247(n81), 262(n1, n18)
Hitler, Adolf 157, 161, 242(n39)
Hoare, Samuel 107, 156
Hobson, Bulmer 234(n59)
Hogan, Conor 254(n20)
Holland see Netherlands
Holsti, Kalevi J. 196, 197, 198, 199
Holy See App. 2
Home Office 107, 108
Home Rule 24, 67; and Boer War 38; and Butt 27; external support for 28-29; foreign policy images of 32-35; and Irish Convention (1917) 46; and Parnell 27-29; and Redmond 29; and separatism 31; and unionists 40; see also Irish Parliamentary Party
Home Rule Bill (1886) 28, 33, 34
Home Rule Bill (1893) 29
Home Rule Bill (1912) 29
Home Rule League 27
Human rights 118, 122, 186-188

Human Rights Commission 187
Hume, John 248(n98)
Hungary 30, 36-37, 212, App. 2
Hyde, Douglas 41

Iceland 130
Images 23, 233(n30); catholic values in 39-40; definition 31-32; and Home Rule 32-35; and missionary activity 40; and Ulster 40-41
Imperial Conference (1926) 66
Imperial Conference (1930) 66
Imperial Conference (1937) 239(n33)
Imperialism, in Irish attitudes 20, 33, 37, 38, 40, 176; see also Anti-imperialism
Independence, as a foreign policy value 61-80, 91, 194-196, 237-240, 250(n13); in Anglo-Irish negotiations (1921) 57-58; and freedom of choice 201; and manipulation of symbols 74-77
India 13, 20, 50, 163, 236(n29), App. 2
Industrial Credit Company 136
Industrial Development Authority (IDA) 138, 140
Industrial Development (Encouragement of External Investment) Act (1958) 140
Industry and Commerice, Department of 209, 210, 214, 219
Institute of Public Administration (IPA) 260(n58)
Intergovernmental organisations: and international order 152; Irish attitudes towards blocs 75-76; leadership roles 76-77; membership 75; at the regional level 165-166; see also British Commonwealth; European Community; League of Nations; United Nations Organisation
International Bank for Reconstruction and Development (IBRD) 139, 183; see also World Bank
International Commission of Jurists 254(n30)
International Convention on the Elimination of Forms of Racial Discrimination 188
International Covenant on Economic, Social and Cultural Rights 188
International justice, as a foreign policy value 151, 170-190, 194-196, 257-

261
International Labour Organisation (ILO) 187, 256(n59), 261(n70)
International law and the Constitution (1937) 152-153
International Law of the Sea Conference 145
International Monetary Fund (IMF) 139, 165, 251(n46)
International order, as a foreign policy value 151-169, 194-196, 253-257
International Socialist Conference (1919) 48
International system, general trends 223-226
Internment crisis (1971) 118-119
Iran 213, App. 2
Ireland Act (1949) 112, 246(n56)
Irish-Americans see United States of America
Irish Anti-Apartheid Movement 174-175
Irish Association for European Studies 266(n52)
Irish Christian Front 177
Irish Citizen Army 43
Irish Commission for Justice and Peace 184, 260(n60)
Irish Confederation 25
Irish Convention (1917) 46, 55, 235(n14)
Irish Council for Civil Liberties 188
Irish Council of the European Movement 243(n72)
Irish Farmers Association (IFA) 260(n59)
Irish League of Nations Society 154, 254(n19)
Irish National League of America 28
Irish Neutrality League 45
Irish Parliamentary Party 28, 42, 44, 47, 55, 235(n17)
Irish Press, The 108
Irish Race Convention 48, 49
Irish Republican Army (IRA) 84, 89, 109, 113, 114, 116, 118, 120, 122, 124-125, 240(n11), 258(n33), 261(n71)
Irish Republican Brotherhood (IRB) 26-27, 28, 30, 45, 46, 48, 51, 233(n14)
Irish situation committee 69, 238(n18)
Irish Socialist Republican Party 30
Irish Sovereignty Movement 243(n72)

Irish United Nations Association 256(n65), 261(n73)
Irish Volunteers 43, 44, 45
Israel 212, App. 2
Issue-areas: definition 3-4, 231(n1); interactions between 194-196
Italy 18, 40, 70, 76, 147,(Table 4), 154, 156, 177, App. 2.

Jacobson, David 250(n22)
James I, King 14
James II, King 11, 16
Japan 30, 72, 143, 154, 155, 213, 225, App. 2
Johnson, Thomas 85, 86, 154
Joint Committee on the Secondary Legislation of the European Communities 220-221, 265(n46,n47,n48, n50)

Katanga 159, 161, 255(n45)
Kellogg-Briand Pact 154
Kelly, John 211
Kennedy, Edward 125
Kennedy, Kieran A. 129(Table 1)
Kent, William 258(n30)
Keynes, John Maynard 137, 251(n37)
Killala Bay 12
Kinsale, Battle of 11
Korean War 139
Kuwait 212, App. 2

Labour, Department of 214
Labour Party 85, 93, 120, 123, 143, 154, 180, 186, 219
Lagos 175
Lamartine, Alphonse de 26
Laval, Pierre 156
Law, Andrew Bonar 42
Law, Hugh A. 61(epigram)
Lawless, Gerard 187, 261(n71)
League of Nations 9, 49, 62, 64, 81, 85, 87, 205, 223, 254(n14), 255(n39); and anti-imperialism 172-173; Assembly 77, 155, 162, 245(n34), 254(n29); Council membership 66, 75-77, 155; de Valera's attitude towards 155-158; as diplomatic forum in the nineteen-twenties 65-66; and disarmament 162; and international order 153-158; Irish attitude towards blocs 75-76; Irish leadership in 76-77; membership of Soviet

Union 76, 156, 176-177; and Northern Ireland 105, 108, 187, 244(n16), 245(n34); and Séan Lester 77, 155, 239(n46), 255(n39); and public opinion 154-155; significance of membership 75; see also Collective security
Lebanon 213, App. 2
Lemass, Seán 94, 100(epigram), 107, 113-115, 117, 127(epigram), 140-141, 155, 175, 179, 189, 207, 208, 209-210, 214, 216, 246(n63), 251(n25,n32), 252(n53)
Lenihan, Brian 262(n18)
Lesotho 184
Lester, Seán 77, 155, 239(n46), 255(n39)
Liberal Party 28, 33, 40, 41, 42, 43, 44
Libya 125, 212, App. 2
Limerick 266(n52)
List, Friedrich 37
Lloyd George, David 10, 54, 55, 58, 63, 103, 104
Local Defence Force 90
Local Government, Department of 214
Local Security Force 90
Locarno 84
Lomé Convention 77, 260(n56)
London 37, 54, 69, 102, 104, 113, 118, 121, 196, 229, 263(n12)
Louis XIV, King 11
Luxembourg 98, 213, App. 2
Lynch, John A. (Jack) 94, 115-120, 123, 248(n101,n107)

McAleese, Dermot 130(Table 2), 146 (Table 3)
MacBride, Seán 92, 113, 188, 209, 254(n30)
McCartan, Patrick 50, 52, 53, 236(n31, n40,n42)
McClusker, John 248(n91)
MacDermot, Frank 156, 177
McDermott, Seán 45
MacDonald, Malcolm 69, 70, 88, 106, 108, 206, 238(n19)
MacEntee, Seán 207, 245(n31)
MacEoin, Seán 159
McGilligan, Patrick 154, 162, 241(n15), 256(n54), 259(n43)
McKenna, Dan 263(n19)
MacNeill, Eoin 20, 39, 45, 104, 188, 205, 244(n16), 263(n6)

McQuillan, Jack 161

Madrid 189
Maffey, Sir John 87
Malaysia App. 2
Manchuria 155
Maritime interests 145-146, 253(n72, n74,n75); and naval defence 82-83, 85, 88-89, 98, 243(n78)
Mark Press 119
Marshall Aid 138, 209, 251(n45)
Marx, Karl 234(n50)
Mazzini, Giuseppe 257(n3)
Meenan, James 191(epigram)
Message to the Free Nations of the World (1919) 9(epigram), 47, 48
Mexico 50, 212, App. 2
Middle East 46, 159, 160, 212, 213, 264(n28), App. 1
Middle power role 158, 166, 168, 189, 255(n41)
Minister of State 211
Missionary activity overseas 20, 40, 176; and development aid 182-184
Mitchel, John 25-26, 35
Monaghan 121, 159
Monday Club 243(n74)
Monroe Doctrine 52
Morocco 34, 212, App. 2
Moscow 53, 163, 176, 213
Moynihan, Maurice 208
Mulcahy, Richard 92
Munich 88, 107, 157
Murphy, Seán 205
Mussolini, Benito 156, 157, 177, 258(n30)

Nairobi 186
Nation 25
National Committeee for the Study of International Affairs (Royal Irish Academy) 222
National identity and independence 74
National Repeal Association 24
National Volunteers 44
Nationalists, in Northern Ireland 102, 105, 107-108, 115, 244(n26), 245(n31); see also Social Democratic and Labour Party
Nationality and Citizenship Act (1935) 68
Navy see Defence Forces
Netherlands 39, 96, 130, 147(Table 4),

168, 169, 175, 198, App. 2

Neutrality: analogy with Cuba 52; and anti-imperialism 173; and defence policy in the nineteen-twenties 86, 241(n18); as doctrine 73-74, 92-93; and de Valera 71-74; and the European Community 78, 94-98, 168-169, 228; and exclusion from the United Nations 75; and external association 58; and freedom of choice 201; and Germany 89-90; and Great Britain 56-57, 83, 88, 90, 91; and independence in World War II 71; and international order 166; and Irish unity 92, 94, 109-112; and the League of Nations 87; as legal status 262(n8); and moral issues in World War II 178; and NATO 91-98; and neutrality 174; and non-alignment orientation 197-198; and public opinion 47, 72-73, 90-91, 93, 137; and security in World War II 88-91; sources of 38, 39, 44, 45, 47; and the Spanish civil war 156-157; and the United States 72, 90

New York 209

New Zealand 29, 64, App. 2

Newry 94

Nigeria 174, 259(n47), 260(n59), App. 2

Nixon, Richard 119

Nobel Prize for Peace 254(n30)

North America 18, 29

North Atlantic Treaty Organisation (NATO) 168, 229; and anti-communism 179; Ireland remains outside 73, 92; and Irish neutrality 94-98; and Irish unity 112, 246(n53)

Northern Ireland 2, 195, 199, 230, 247(n85), 248(n94, n107); and the European Community 117, 123, 124; executive (1973-74) 120-121; government established 55; as independent state 228-229; and the issue of Irish unity 100-125, 246(n66); and tourism 142; trade with 130 (Table 2), 136; and United Nations peace-keeping 159-160; see also Nationalists in Northern Ireland; Ulster; Unity

Norway 130, 141, 158, 168, App. 2

Nuclear Proliferation Treaty 163, 168, 256(n56)

O'Brien, Conor Cruise 93, 120, 123, 159, 161, 247(n86), 248(n98), 255(n45)

O'Connell, Daniel 24-25, 27, 32

O'Duffy, Eoin 177, 258(n33)

O'Higgins, Kevin 86, 153, 205

O'Higgins, Thomas F. 93, 242(n50)

Oil see Maritime interests

O'Kelly, Seán T. 48, 155

O'Kennedy, Michael 197, 260(n67)

O'Leary, Michael 219

O'Neill, Terence 114, 210

O'Neill, Tip 125

Orange Order 108

Organization for Economic Co-operation and Development (OECD) 142, 165, 215

Organisation for European Economic Co-operation (OEEC) 140, 165, 166

Orientations 196-198, 233(n30), 262(n4, n11)

Palestine 190, 245(n34)

Paraguay 155

Paris 25, 48, 79

Paris Peace Conference (1919) 48-50, 154

Parliamentary Secretary 211, App. 1

Parnell, Charles Stewart 22(epigram), 27-29, 33, 34-35, 112, 174, 234(n40)

Parsons, Sir Lawrence 7(epigram)

Partition see Unity

Peace-Keeping see United Nations Organisation

Pearl Harbor 111

Pearse, Patrick 45

Peking 174

Persia 34

Peru 155

Philadelphia 48, 49

Poland 180, 212, App. 2

Policy-making 203-222; and the cabinet 204-208, 219-220, 263(n6); and change in the international system 224-225; and civil servants 205-218; coordination of 204, 211, 213-220; and Dáil Éireann (1919-21) 50-54; fragmentation 208-210, 216-217; and information 204, 215-216, 230; models 203-204, 263(n2); and policy planning 230, 267(n8, n9); and public control 204, 205-206, 207, 216, 220-222, 263(n11), 265(n46, n47,

n48,n49,n50)
Political co-operation see European political co-operation
Political culture 31
Pompidou, Georges 142
Portugal 96, 228, App. 2
Privy Council, Judicial Committee of 68
Priorities in foreign policy 200
Propaganda: and Dáil Éireann (1919-1921) 49-50; and Irish unity 107-109, 112-113, 119, 245(n33,n40)
Prosperity, as a foreign policy value 127-148, 194-196, 249-253; in Anglo-Irish negotiations (1921) 54-55; and freedom of choice 201; see also Economic policy; Trade
Protection see Economic policy
Protestants 40
Provisional Government (1916) 42(epigram), 235(n6)
Provisional Government (1922) 63-64, 102, 153
Public opinion: and the British Commonwealth 67; and defence policy 82; and development aid 186; and Great Britain 74, 239(n37); and Irish unity 123-124; and the League of Nations 154-155; and neutrality 47; 72-73, 90-91, 93, 137; and policy-making 216, 220-222; and United Nations peace-keeping 161; and World War II 178; see also Elections; Referendum (1972)

Qatar 212, App. 2
Queenstown see Cobh

Recognition 50
Redmond, John 28, 29, 33, 37, 41, 42, 43-45, 71, 110, 112, 233(n35), 235(n3,n17)
Referendum (1972) 78, 94-95, 142-144
Regional policy see European Community
Regions, international 165
Religious divisions 10-11, 16, 40, 102, 115, 246(n67)
Religious values 20, 39-40, 176-181, 258(n28,n33), 259(n39,n41)
Representation overseas 52-53, 71, 74, 212-213, 239(n38), 264(n29), App. 2
Republican Party 50
Resources see Economic policy

Resources Protection Group 253(n71)
Rhodesia 175
Rising (1916) 46
Rockall 146
Roles 199-200, 262(n14); see also Middle power role
Rome 178
Rome, Treaties of. 95
Ronan, Seán 163
Roosevelt, Franklin D. 72, 108
Rosenau, James N. 231(n1)
Royal Irish Academy see National Committee for the Study of International Affairs
Russia 29; see also Soviet Union
Ryan, Richie 180

Salisbury, Lord 13
Saorstát Éireann Gloss.
Saudi Arabia 212, 213, App. 2
Schumann, Maurice 96
Scotland 27, 228-229
Scottish Nationalist Party 266(n7)
Seanad Gloss.
Security, as a foreign policy value 81-99, 194-196, 240-243; in Anglo-Irish negotiations (1921) 56-57; and the European Community 228; and freedom of choice 201; see also Defence Forces; Maritime interests; Neutrality
Self-sufficiency 134-138, 201
Separatism: and foreign policy images 35-39; and Home Rule 31; and the Irish Reublican Brotherhood 26-27; revival in the eighteen-nineties 29-30; and Sinn Féin 30; and World War I 45-47; and Young Ireland 25-26
Sherwin, Frank 261(n76)
Singapore 212, App. 2
Sinn Féin Gloss., 30, 38, 41, 45, 47, 48, 55, 113, 143
Social Democratic and Labour Party (SDLP) 118, 120, 123, 248(n98)
Socialism 38, 48
South Africa 65, 66, 174-175
South America 38
Sovereignty 61-62, 77-78, 128, 153-154; see also Independence
Soviet Union 161, 163, 174, 225, 242(n39), App. 2; draft treaty with (1920) 50, 53, 236(n31,n32); Ireland establishes diplomatic relations

with 180, 259(n44); Ireland supports admission to the League of Nations 76, 156, 176-177, 258(n28); opposes Irish admission to the United Nations 75, 158; and security 97
Spain 18, 29, 41, 167, 189, 228, App. 2
Spanish civil war 109, 157, 177-178, 207
Spencer, John 130(Table 2), 146 (Table 3)
Standard, The 178
State Department 111
Statute of Westminster 66-67
Stepinac, Archbishop 178
Sterling see Economic policy: monetary policy
Stormont 105, 112, 119
Strategic Arms Limitation Talks (SALT) 163
Sunningdale agreement (1973) 93, 120-121, 122, 123, 247(n88), 248(n91)
Supplies, Department of 208
Supreme Court 121
Sweden 95, 158, App. 2
Swilly, Lough 85
Switzerland 95, App. 2
Symbols, and independence 74-77

Taft, William Howard 37
Taoiseach Gloss.
Taoiseach, Department of 211, 214, 218, 219, 264(n27), 265(n43)
Tariffs see Economic policy: protection
Tariff Commission 133
Thailand 212, App. 2
Thorn, Gaston 167
Tibet 174, 257(n10)
Tindemans, Léo 95, 219
Tone, Wolfe 12, 24, 30
Trade 132-133, 136, 138; dependence 88, 130-131, 146-147, 250(n11,n12); and development aid 185-186; and the economic war 135; historical development 15; and international order 165; see also Economic Policy
Transgovernmental relations 217
Transnational relations 23
Transport and Power, Department of 214
Trinity College Dublin 266(n52)
Trócaire Gloss., 184
Tunisia 212, App. 2
Turkey App. 2

Ulster 14, 40-41; see also Northern Ireland; Unity
Ulster Volunteer Force 43
Union of Soviet Socialist Republics (USSR) see Soviet Union
Unionists: and Home Rule 33, 40, 42-44; and independence 63; and the Irish Convention (1917) 46-47; and the issue of Irish unity 100-125; and negotiations with Britian (1921) 53; and Ulster 40-41; 42-44
Unionist Party 120
United Arab Emirates 212, App. 2
United Irish League 29
United Kingdom, see Great Britain
United Nations Conference on Trade and Development (UNCTAD) 186, 260(n65)
United Nations Congo Operation (ONUC) 159, 255(n43,n44,n50)
United Nations Emergency Force (UNEF) 159, 160, 168
United Nations Freedom from Hunger Campaign see Gorta
United Nations Force in Cyprus (UNFICYP) 159, 255(n43)
United Nations Organisation (UNO) 3, 149, 153, 195, 199, 200, 209, 215, 254(n30), 255(n39), 260(n57), 264(n28); and anti-communism 179; and anti-imperialism 173-175; and development aid 182, 184; and disarmament 162-164, 168; and European political co-operation 165-169, 256(n70), 261(n81); General Assembly 77, 163, 167, 173, 174, 175; and human rights 188; and independent stance 76; and international order 156-168; Ireland excluded 75; Irish attitudes towards blocs 76; Irish leadership in 77; and Irish unity 117, 119, 123, 125, 246(n61), 247(n73); peace-keeping operations 82, 93, 158-161, 168, 255(n40,n48); and religious values 178; Security Council 77, 117; specialised agencies 150
United States of America (USA) 37, 39, 45, 47, 71, 88, 89, 91, 96, 137, 141, 146(Table 3), 163, 225, 226, 230, 250(n12), 254(n29), 264(n28), App. 2; and Constitution (1937) 70; as counterweight to Britain 198; econo-

mic relations with 143; and Ireland in the United Nations 76, 174, 178-180; and Irish neutrality 72-73, 238(n29); and Irish unity 108, 109, 111-112, 119, 125, 238(n29), 245(n51), 249(n109); Irish-American community 18-19, 232(n15); and recognition of Dáil Éireann (1919-21) 50; as source of support for Irish nationalists 25-30, 44, 46, 48-49, 233(n21), 235(n3,n8), 236(n26,n27, n34); and strategic value of Ireland in World War II 90, 238(n29); and truce of 1921 54

Unity, as a foreign policy value 88, 100-125, 194-196, 246(n66); and Anglo-Irish negotiations (1921) 55-56; attitudes before 1914 40-41, 42; and the Boundary Commission 102-104; and the coalition government (1973-77) 120-123; and the Constitution (1937) 70; and defence policy 89-90, 91, 92, 93-94, 97; and de Valera 105-113; and external association 73, 246(n53); and federalism 109; and freedom of choice 201; and functional co-operation 107, 114, 117-118, 120-121, 124-125, 245(n29), 246(n63), 248(n107); and the Government of Ireland Act (1920) 102-103; and human rights 118, 122, 187; and the League of Nations 105, 108, 187, 244(n16), 245(n34); and the IRA 109, 113, 114, 116, 118, 120, 124-125; and Seán Lemass 107, 113-115, and Jack Lynch 115-120; 123; and neutrality 109-112; and policy-making 204, 210, 212, 221; and propaganda 107-109, 112-113, 119, 246(n58); prospects 228-230; and public opinion 123; and the United Nations 117, 119, 123, 125, 246(n61), 247(n73); and the United States 108, 109, 111-112, 119, 125, 238(n29), 245(n51), 249(n109)

University College Dublin 266(n52)

Values, in foreign policy 4; and milieu

goals 150-151; and possession goals 149-150; see also Independence; International justice; International order; Prosperity; Security; Unity

Vatican 25, 39, 176
Versailles 49
Vienna 37
Vietnam 180
Vinegar Hill, Battle of 12
Volunteers (1782) 16
Voluntary Agencies Liaison Committee 185

Wales 27, 229
Walshe, Joseph P. 205, 208
Washington D.C. 29, 53, 263(n12)
Washington naval agreements 54
Webster, Charles K. 256(n60)
Westminster Gazette 236(n39)
Whitaker, T. K. 129(Table 1), 140, 147(Table 4), 210, 214, 264(n24)
William of Orange, King 11
Wilson, Harold 117
Wilson, Woodrow 48, 49, 51
Wolfers, Arnold 149, 150
World Bank 252(n57); see also International Bank for Reconstruction and Development
World War I 21, 24, 33, 38, 41, 61-62, 64, 103, 111; and Anglo-Irish relations 43-47
World War II 94-165, 216, 225; and Anglo-Irish relations 70-73; 87-91, 137; and ideological positions 178; and interactions between issue-areas 194; and the Irish economy 137, 251(n38); and Irish neutrality 88-91; and Irish unity 109-112; and the League of Nations 157-158; and policy-making 208-209; and trade 130

Yeats, William Butler 100(epigram)
Young Ireland 25-26, 32, 35
Yugoslavia 178, 212, App. 2

Zambia 184, 260(n58), App. 2
Zimmermann, Artur von 45